ANCIENT ROME

HISTORY OF A CIVILIZATION
THAT RULED THE WORLD

MetroBooks

ANCIENT ROME

HISTORY OF A CIVILIZATION THAT RULED THE WORLD

Texts and captions
Anna Maria Liberati
Fabio Bourbon

Editor
Valeria Manferto De Fabianis

Graphic design
Patrizia Balocco Lovisetti

Editorial coordination
Fabio Bourbon

**Color and black
and white drawings**
Roberta Vigone
Monica Falcone

Translation
A.B.A., Milan

CONTENTS

1 The Capitoline She-Wolf symbolizes the mythical origins of Rome. This bronze of Etruscan manufacture dates from the 5th century B.C., while the twins are a 15th-century addition by Pollaiolo.

2-3 For centuries the Roman Forum, standing in the valley at the foot of the Palatine Hill, was the heart of public life in Rome. Temples, basilicas, triumphal arches and votive columns were built there on various occasions.

4-5 The Column of Marcus Aurelius, which stands in front of Palazzo Chigi in Rome, was erected between 176 and 193 A.D. to celebrate the Emperor's victories against the Germans and the Sarmatians. It is just under 100 feet tall and embellished with a spiral decoration, the reliefs of which portray the various stages of the military campaigns.

6-7 The Temple of Ba'alshamin is one of the most outstanding monuments in Palmyra, the splendid Syrian caravan town which became part of the Roman Empire under Hadrian in the 2nd century A.D.

8 This delicate Pompeiian fresco shows a girl in a pensive attitude; because of the quill pen resting on her lips and the wax tablet in her left hand, she has become known as the "Poetess."

9 This intense portrait of Augustus, a detail of the Prima Porta statue, shows the founder of the Roman Empire at the peak of his strength, wearing his commander's breastplate.

10-11 The Villa of Mysteries in Pompeii contains the most famous cycle of frescoes surviving from Roman times.

12-13 The "Pugilist" is a masterpiece of the Neo-attic school of the 1st century B.C., which exerted great influence on Roman statuary.

14-15 This superb 2nd century mosaic from Hadrian's Villa portrays two theatrical masks; worn by actors, they emphasized the more grotesque features of the various characters to define their personalities.

© 1999 White Star S.r.l.
Via C. Sassone, 24 13100 Vercelli, Italy
www.whitestar.it

MetroBooks
An Imprint of the Michael Friedman
Publishing Group, Inc.

This edition published by Metrobooks by
arrangement with White Star S.r.l.

ISBN 1-58663-767-3
3 5 7 9 10 8 6 4

For bulk purchases and special sales,
please contact:
Michael Friedman Publishing Group, Inc.
Attention: Sales Department
230 Fifth Avenue, Suite 700
New York, NY 10001
212/685-6610 FAX 212/685-3916

Visit our website: www.metrobooks.com

Printed in Italy by Grafedit

White Star would like to thank the Commander Vincenzo Calabrese and Augustín Velázquez Jiménez, Director of the Museo Nacional de Arte Romano of Merida, Spain, for their valuable contributions to this book.

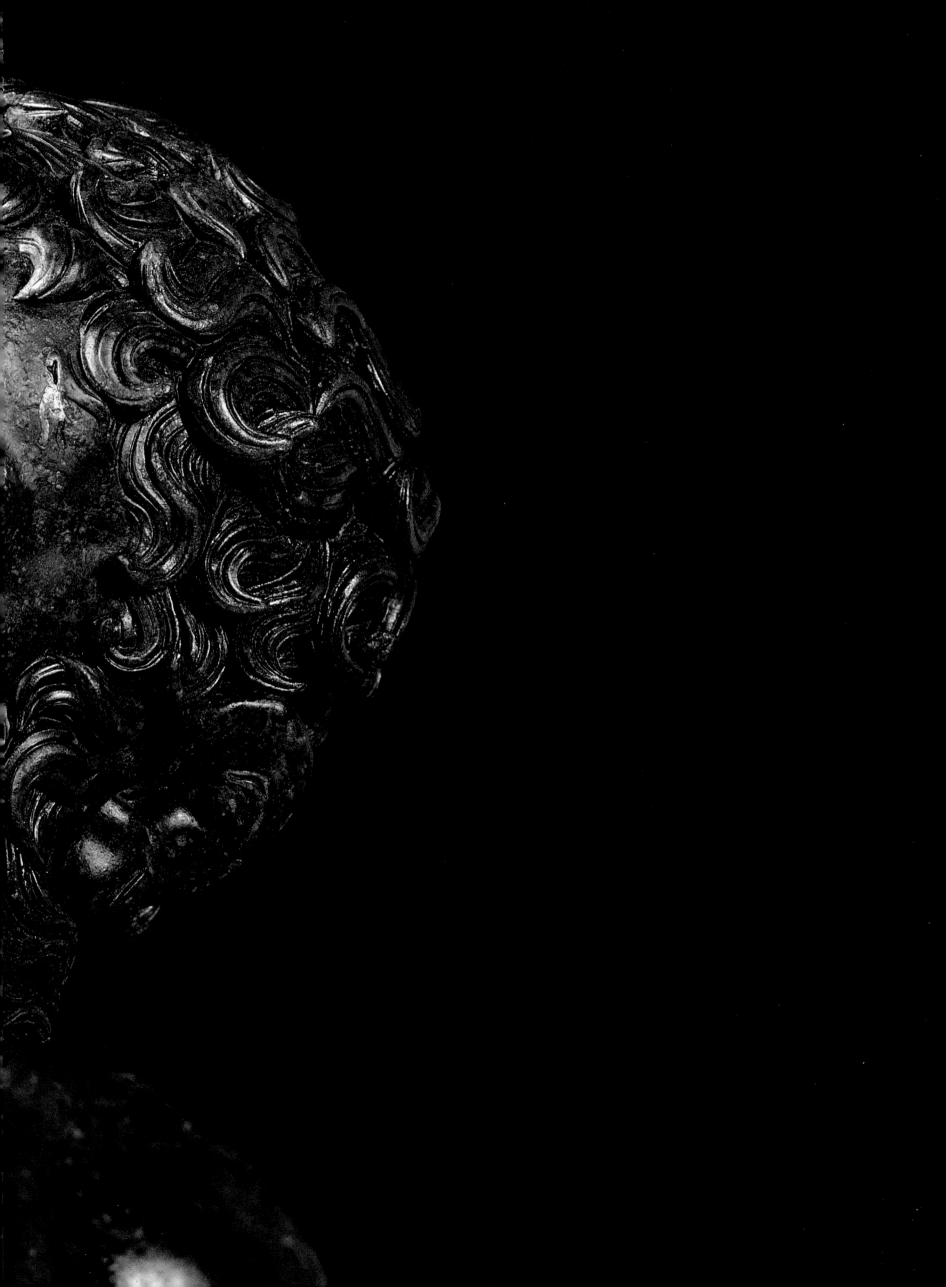

FOREWORD

Roman civilization still holds an irresistible attraction, even in this technological era. It has survived over the centuries not only in the form of archaeological remains or abstract ideas forming the subject of learned dissertations, but above all as a tangible heritage, which is still active in the world we live in, and which is all the more surprising the closer it comes to us. The residential districts discovered in Ostia, the engineering systems, the complex water supply systems found from Britannia to Syria, and the efficient road network which connected even the most distant towns to the heart of the Empire bear witness to a society which was highly technically advanced. The types of construction, architectural styles and decorative tastes of the Roman world are extensively reflected in the artistic languages we know best, from Renaissance to Post-modern. Even the social issues, the constant struggle for political power, the excesses and decadence of the ancient Roman lifestyle are by no means foreign to us. For better or worse, the long shadow cast by Rome permeates many aspects of our daily lives. We are often only subconsciously aware of this heritage, but it would obviously be impossible to consciously remember every time we turn on a tap to quench our thirst that we have just used a mechanism designed 2,000 years ago. Equally, we do not daily consider that the origins of the legal system that protects our rights date back to the work of the Roman jurisconsults. Recounting the history of Rome and its civilization, which influenced the culture of a large part of the world for over 1,000 years, is no easy task. We have therefore tried to bring ancient Rome to life by describing all its social, political, cultural and artistic aspects as clearly and directly as possible. The various chapters are structured in such a way as to familiarize even the least expert readers with this highly complex world, though without boring the more demanding readers who, we trust, will still find plenty of interest in this volume. The basic characteristics of Roman civilization are particularly emphasized by an analysis of the various stages of its history (from archaic times to the decline of the Empire) and the most interesting

16 bottom Cameos, made using a very complex technique, were designed to immortalize leading personalities and salient facts of Imperial court life. The "Gemma Claudia" portrays the Emperor Claudius with his wife Agrippina the Younger on the left, and Germanicus, a valiant commander and adopted son of Tiberius, with his wife Agrippina the Elder, on the right.

aspects of its everyday life, in order to give an overview which is neither too complex nor too simplistic, but as interesting as possible. The remains of Roman civilization in Italy and the various provinces of the Empire are given particular attention, by means of a detailed review of the archaeological sites in each region which best demonstrate the influence exerted by Rome, sometimes overlapping with and suffocating the local cultures, and sometimes incorporating them with admirable results. The extensive pictorial documentation performs an important function in this context and includes many new pictures, including aerial photos specially taken to highlight structural characteristics and other details of monuments or town planning that would otherwise be difficult to appreciate. We are sure that the dozens of diagrams, plans, black-and-white drawings and complex color tables in this volume will evoke, better than many learned tomes, the splendors of a civilization that conquered the world.

17 This sardonyx masterpiece dating from the 1st century A.D., known as the "Great Cameo of France," portrays the Emperor Tiberius surrounded by his mother Livia and other members of the Julio-Claudian family.

18-19 The exceptional size of the Coliseum, which was destined for gladiatorial games and wild beast hunts, makes it the largest of the Roman amphitheaters. This aerial photo shows the inner structure of the

building whose load-bearing structures, entirely made of travertine blocks, were connected by tufa and brick masonry. The complex system of cellars which ran under the arena can be seen clearly from above.

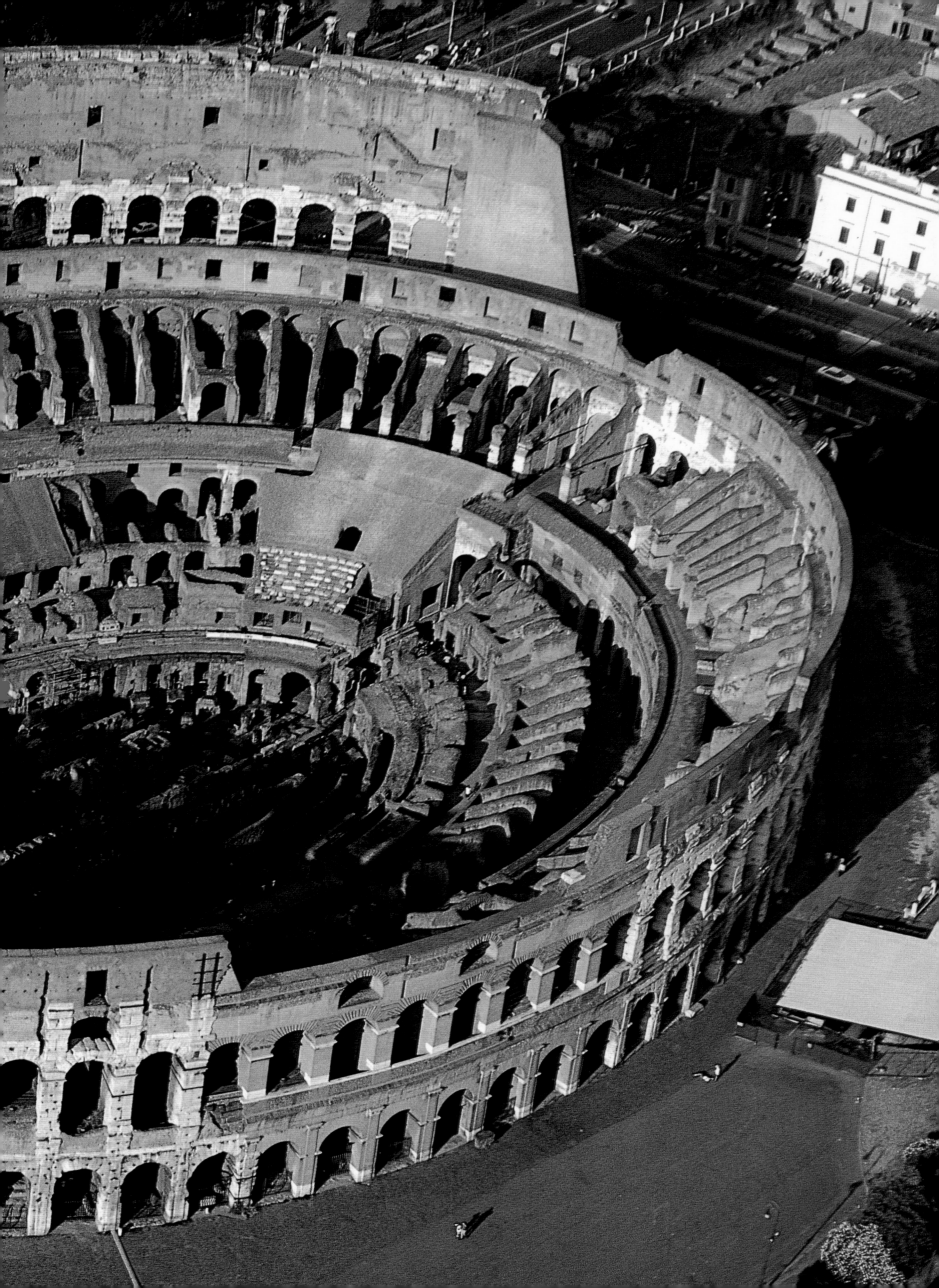

ROME:

FROM ITS ORIGINS TO THE FALL OF THE EMPIRE

20-21 Because of the legend of Romulus and Remus, the she-wolf was considered a sacred animal in ancient Rome, and became the symbol of the city.
It is known from an inscription that a statue (which often appeared on coins in the Republican and Imperial ages) was dedicated to the Capitoline She-Wolf in 296 B.C., and that there was already another in the Capitol. The date commonly attributed to the sculpture now displayed in the Museo dei Conservatori in Rome suggests that it is the latter, perhaps commissioned from the bottega of an Etruscan craftsman. However, the riddle is remains unsolved.

In the 8th century B.C., Latium (now known as Lazio) was inhabited by a population of shepherds and farmers, the Latins. They occupied the plains and coastal areas of the region and were scattered among numerous villages that were independent from one another, but united in religious associations and open to cultural influences from the Etruscans and Greeks who had settled in the neighboring areas. One of these villages, called Rome, was built in a favorable position for trade; it was situated near the Tiber at a point where it was particularly easy to ford the river. Even before it came under Etruscan dominion, Rome, ruled by a king, had reached a level of development that distinguished it from the other Latin communities. The four pre-Etruscan kings of which tradition tells are said to have performed numerous acts that, though difficult to date, paved the way for the future power of Rome. Tradition has it that Romulus, as well as founding the city in 753 B.C. (the conventional date proposed by M. Terentius Varro, a scholar of the Caesarean period), instituted the Senate and increased the population by allowing the Sabines to settle in Rome; Numa Pompilius organized religious life, worship and the Colleges of Priests and reformed the calendar by dividing the year into 12 months; Tullius Hostilius (673-642 B.C.) destroyed the rival city of Alba Longa, thereby extending the rule of Rome; and Ancus Martius (641–617 B.C.) built the first bridge over the Tiber and founded the colony of Ostia at its mouth, thus creating an outlet to the sea for Rome. Towards the end of the 7th century B.C., Rome fell under the dominion of the Etruscans, who pushed through Latium to Campania. Tradition tells of three Etruscan kings: Tarquinius Priscus (616–579 B.C.), Servius Tullius (578–535 B.C.) and Tarquinius Superbus (Tarquin the Proud) (534–510 B.C.).

22 top The origins of Rome are still shrouded in mystery. Greek historians included Rome among the towns founded by Trojan hero Aeneas, who fled to Italy after the fall of Troy, while the first Roman historian, Fabius Pictor, gave credit to the legend of Romulus and Remus, illustrated on this altar, which dates from the 2nd century A.D. The twins, who were the sons of Mars and Vestal Virgin Rhea Silvia, were abandoned in a basket on the Tiber, saved by a she-wolf, and brought up by the shepherd Faustulus. When they grew up they punished the usurper Amulius, and Romulus, who laid the foundations of Rome, became the first king of the city.

22 bottom Numerous hut-shaped urns similar to this one have been found in the cremation tombs excavated in the area of the Roman Forum. Dating from the 10th to 8th centuries B.C., they are of particular interest because they portray, albeit in a stylized fashion, the homes typical of the most archaic Roman settlement.

23 The famous Apollo of Veii is attributed to Vulca, the only Etruscan artist whose name survives; he was summoned to Rome by Tarquinius Priscus to sculpt the statue of Jupiter for the Capitoline Temple.

During this period the city prospered, and was transformed from a purely agricultural-pastoral town into a center of trade and commerce. The society was made up of patricians, members of the richest and most powerful families, and plebeians, who constituted the humbler sections of the population. The king exercised power in the religious, political, military, legislative and judicial fields, but left a degree of authority to two consultative bodies: the Senate (consisting of representatives of the leading families) and the comitia curiata, which constituted the General Assembly of citizens that was divided into 30 curiae, grouped into 3 clans and controlled by the patricians. By setting up the comitia centuriata, based on the division into "centuries" according to the census, Servius Tullius tried to limit the power of the patricians to some extent and help the nouveaux riches to improve their social status. At the same time Rome was extending its rule to the

surrounding territory of Latium. The city center, fortified by strong walls, was embellished with temples and public buildings and grew much larger than the other major cities of Latium and Etruria of the same period. The expulsion of Tarquin the Proud (509 B.C.) marked the end of Etruscan rule and the advent of a patrician regime hostile to the rise of the new classes that the monarchy had favored.

24 Although the last kings of Rome were of Etruscan origin, the city always maintained its independence. However, it is clear that the original Roman culture, art and architecture were strongly influenced by their Etruscan counterparts. As well as adopting Etruscan ceremonies, power symbols and some religious practices, the Romans imported many goods from Etruria, and it is certain that numerous Etruscan craftsmen were summoned to Rome to construct public works and decorate the main temples.
The two antefixes and the multicolored terra-cotta frieze shown here give some idea of what these decorations must have looked like. It was not until the 4th century B.C. that Roman art began to break away from Etrusco-Italic art and manifest original features. However, especially in the case of statuary, it long retained (and indeed emphasized) the latter's strong tendency to realism.

IMPERIAL ROME IN THE FOURTH CENTURY A.D.

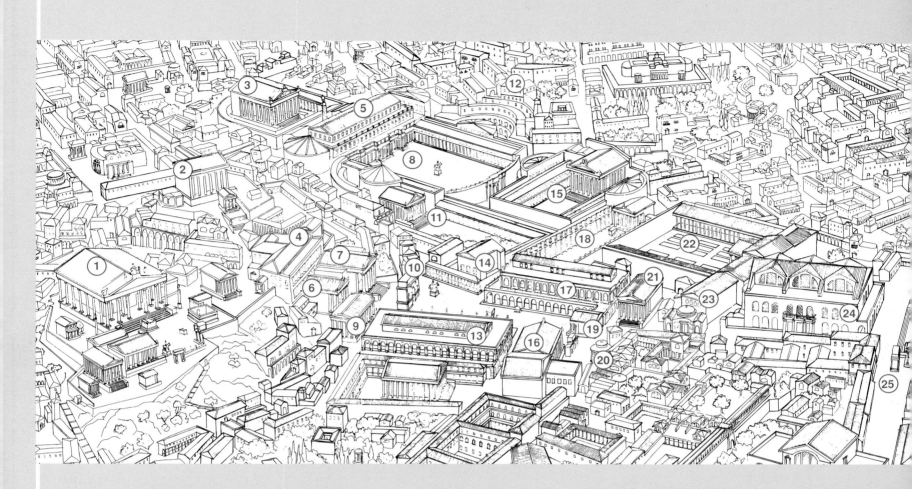

The large color plate inserted in the following pages is inspired by the relief model made by Italo Gismondi in the Thirties on the basis of the Forma Urbis, a plan of Rome engraved on marble slabs dating from the age of Septimius Severus, which has survived in fragments. This bird's-eye view reconstructs with considerable accuracy the heart of the Eternal City, i.e., the Forum area between the Capitol and the Coliseum during the reign of Constantine. The dates shown in the key alongside the names of the major monuments relate to the year in which each building was completed; in many cases the second date is that of the last known reconstruction of the building. However, as the plate relates to Rome in the age of Constantine, in some cases dates later than A.D. 337 have been omitted. For example, the Julian Basilica, commenced in 54 B.C. and inaugurated in 46 B.C., was rebuilt first by Augustus, then by Diocletian, and finally by Gabinius Vettius Probianus in A.D. 416. This last date has been excluded, as it does not relate to the reconstructional view.

1 Temple of Jupiter Capitoline (509 B.C.– A.D. 82)
2 Temple of Juno Moneta (344 B.C– I century A.D.)
3 Temple of Trajan (A.D. 122)
4 Tabularium (78 B.C.)
5 Basilica Ulpia (A.D. 113)
6 Temple of Vespasianus and Titus (A.D. 81)
7 Temple of Concord (367 B.C.– A.D. 10)
8 Trajan's Forum (A.D. 112)
9 Temple of Saturn (493 B.C.–A.D. 283)
10 Arch of Septimius Severus (A.D. 203)
11 Caesar's Forum (42 B.C.)
12 Trajan's Markets (A.D. 112)

13 Julian Basilica (46 B.C.–A.D. 286)
14 Curia (29 B.C.–A.D. 303)
15 Forum of Augustus (2 B.C.)
16 Temple of Castor and Pollux (484 B.C.–A.D. 6)
17 Basilica Aemilia (179 B.C.–A.D. 12)
18 Nerva's Forum (A.D. 97)
19 Temple of Caesar (29 B.C.)
20 Temple of Vesta (VII century B.C.– A.D. 193)
21 Temple of Antoninus and Faustina (A.D. 141)
22 Vespasianu's Forum (A.D. 75)
23 Temple of Romulus (IV century A.D.)

24 Basilica of Maxentius and Constantine (A.D. 312)
25 Arch of Titus (A.D. 82)
26 Temple of Caesars
27 Temple of Venus and Rome
28 Meta Sudans (I century A.D.)
29 Colossus of Nero (I century A.D.)
30 Arch of Constantine (A.D. 315)
31 Flavian Amphitheater or Coliseum (A.D. 80)
32 Baths of Titus (A.D. 81)
33 Baths of Trajan (A.D. 109)
34 Ludus Magnus (A.D. 96– IV century A.D.)

| The foundation of Rome and the Royal age: 753–509 B.C. | The Republic and the patrician-plebeian conflict: 509–343 B.C. | The conquest of Italy and the Punic Wars: 343–146 B.C. | The crisis facing the Republic: 146–78 B.C. | The age of Caesar and the end of the Republic: 78–44 B.C. |

Legend has it that Rome was founded by Romulus, brother of Remus, on 21 April 753 B.C. From that date until 509 B.C., seven kings are traditionally said to have reigned. However, archaeological excavations date the remains of the first settlement of huts on the Palatine Hill, the original nucleus of the Urbs, at the 10th century B.C. Around 575 B.C. two marshy areas by the Tiber were leveled for the construction of the Roman Forum and the Cattle Market. Rome began to expand into Latium, destroying rival city Alba Longa. The colony of Ostia was founded at the mouth of the Tiber. Under Tarquinius Priscus, Etruscan domination of Rome and expansion towards Campania began. The society was divided between patricians and plebeians.

Foundation of Rome
(753 B.C.)

Reign of Romulus
(753–715 B.C.)

Reign of Numa Pompilius
(715–673 B.C.)

Reign of Tullius Hostilius
(673–642 B.C.)

Reign of Ancus Martius
(642–617 B.C.)

Reign of Tarquinius Priscus
(617–579 B.C.)

Reign of Servius Tullius
(579–535 B.C.)

Reign of Tarquin the Proud
(535–509 B.C.)

Expulsion of Tarquin the Proud and commencement of the Republic
(509 B.C.)

After the expulsion of the Etruscans from Rome and the election of the first consuls, Lucius Junius Brutus and Lucius Tarquinius Collatinus, the Roman Republic was introduced. A long period of serious social strife between patricians and plebeians began. In 493 B.C., Rome joined the Latin League. In 494 B.C. the Tribunes of the Plebs were created and the comitia tributa instituted to defend the rights of the less wealthy classes. The organization of the army into "centuries" dates from 451 B.C. In the same year the first decemvirs were elected, and the laws of the Twelve Tables were enacted. The rival city of Veii was destroyed in 396 B.C. Rome was plundered by the Gauls in 390 B.C., but soon recovered and continued to pursue its expansionist policy. In 367 B.C., the plebs obtained the right to appoint their own consuls and, within a few years, gained admission to the main magistratures.

Roman victory against the Latins at Lake Regillus
(496 B.C.)

Creation of the Tribunes of the Plebs
(494 B.C.)

Enactment of the laws of the Twelve Tables
(451 B.C.)

Marriage between patricians and plebeians allowed
(445 B.C.)

Destruction of Veii
(396 B.C.)

The Gauls burn Rome
(390 B.C.)

Plebeians allowed to hold consular office
(367 B.C.)

Between 343 and 341 B.C. the Romans fought the first war against the Samnites, whose rule extended over southern Italy. In 338 B.C., the dissolution of the Latin League was imposed by Rome. During the Second Samnite War the Romans were defeated at the Caudine Forks, but the third and decisive war concluded in 290 B.C. with the victory of Rome. Pyrrhus, King of Epirus, summoned to Italy by Tarentum in 280 B.C., was defeated five years later at Beneventum. Rome, now expanding rapidly, clashed with Carthage; at the end of the Second Punic War in 201 B.C., Rome controlled the Mediterranean. In 146 B.C., Carthage was razed to the ground; Rome annexed Greece and Macedonia.

Samnite Wars
(343–290 B.C.)

Victory over Pyrrhus
(285 B.C.)

The 1st Punic War
(264–241 B.C.)

The Romans occupy Sardinia and Corsica
(238 B.C.)

The Romans occupy Cisalpine Gaul
(222 B.C.)

The 2nd Punic War
(218–201 B.C.)

The Romans institute the Hispanic provinces
(197 B.C.)

The 3rd Punic War and the destruction of Carthage
(149–146 B.C.)

The destruction of Corinth; Macedonia and Greece become Roman
(146 B.C.)

The province of Asia was instituted in 130 B.C. The republic was racked by social conflict. The tribune Tiberius Gracchus challenged the authority of the Senate and endeavored to introduce some agricultural reforms, but was assassinated. Caius Gracchus, Tribune of the Plebs in 119 B.C., confirmed the laws proposed by his brother, but was also murdered. Southern Gaul was conquered between 121 and 125 B.C. The Jugurthine War was won in 105 B.C. by Caius Marius, who reorganized the army in the same year. Between 91 and 88 B.C. Rome fought the Allies' War against its Italic allies, to whom Roman citizenship was eventually granted. General Lucius Cornelius Sulla became dictator and reformed the constitution, reestablishing the absolute authority of the Senate.

Assassination of Tiberius Gracchus
(133 B.C.)

Assassination of Caius Gracchus
(121 B.C.)

War against Jugurtha
(118–105 B.C.)

Marius defeats the Teutons and Cimbrians
(102–101 B.C.)

Allies' War (91–88 B.C.)
Death of Caius Marius
(86 B.C.)

Sulla wins the 1st Mithradatic War
(87–85 B.C.)

Sulla becomes dictator
(82 B.C.)

Sulla dies at Pompeii
(78 B.C.)

Rome underwent a period of great social upheaval, while the senatorial oligarchy was increasingly weakened. Pompey, elected consul in 70 B.C., conquered Pontus, Bithynia and Palestine in 64 B.C. In 63 B.C. Cicero foiled Catiline's conspiracy. Caesar, Pompey and Crassus set up the First Triumvirate, a coalition against the power of the Senate, in 60 B.C. Between 58–51 B.C. Caesar conquered Gaul. On the death of Crassus in 52 B.C., Pompey became sole consul, with the support of the senatorial party. In 49 B.C. the Senate ordered Caesar to dissolve the legions, but he crossed the Rubicon and marched on Rome, thus initiating the Civil War. Pompey was defeated at Pharsalus and fled to Egypt, where he was killed. In 45 B.C. Caesar finally defeated Pompey's supporters at Munda. In February of 44 B.C. he was appointed dictator for life, but was assassinated on 15 March by conspirators led by Brutus and Cassius.

Consulship of Pompey and Crassus
(70 B.C.)

Catiline's conspiracy
(63 B.C.)

First Triumvirate
(60 B.C.)

Caesar conquers Gaul
(58–51 B.C.)

Civil War breaks out
(49 B.C.)

Battle of Pharsalus and death of Pompey
(48 B.C.)

Caesar defeats Pompey's supporters at Munda
(45 B.C.)

Caesar assassinated
(44 B.C.)

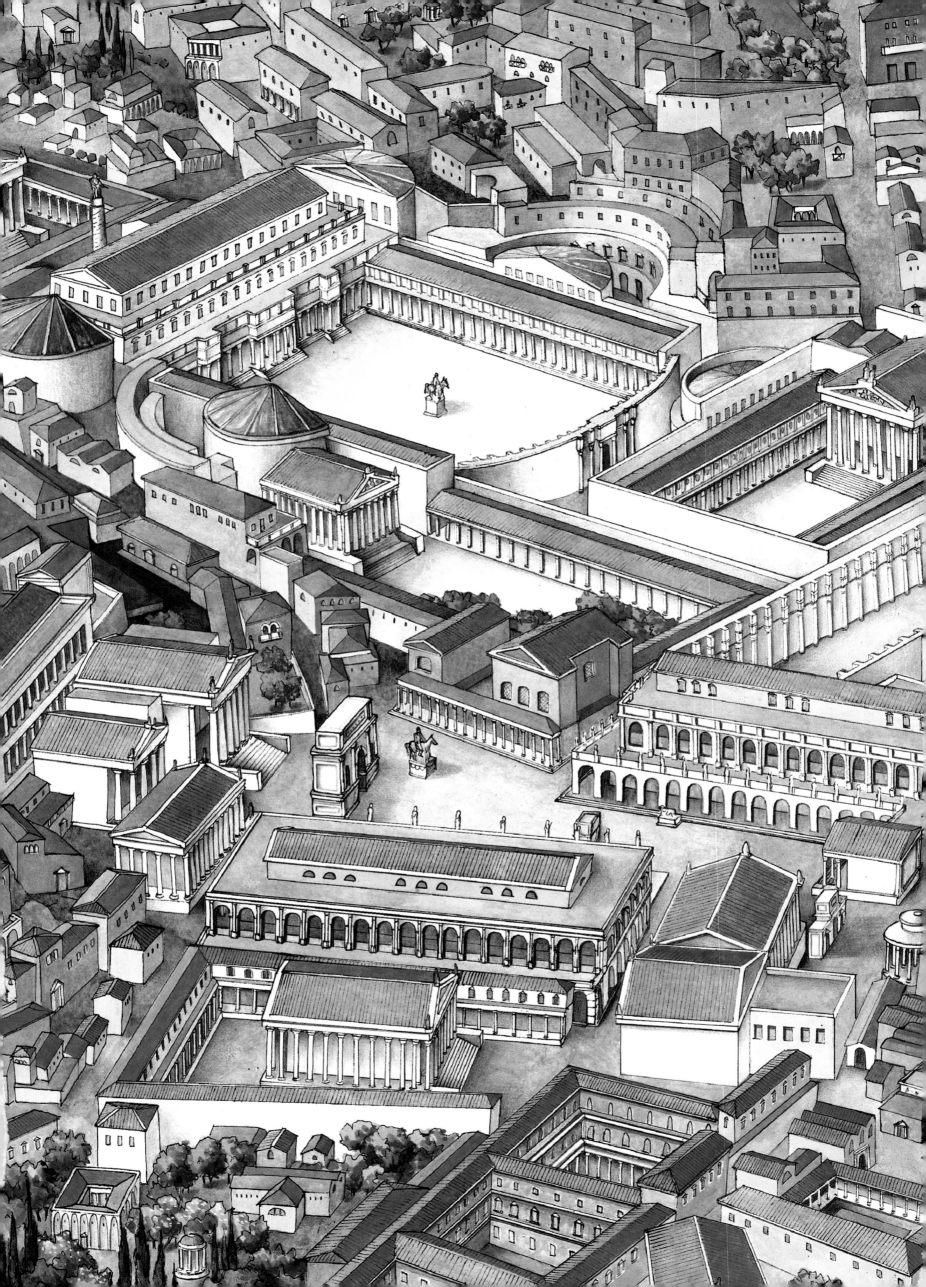

25 This clay head of the god Hermes, dating from the 6th century B.C., was part of a statuary group that ornamented a temple at Veii, a large Etruscan city hostile to Rome that was stormed and destroyed by M. Furius Camillus in 396 B.C. This work is also traditionally attributed to Vulca.

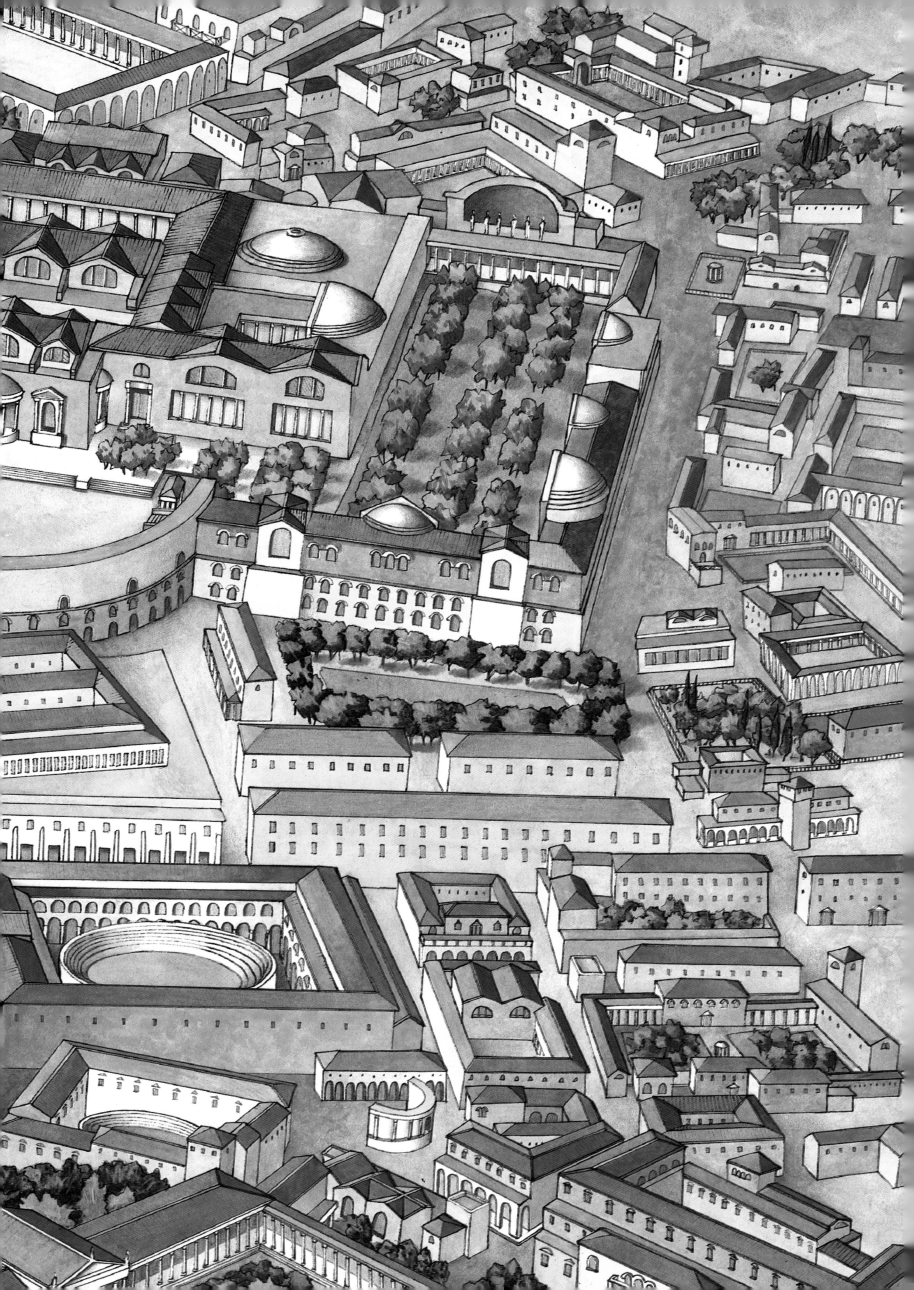

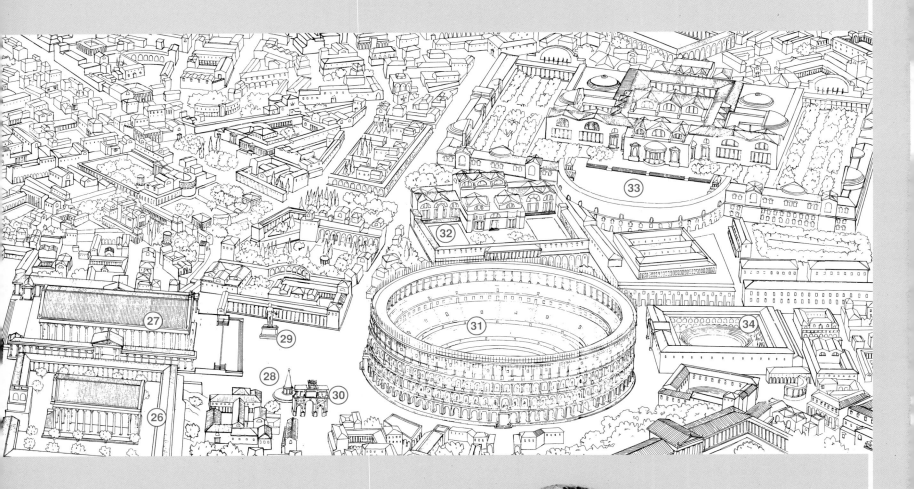

34 The deification of the city of Rome took place at quite a late date. It only acquired political and religious significance with the advent of Augustus and was later elevated to the highest honors of worship under Hadrian.
In iconographic terms, personifications of the goddess Rome usually emphasized her warlike nature, as in this relief, that decorates the base of the column of Antoninus Pius.

Augustus and the Julio-Claudian dynasty: 44 B.C.–A.D. 68

With the battle of Actium, fought between the armies of Octavian and those of Antony and Cleopatra, the battle for the succession to Caesar ended and the Imperial age began. Octavian, who received the title of Augustus from the Senate in 27 B.C., totally reorganized the political structures of the State and concentrated all the major powers in his own hands; he limited the role of the Senate, reorganized the provinces, strengthened the borders and boosted the economy. On his death in A.D. 14 he was succeeded by Tiberius, a good administrator and skilled diplomat. After the insane reign of Caligula, Claudius undertook the bureaucratic and financial reform of the State and the Romanization of the provinces. His successor, Nero, is infamous for his excesses and the burning of Rome.

Second Triumvirate (43 B.C.)

Battle of Actium (31 B.C.)

Octavian receives the title of Augustus (27 B.C.)

Death of Augustus (A.D. 14)

Reign of Tiberius (A.D. 14–37)

Crucifixion of Jesus Christ (A.D. 33)

Reign of Caligula (A.D. 37–41)

Reign of Claudius (A.D. 41–54)

Reign of Nero (A.D. 54–68)

The Flavian dynasty and the adopted emperors: A.D. 68–192

On the death of Nero a period of military anarchy began, during which the Emperors Galba, Otho and Vitellius reigned in succession. After Vespasian seized power, he conquered Judaea and reorganized the administration of the State. After the brief reign of Titus, Domitian consolidated the Roman conquests in Britannia and Germanys. By adopting Trajan, Nerva initiated the series of adopted emperors. Trajan's victorious military campaigns brought the Empire to the peak of its expansion. Hadrian renounced the expansionist policy of his predecessor and built Hadrian's Wall in Britannia. The reign of Antoninus Pius coincided with a long period of peace, while Marcus Aurelius had to put down a number of revolts in Africa, Spain and Britannia. With the accession of Commodus, a serious political crisis began.

Reign of Vespasian (A.D. 69–79)

Reign of Titus (A.D. 79–81)

Eruption of Vesuvius (A.D. 79)

Reign of Domitian (A.D. 81–96)

Reign of Trajan (A.D. 98–117)

Dacian Wars (A.D. 101–106)

Reign of Hadrian (A.D. 117–138)

Reign of Antoninus Pius (A.D. 138–161)

Reign of Marcus Aurelius (A.D. 161–180)

Reign of Commodus (A.D. 180–192)

The Severus dynasty and the period of anarchy: A.D. 193–284

After the short-lived reign of Pertinax, Septimius Severus became emperor with the support of his legions. He accentuated the policy of appointing Romanized provincials to government office, but this reform and the increase in military expenditure created discontent and weakened the economy. On his death, his despotic, bloodthirsty son Caracalla, became emperor. In order to rule he bought the favor of the army, thus further depleting the State coffers. In A.D. 212, with the Constitutio Antoniniana, he granted Roman citizenship to all free citizens of the Empire.
His assassin, Macrinus, only reigned for a short time. Heliogabalus introduced the worship of Eastern gods to Rome. The rule of the mild Alexander Severus was marked by wars against the Persians. In A.D. 235 a long period of military anarchy began; the title of emperor was disputed by numerous generals, while barbarians massed at the borders.

Reign of Septimius Severus (A.D. 193–211)

Reign of Caracalla (A.D. 211–217)

Enactment of the Constitutio Antoniniana (A.D. 212)

Reign of Macrinus (A.D. 217–218)

Reign of Heliogabalus (A.D. 218–222)

Reign of Alexander Severus (A.D. 222–235)

Period of anarchy and disorder (A.D. 235–284)

The Late Empire and the division of power: A.D. 284–337

In A.D. 284 the reign of Diocletian began. He initiated a series of reforms, culminating in the division of the Empire and the institution of the Tetrarchy. However, when he retired to Split, persuading Maximian (to whom he had entrusted the West) to abdicate too, the succession mechanism failed to work, and a struggle for power began.
The usurpers Constantine and Maxentius took to the field of battle (A.D. 312); the victor, Constantine, proclaimed freedom of worship for the Christians in the Edict of Milan. His agreement with Licinius, Augustus of the East, was short-lived. The rivalry between the two degenerated into civil war, and in A.D. 324 Constantine eliminated his rival and took the title of the sole Augustus. In A.D. 330 he proclaimed Constantinople the capital of the Empire. On his death, the Empire was divided between his sons.

Reign of Diocletian (A.D. 284–305)

Diocletian institutes the Tetrarchy (A.D. 293)

Collapse of the Tetrarchy (A.D. 306)

Battle of the Milvian Bridge (A.D. 312)

Edict of Milan (A.D. 313)

Constantine unifies East and West (A.D. 324)

Constantinople proclaimed capital (A.D. 330)

Death of Constantine; division of the Empire between Constantius II, Constantine and Constans (A.D. 337)

The decline and fall of the Empire in the West: A.D. 337–476

Constantius II, who long fought the Persians, was succeeded by Julian the Apostate, who attempted to restore paganism. Valens was killed at the battle of Hadrianopolis (A.D. 378) against the Goths. Theodosius reunited the Empire and allowed numerous barbarian communities to settle inside its borders as foederati (allies). In the Edict of Thessalonica (A.D. 380) he proclaimed Christianity to be the only state religion. On his death, the Empire was divided between his sons: Honorius took the West, and Arcadius the East.
The western capital was transferred to Ravenna (A.D. 402). Rome was sacked by the Goths in A.D. 410. Valentinian III reigned under the regency of his mother, Galla Placidia, but by this time, the unity of the Empire in the West was falling apart.
In A.D. 452 the Huns invaded Italy. The deposition of Romulus Augustulus (A.D. 476) marked the end of the Roman Empire in the West.

Constantius II reunites the Empire (A.D. 353–361)

Reign of Julian the Apostate (A.D. 361–363)

Valens defeated at Hadrianopolis (A.D. 378)

Reign of Theodosius (A.D. 379–395)

Alaric sacks Rome (A.D. 410)

Attila invades Italy (A.D. 452)

The Fall of the Roman Empire in the West (A.D. 476)

THE BATTLES BETWEEN PATRICIANS AND PLEBEIANS - ROME CONQUERS ITALY

This period was marked by a series of major internal and external conflicts. Internally, a struggle took place between the patricians, who had gained power by sending the king into exile, and the plebeians who, having lost the support of the monarchy, were becoming aware of their abilities and the methods they could use to assert themselves. In addition to the economic power based on their greater wealth, the patricians held political power through the Senate, the civil and religious magistratures and control of the law, which was handed down by oral tradition. The basic stages in the plebeians' campaign to participate in political life were the election of their own assembly and their own magistrates, the Tribunes of the Plebs; the appointment of the decemvirs to draft a code of written rather than arbitrary laws, called the Twelve Tables; the institution of comitia tributa open to the plebeians, which had a legislative function; and access to various magistratures. A series of laws also limited the power of the rich by aiding gradual elimination of the patricians' political/economic domination and the indiscriminate rise of the nobility that included the wealthier plebeian families.

The young republic was immediately forced to defend itself against its neighbors, and soon manifested an expansionist drive that overlapped with defensive wars and enabled it to dominate the entire peninsula in just over two centuries. The political and military rise of Rome took place in two stages: first in Latium, between the fall of the monarchy and the Gallic invasion (509–390 B.C.), and then in the entire peninsula, against the Etruscans and Gauls in the north, and the Sabellians, Umbrians, Campanian Samnites and Greek towns in the south. The fundamental stages in this historical process were the defeat of the Latins at Lake Regillus in 496 B.C., followed by gradual domination of the neighboring populations (the Aequi, Volsci and Hernici), the elimination of the Etruscan threat culminating with the destruction of Veii in 396 B.C., and finally the three Samnite wars which, between 343 and 290 B.C., led to the constitution of a Roman-Latin federal state and consequent rule over a huge territory containing numerous flourishing colonies. The conquest of the Samnites brought the Romans into contact with the Greek towns of the Ionian on which the nearby Hellenistic kingdom of Epirus had also set its sights. In 280 B.C. King Pyrrhus of Epirus landed in Italy with his army to support Tarentum and other minor towns. However, the Romans were equal to the challenge, and despite some setbacks eventually prevailed, forcing the enemy to return to their own country and the Greek towns to submit to the Roman alliance. By the second half of the 3rd century B.C., Rome had become the ruler of peninsular Italy, from the mouths of the Arno and the Rubicon in the north to the Strait of Messina in the south, and was pushing on towards the Mediterranean. During this period, the power struggle between patricians and plebeians and the transformation of Rome from a small city-state to the capital of a large confederation of populations radically modified the Roman state. The power base was theoretically held by the various people's assemblies, the comitia curiata, comitia centuriata, comitia tributa and the Council of the Plebs; in practice, however, the real power was exercised by the Senate, the assembly constituted by the members of the richest and most important families. Executive power was held by the magistrates: consuls, praetors, censors, aediles, quaestors and tribunes of the plebs.

36 The head of this Republican gold coin, minted in Rome, portrays Mars, lord of war, while the reverse shows the eagle. Mars was originally the god of spring and the harvest, and his transformation from tutelary deity of agriculture to war god graphically represents the development of the Roman people from a settled population of farmers to an expansionist race.

37 Lucius Junius Brutus was honored as the man who freed Rome from the tyranny of the Etruscan kings and initiated the Republic. This portrait, by an Italic bronze worker of the 4th century B.C., is traditionally attributed to him; in practice, as with all the alleged images of leading figures from the most ancient period of Roman history, this hypothesis is based solely on suppositious dates.

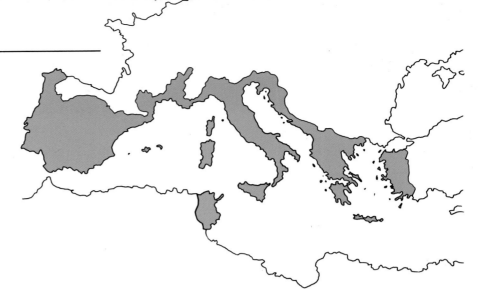

THE PUNIC WARS AND DOMINION OF THE MEDITERRANEAN

Having extended its rule to the Greek towns in Italy, Rome soon found that a radical transformation was needed to deal with changing economic and political conditions, which inevitably forced it to clash with the power that held sway over most of the Mediterranean – Carthage. By the beginning of the 3rd century B.C., that city dominated the African coast as far as Egypt and the Spanish coast of the Mediterranean; its dominions reached south along the Atlantic coast of Africa and north as far as Cornwall. The interests of Carthage mainly revolved around trade. Its trading interests were served by a great fleet, also equipped for military actions, which was ready to intervene as required. Sardinia, Corsica and Western Sicily were under Carthaginian control, but Carthage left the coasts of mainland Italy alone under the terms of treaties concluded first with the Etruscans and then with the Romans. The conflict between the two powers began in Sicily, the home of Greeks who had been rivals of the Carthaginians for centuries and were allied with their fellow citizens in southern Italy, now ruled by Rome. A direct clash with the Carthaginian empire was inevitable. The Punic Wars were fought over several decades, and the Romans gained the upper hand on land and sea. During the first war, the naval battle of Mylae in 260 B.C. was of great importance; together with the battle of the Aegates in 241 B.C., it enabled the Romans to conquer Sicily and later, Sardinia and Corsica. The Second Punic War was dominated by the genius of Carthaginian general Hannibal; the Roman armies achieved some victories but also suffered some resounding defeats, culminating in the bloody Battle of Cannae in 216 B.C. Only the intervention of the Scipio family,

specifically Publius Cornelius Scipio, decisively reversed the fortunes of the war in favor of Rome, which finally defeated Carthage at Zama in 202 B.C. The Roman victory established a new balance of power in the Mediterranean. In the Western sector, Rome replaced Carthage in the control of Spain, while the Eastern part remained dominated by the kingdoms of Macedonia, Syria and Egypt, which often fought one another. Greece was also divided between city-states and leagues of towns, which constituted a very unstable system of alliances. Rome could not remain indifferent to such an international situation that, though it presented cause for concern, also offered great opportunities for intervention and expansion. The Romans thus initiated a

series of diplomatic and military operations that, in just a few years (between 201 and 133 B.C.), made them the rulers of the entire Mediterranean. These included the Macedonian Wars, which culminated in 168 B.C. with the victory of Pydna, the destruction of Corinth in 146 B.C., and the siege of Numantia in 133 B.C.

Initially, Rome governed with a degree of tolerance for the independence and interests of the populations that came under its rule. However, after 168 B.C., it adopted an unscrupulous policy of direct annexation of territories in line with the capitalist interests of the dominant Roman groups, which involved the subjugation and destruction of possible competitors and intensive exploitation of the lands conquered.

38 War elephants, one of which is portrayed on this Campanian plate dating from the 3rd century B.C., were used for the first time against the Romans by Pyrrhus, King of Epirus. They were also used later by Hannibal, the Carthaginian general who invaded Italy after crossing the Alps during the Second Punic War.

39 Publius Cornelius Scipio, shown here in a portrait that emphasizes his strong character, was nicknamed "The African" after he defeated Hannibal at the Battle of Zama, south of Carthage, on 19 October 202 B.C.

THE REPUBLIC FACES A CRISIS: FROM THE GRACCHI TO THE FIRST TRIUMVIRATE

40 top This bronze statue by a Romanized Etruscan craftsman, dating from the 2nd or 1st century B.C., portrays a virile character in an oratorical pose, as can be deduced from his raised right arm. This gesture was common among Roman politicians, and we can imagine Tiberius Gracchus in the same attitude.

40 bottom The great orator and author Marcus Tullius Cicero became the champion of the senatorial oligarchy when he thwarted a conspiracy led by Catiline, who was supported by the lower classes. On Caesar's death he mistakenly supposed that he could defend the Republic against Antony, who had him killed.

The republic, which had been transformed in a short time from a small state to a great Mediterranean power, was unable to cope with the growing social inequality caused by its conquests. This soon caused a series of civil clashes that paved the way for a radical social and institutional transformation. In 133 B.C. Tiberius Gracchus, a tribune of the plebs, was assassinated together with many of his supporters following a violent reaction by the Senate. This episode marked the beginning of a serious crisis in Roman society. The provincials and Italics aspired to political power, and even the Roman citizens, especially the small landowners, forced into debt by an economic policy that ran contrary to their interests, were pressing for the extension of privileges that had so far only been granted to a few groups. Two personalities emerged during this difficult period: Marius and Sulla. Marius, an energetic man unconnected with the interests of the senatorial class, had been elected consul by the People's Party, while Sulla represented the conservatives (optimates).

Sulla was responsible for a reform of the state that took an authoritarian, conservative direction. This reform, which was imposed by force and ignored the serious social problems of the period, was destined not to last long after the death of its creator (in 78 B.C.). The subsequent period was one of extraordinary vitality for Roman society; major socio-political transformations took place and there was a great development of the economy, the arts and intellectual life. Sulla's constitution had represented the last attempt to organize the state on the basis of domination by the senatorial oligarchy. But the state could not survive without the

41 top Sulla, of ancient patrician origins, had already demonstrated his skills as a general when he was elected consul. In 87 B.C. he had to lead a Roman expedition against Mithridates, and in his absence, the People's Party maneuvered so as to bring him into conflict with Caius Marius. At the end of the war, after eliminating his opponents (partly with the use of the dreaded proscription lists), he reformed the constitution in the direction of oligarchy.

41 center Able general Gnaeus Pompey obtained major military appointments from Sulla, and achieved a series of outstanding victories against the supporters of the democratic party. On Sulla's death in 78 B.C., Pompey still defended his policies, fighting in Spain, but having reached an agreement with Licinius Crassus in 72 B.C., he became consul and undertook to abolish Sulla's constitution. He then set up the First Triumvirate with Crassus and Caesar, with whom he soon came into conflict.

representation of the other social forces—
the proletariat, the soldiers, the small
businessmen and the provincials—all
excluded from the exercise of power, to
which they could only obtain access by
joining the dominant class.

A different balance was thus required,
but it could only be achieved by creating
a new center of power to control the
Senate and guarantee that the new
emerging groups could participate in the
benefits of social life. Slowly but surely,
despite resistance from the senatorial
class which did not want to give up its
powerful status, all this was achieved,
partly by men who were appointed by the
Senate to protect its interests. But this
eventually created an external consensus,
often in conflict with the Senate.

The figure of Pompey is emblematic of
this difficult period. He was responsible
for the abolition of Sulla's constitution,
which allowed the traditional political
forces to take the field again.
Following some major foreign
policy appointments
obtained from the
Tribunes of the Plebs,
whose role had been
restored, Pompey
also made a major
contribution to
extending the
supremacy of Rome by
annexing new
territories. In 63 B.C. the
consul Cicero was the
leading representative of the
declining senatorial domination. An
attempt by Catiline to seize power was
defeated by the great orator with a
determination that has gone down in
history. However, this still did not
prevent the men who held the real power,
with the support of the People's Party
and their armies, from forming an
alliance against the Senate.

The First Triumvirate of Julius Caesar,
Crassus and Pompey was formed
whereby, with the formal consent of the
Senate, power was shared with the
support of the knights, the people and the
army. The immediate outcome of this
political move was the appointment of
Caesar as Proconsul of Gaul for five years.

*41 bottom Caius
Marius, who hailed
from a peasant family,
won major victories
against the Cimbrians
and Teutons and in the
political sphere aimed
at striking a balance
between the opposing
forces. He became a
symbol of the
democrats and found
himself in conflict with
Sulla (against whom he
triumphed for a short
period) in a tragic
climate of violence.
Marius's death in
86 B.C., shortly after
his election as consul,
left a clear field to
Sulla, who brutally
eliminated the
opposition and
initiated a reign of
terror.*

THE AGE OF CAESAR

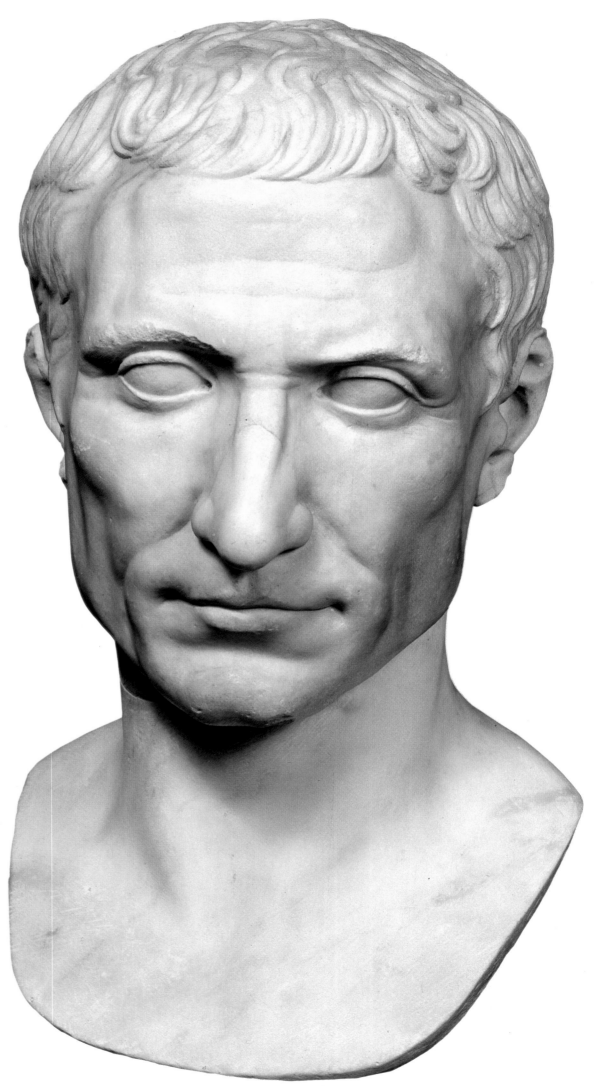

The conquest of Gaul constituted a major extension of Roman rule, and also the military base of Caesar's political power; he obtained a five-year extension of his appointment, following which he won some brilliant military victories, even leading his troops into Britannia and across the Rhine.

In the meantime, the conditions that would soon lead to civil war between the senatorial faction and the people's faction were worsening. After the death of Crassus in the Battle of Carrhae against the Parthians in 53 B.C. the Triumvirate was dissolved and conflict began between Caesar, whose strength lay in his victories and the support of the People's Party, and Pompey, allied with the senatorial party, whose leading representatives included Cicero and Cato. In 49 B.C. civil war broke out. The first act was the symbolic crossing of the Rubicon by Caesar, who marched on Rome with an army. The rapid victories obtained by Caesar in various Mediterranean theaters made him the unchallenged victor and enabled him to concentrate all power on himself, resulting in the demise of the senatorial class. However, he was assassinated on 15 March 44 B.C. by a group of conspirators led by Brutus and Cassius. The conspirators were endeavoring to terminate a historical process, but now that the ball was rolling, it could not be stopped merely by the physical elimination of one man, however outstanding. Caesar's heirs were his lieutenant Mark Antony and his nephew and adopted son Octavian, who had very different temperaments. Octavian, in particular, considered that the power of a single man should not be based on the Hellenistic type of monarchy, but supported by a wide consensus and

formal obedience to the Senate and the republican magistratures. The great orator Cicero made an anachronistic attempt to reestablish the authority of the Senate by declaring Antony an enemy of the state, but paid for it with his life. Octavian and Antony, together with Aemilius Lepidus (who was soon excluded), formed a Second Triumvirate. After defeating the conspirators at Philippi in 42 B.C., they divided the empire: Octavian took the west, and Antony the east. The time was now ripe for government by one man – the most able. Octavian won by defeating Antony at Actium in 31 B.C., and skillfully began the task of reconstructing the state.

42 Julius Caesar, born in 100 B.C., came from an ancient patrician family. He soon attracted the enmity of Sulla, but after the latter's death he embarked on an outstanding political and military career. In 60 B.C. he joined forces with Pompey and Crassus, and two years later began the Gallic campaign, which ended victoriously in 52 B.C. After the death of Crassus he came into conflict with Pompey, who died in the attempt to oppose him. He won the civil war at the battle of Munda, and was assassinated by conspirators in 44 B.C. after obtaining a lifetime dictatorship.

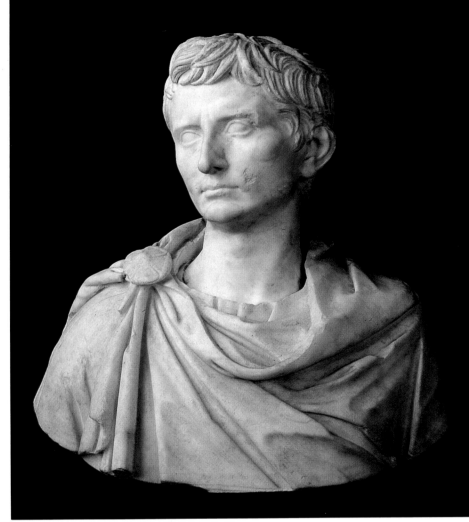

43 bottom After Caesar's death, Mark Antony consolidated his position as the dictator's political heir. He set up the Second Triumvirate with Lepidus and Octavian, and after defeating the conspirators, he obtained the East. In Egypt he fell in love with Cleopatra; he came into conflict with Octavian and committed suicide immediately after his defeat at the battle of Actium.

43 top Octavian, born in 63 B.C., was still very young when he found himself leading the forces that opposed Antony after Caesar's death. After the first conflict, he reached a short-lived agreement with his opponent in order to save Caesar's party. This marble bust shows the young Octavian at the time of the Battle of Actium.

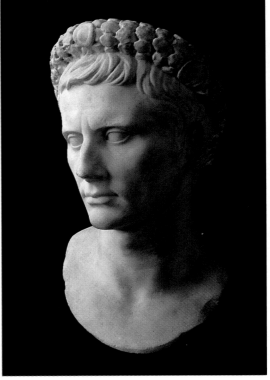

44 top After defeating Mark Antony in battle, Octavian returned to Rome, celebrated the victory and declared the period of the civil wars over. From that time on he worked to consolidate his personal power, moving the Roman state towards the status of an empire. The title of Augustus, taken from religious vocabulary and bestowed on him by the Senate in 27 B.C., remained the official title for all of the Roman emperors.

44 bottom This magnificent onyx cameo dating from the reign of Augustus portrays an eagle grasping the symbols of victory in its claws. The great bird of prey was considered the emblem of Imperial strength. The gold and silver frame dates from the second half of the 16th century.

45 In Rome alone, over 80 statues were erected in honor of Augustus, the most famous of which is the Prima Porta statue, named after the place of its discovery. The reliefs on the breastplate allegorically evoke his feats of arms; in particular, the central scene portrays a defeated barbarian delivering a Roman banner, probably lost in battle by another commander, into the hands of the emperor. Octavian's rise to power was facilitated by his influence over the army; his prestige was won on the battlefield, where he always demonstrated his gifts as a great strategist. By the time of his death in A.D. 14, the Roman empire was firmly consolidated.

Thanks to Octavian's skill, the transformation of the Roman state took place without bloodshed and led to an era of internal peace that facilitated the economic and cultural development of the entire empire. As Julius Caesar had already done, Octavian apparently maintained the functions of all the magistratures, but actually held all the reins of power by conferring a number of titles and functions on himself; the most important were the **potestas tribunicia**, *which gave him all the rights of the tribunes such as inviolability and the prestige of representing the people, and command of the army, called* **imperium**, *hence the title of* **imperator** *(emperor). He adopted the name of Augustus to symbolize his exceptional role. Augustus reorganized the senatorial and equestrian orders and divided the provinces into senatorial and imperial provinces. He set up a special corps of personal bodyguards called the Praetorian Guard, and undertook the maintenance and decoration of Rome, which had been neglected for years due to the civil wars. Apart from an unsuccessful attempt at invading Germany he limited his military activities to consolidating the borders, only intervening where pockets of resistance still existed.*

As the success of the complex political and administrative reorganization of the state required the maximum support from its citizens, instead of focusing on his

innovations Augustus emphasized the continuity of his political views with those of republican Rome, presenting himself as the restorer of traditional values. In this context he promoted the worship of specifically Roman divinities, and forgotten practices and ceremonies were revived. However, this did not prevent the dissemination of new religious sects in Rome, including Christianity, which was destined, in time, to change the face of the Empire and leave an indelible mark on Western civilization. Augustus's program of peace and restoration was widely supported, even by the intellectuals of the age. The universal peace offered by Augustus (celebrated by the altar of peace called the **Ara Pacis Augustae** *dedicated to him by the Senate in 13 B.C.) greatly appealed to them, and at the same time enhanced the civil and moral role that they felt to be their due. Some of the greatest Latin literature was written during this period: Virgil, Ovid, Horace, Propertius, Tibullus and historian Livy were its leading representatives. By the death of Augustus in A.D. 14, Rome had been transformed into an Empire, and the guidelines that were to support it in the centuries to come had already been laid down.*

THE JULIO-CLAUDIAN DYNASTY

The unknown factor in the newly adopted political system was constituted by the succession, because of the unusual position of the prince, who formally received his powers from the senate. This state of crisis was overcome by Augustus, who introduced a cleverly concealed system of dynastic succession that enabled four members of the Julio-Claudian family to rule the empire. Tiberius (A.D. 14–37) came to power on the designation of Augustus; Caligula (A.D. 37–41) on the proposal of the Prefect of the Praetorian Guard; Claudius (A.D. 41–64) was imposed by the Praetorian Guard; and Nero (A.D. 54–68) was proposed by Claudius's wife Agrippina, supported by the Praetorian Guard.

The positions of these early successors of Augustus were somewhat precarious. Caligula and Nero died as a result of conspiracies by the Praetorian Guard and Claudius is believed to have been poisoned. Nevertheless, the expansion of the Empire continued during this period with consolidation in the economic and social field and a particular expansion of agriculture, trade and commerce. The roads, built for commercial and military purposes, now formed a close-knit network covering the whole Empire, connecting the provinces with one another and with Rome. Under Claudius, not only did the organization of the imperial administration considerably improve, but a new province was added to the Empire—Britannia.

46 top In the "Gemma Augustea," an onyx cameo dating from the 1st century A.D., Tiberius is portrayed in triumph in the presence of Augustus and the personification of Rome. At the bottom, some Roman soldiers are hoisting aloft the spoils won from defeated enemies in front of a group of prisoners. Tiberius (A.D. 14–37) had already shown himself to be a brave commander before Augustus designated him as his successor.

46 bottom Nero (A.D. 54–68) became emperor as a result of intrigues by his mother, Agrippina, who did not hesitate to assassinate Claudius in order to achieve her purpose. He originally reigned with moderation, but soon indulged in every kind of excess. Encouraged by Tigellinus, prefect of the Praetorian Guard, he initiated a reign of terror and embarked on exorbitant spending that dealt a crippling blow to the economy of the state. After the Fire of Rome, a series of conspiracies and revolts against him began and he eventually found it prudent to commit suicide.

THE FLAVIAN DYNASTY

After Nero's death, the political situation once again become complex. During the year A.D. 69 the Empire was racked by military anarchy, which led to civil war. Three emperors, elected on each occasion by the legions stationed in various parts of the Empire, were assassinated in turn. Eventually, T. Flavius Vespasian (A.D. 69–89) prevailed, with the support of the Eastern and Danube legions, and his proclamation was ratified by the Senate. Vespasian thus founded the Flavian dynasty, and proved an excellent administrator, reorganizing the state treasuries and giving special priority to the provinces, improving the army, and strengthening the borders.

He was succeeded by his sons: first Titus (A.D. 79–81), then Domitian (A.D. 81–96). During the brief reign of Titus, which marked the beginning of the Jewish Diaspora, the Temple of Jerusalem was destroyed and the eruption of Vesuvius razed Pompeii, Stabia and Herculaneum to the ground.

Domitian attempted (like Caligula before him) to institute a true absolute monarchy. During this period the Senate finally lost its characteristics as a decision-making body, increasingly becoming an elite group from which the emperors obtained useful candidates for administrative office. Numerous members of the equestrian order who were natives of Italic municipalities, and even the provinces, were given high office. This policy, designed to introduce new blood into the Roman administration, was continued by subsequent emperors.

Some major new monuments were built in Rome under the Flavians, the most famous being the Coliseum. The borders were strengthened by some modest conquests and the Empire experienced a fairly quiet period. However, there was no lack of strong opponents to the policies of the Flavians, especially under Domitian; his attempt at self-deification was strongly opposed in cultural circles and by believers in Christianity, against which the emperor unleashed a ruthless persecution. In A.D. 96, Domitian was assassinated by conspirators.

47 top left Titus demonstrated his outstanding military abilities during the Judaic War conducted by his father Vespasian. He became Emperor in A.D. 79, but died only two years later, after strengthening the Roman hold on Britannia.

47 top right Domitian (A.D. 81–96), son of Vespasian and younger brother of Titus, was acclaimed Emperor although he had demonstrated little aptitude for command. His reign was characterized by an accentuated form of absolute rule.

47 bottom right On Nero's death, Vespasian (A.D. 69–79) was acclaimed emperor by his soldiers in Judaea. A man of great character, he energetically defended the borders of the Empire, undertook to replenish the state finances, reorganized the administration of the provinces, and above all, guaranteed the dynastic continuity of power.

47 bottom left This coin was minted by Vespasian in A.D. 70 to celebrate the conquest of Judaea (portrayed as a woman with bowed head) by his son Titus. With the fall of Jerusalem and the destruction of the Temple, commemorated on the triumphal arch erected in the Roman Forum, the second Jewish Diaspora began.

THE ADOPTED EMPERORS

48-49 The reign of Trajan (A.D. 98–117) was long remembered as a golden age; mining and farming activities were greatly expanded, and as a result of the security of the borders, trade flourished. Above all, after his conquests, the Roman Empire reached the peak of its expansion. He succeeded in conquering Dacia and occupying Ctesiphon, the capital of the Parthian Empire, which had been an enemy of Rome for centuries. Trajan also undertook extensive monumental building work in Rome, commissioning the construction of a new forum from architect Apollodorus of Damascus. A triumphal column was erected here to commemorate his victories over the Dacians. The shaft of Trajan's Column, which stands 100 feet tall, is decorated with a spiral frieze with reliefs illustrating the major episodes of the war. The scene reproduced here shows the emperor standing in front of the Roman fortifications as he addresses the troops and receives a delegation.

The 2nd century A.D. was characterized by a general situation of political stability, which led to the increase and expansion of manufacturing and commercial activities and to considerable development, including cultural development, throughout Imperial society. The emperors began to follow the adoptive rather than the dynastic system of succession; each emperor chose his successor from outside his family on the basis of the qualities of the person chosen. The fact that these emperors often came from the provinces (starting with Trajan, a native of Italica in Iberia) demonstrated that the provinces were now on a par with Italy, and constituted one of the reasons for the prosperity and unity of the Empire. The emperor who introduced the new system of succession was Nerva (A.D. 96–98), elected by the Senate when already elderly; he immediately adopted and brought into the government M. Ulpius Traianus (Trajan) (A.D. 98–117), a young consul who had proved to have outstanding political and military gifts. The conquest of Dacia and the defeat of the Parthians can be attributed to Trajan's ability as a general.

His successor, Hadrian (A.D. 117–138), preferred a policy of consolidation. Abandoning the lands beyond the Euphrates, he built a strong system of defensive fortifications along the borders of the Empire, including the famous Hadrian's Wall in Britannia, and devoted more attention to solving the administrative problems of the Empire and to its total Romanization. The policy of Antoninus Pius (A.D. 138–161) was inspired by that of his predecessor, and he built a new wall north of Hadrian's in Britannia. He was succeeded to the throne by Marcus Aurelius (A.D. 161–80), a valiant general

49 top Trajan, born in the part of Spain known as Baetica, succeeded Nerva. An able politician and strategist, he undertook the conquest of Dacia after strengthening the Rhine border. An excellent government and financial administrator, he was popular with all classes of society. He died during the campaign against the Parthians.

49 bottom Hadrian (A.D. 117–138), acclaimed emperor after Trajan's death, immediately made peace with the Parthians and pursued a policy designed to strengthen the borders of the Empire, renouncing the expansionism of his predecessors. An admirer of Greek civilization, he delighted in poetry and meditation.

and philosopher who was a disciple of Stoicism. He abandoned the adoptive principle of succession, and returned to the dynastic system. His decision turned out to be a serious mistake because his son Commodus (A.D. 180–192), who succeeded to the throne at an early age, interrupted the tradition of good government of the preceding emperors and was distinguished only by his ambition and cruelty. On the verge of the 3rd century A.D., one of the last periods of splendor of the Roman Empire came to an end.

Although highly complex, the imperial administration had reached a level of unparalleled efficiency. Grants of citizenship in the provinces had been intensified, the general economy was brought to an excellent level and

numerous measures in favor of the poorer classes were instituted, such as benefits for needy children and alms for the plebeians. At the same time, however, there was a growing spiritual restlessness among both the intellectuals and the masses, which led to a move away from political life and a search for inner happiness and salvation of the soul that could find no answer in the official state religion. This led to the spread of the philosophical schools of Stoicism and Cynicism among the educated classes, and the mystical cults of Isis, Serapis and Mithras, especially among the common people.

Christianity was also becoming more and more popular among all sections of society as it met both the needs of the humbler, more deprived classes and the restlessness of the more sensitive, reflective spirits. The political authorities were generally fairly tolerant of all forms of religion and thought, provided that they did not represent a threat to the established order (e.g., by questioning the official state religion). For this reason, despite the climate of tolerance, severe repression was instituted in A.D. 135 against the Jews, who used their monotheism as an ideological weapon against the Empire. Right from the start, the Christian religion appeared different from the others. As it was based on simple, easily understood rites and preached brotherly love between men, it immediately attracted followers from all walks of life. The authorities looked with increasing consternation at the propagation of a religion that considered itself to be the sole repository of truth and viewed membership of and loyalty to the Empire as subordinate to the word of God. The Biblical expression, "Render unto Caesar the things which are Caesar's, and unto God the things that are God's," clearly indicated that although Christians did not reject human laws, they blindly obeyed their faith. This was the real reason for the systematic persecutions conducted beginning in the 3rd century A.D.

50 top Marcus Aurelius (A.D. 161–180) kept the peace within the state and put down the revolts that broke out on the borders of the Empire. A decisive commander and a philosopher of Stoic and Epicurean inspiration, he is remembered as a very humane man. His equestrian statue in the Capitol (a detail of which is shown here) is the only one to have survived intact from the Roman era.

50 bottom Commodus (A.D. 180–192) became emperor at an early age on the death of his father, Marcus Aurelius, whose virtues he failed to inherit. His reign was tragically famous for acts of senseless cruelty and tyranny; an exhibitionist, he identified with Hercules and liked to be portrayed in that guise. Unpopular even with the aristocracy, he eventually fell victim to a conspiracy.

50-51 The base of the triumphal column in Rome dedicated to Antoninus Pius is magnificently decorated; one of the two splendid reliefs on the short sides portrays a parade of Roman soldiers and knights, with chiaroscuro effects. Antoninus Pius (A.D. 138–161), who succeeded Hadrian, was universally admired for his good rule. A decisive man and a capable

government administrator, he consolidated the domestic peace and at the same time firmly crushed uprisings in Africa and in Britannia, where he built a defensive wall to the north of Hadrian's Wall. He also reduced taxes and founded numerous charitable institutions. His long reign marked the height of stability of Rome's institutions and military power.

HADRIAN'S WALL

BRITANNIA

BATH

TRIER

GERMANYS

PARIS

GAUL

AUGST

SAINTES

ORANGE

VERONA

ITALY

NÎMES

AOSTA

ALCANTARA

SEGOVIA

OSTIA

ROME

IBERIAN PROVINCES

TARRAGONA

HADRIAN'S VILLA

MERIDA

CAGLIARI

HERCULANEUM

DOUGGA

SYRACUSE

VOLUBILIS

EL DJEM

AFRICAN PROVINCES

TIMGAD

SABRATHA

LEPCIS MAGNA

THE ROMAN EMPIRE
IN THE 2ND CENTURY A.D.
AT THE HEIGHT OF ITS
EXPANSION

BUDAPEST

PULA

SPLIT

ADAMKLISSI

DANUBE PROVINCES

POMPEII

CONSTANTINOPLE

ASIA MINOR

MILETUS

APHRODISIAS

ATHENS

EPHESUS

SARDIS

PALMYRA

GREECE

BAALBEK

ORIENTAL PROVINCES

CRETE

CAESAREA

JERASH

CYRENAICA

EGYPT

THE SEVERUS DYNASTY

54 In official portraits, Caracalla (A.D. 211–217) liked to be shown with a menacing expression, and his head slightly inclined towards one shoulder.

After the reign of Commodus and the five-year civil war that followed it, at the beginning of the 3rd century A.D. and in a departure from previous policies, the Empire was increasingly taking on a military bias as all authority was now held centrally by the emperor. The Senate was deprived of its legislative and judicial powers, to the advantage of the emperor's private counselors. In society, the forces of production were being organized into guilds and the state began to intervene widely in economic life. In A.D. 197 Septimius Severus, supported by the legions of Pannonia and Germany, became master of the Empire. Thus began the Severus dynasty, which ushered in a new era of prosperity. Septimius Severus (A.D.

197–211) defeated the Parthians, reconstituted the province of Mesopotamia, made the city of Palmyra (an important caravan junction in present-day Syria) into a colony, and generally strengthened the Empire's defenses. In Africa, the frontiers were pushed south to Mauretania and Tripolitania, where flourishing cities such as Sabratha, Oea and Leptis Magna were situated. The latter was the birthplace of the emperor who devoted particular attention to the city, embellishing it with magnificent buildings. Septimius Severus was succeeded by his son, M. Aurelius Antoninus, nicknamed Caracalla (A.D. 211-217). During his brief reign a decree of great civil importance (the

Constitutio Antoniniana) was issued, whereby Roman citizenship was granted to all free inhabitants of the Empire. Caracalla, who had already had his brother, Geta, murdered to avoid having to share the power inherited from their father, was assassinated, and Avitus Bassianus, better known as Heliogabalus (A.D. 217–222), was acclaimed Emperor in his place. His reign was short-lived, and the last descendent of the dynasty, Severus Alexander (A.D. 222–235), soon came to power. This emperor was not a total failure; however, as a result of increasing pressure by the barbarians, it became more and more difficult to defend the borders. This caused such disorder and unrest in the army, that he was assassinated.

THE MILITARY ANARCHY; FROM DIOCLETIAN TO CONSTANTINE.

In the years between A.D. 235 and 284, a profound institutional and social crisis took place. The economy was almost paralyzed and monetary devaluation reached intolerable levels. The border areas came under increasing pressure from numerous barbarian populations. The army, having almost entirely deprived the Senate of its power, became the de facto rulers of the Empire. Among the numerous emperors who ruled during this period were M. Junius Philippus (A.D. 244–249), who celebrated the millennium anniversary of the foundation of Rome with great pomp; Decius, responsible for the first great persecution of the Christians in A.D. 250; Valerian (A.D. 253–260), taken prisoner by the Parthians, and his son, Gallienus (A.D. 260–268) who, like his father, fought to defend the borders; and, finally, Aurelian (A.D. 270–275), who regained and destroyed Palmyra (guilty of rebelling against Rome and creating a powerful independent kingdom) and surrounded Rome with a ring of strong walls. But no sooner had the unity of the Empire been restored than Aurelian was assassinated by a military conspiracy. After other short-lived reigns, the troops of the East proclaimed Diocletian emperor in A.D. 284; he became sole master of the Empire, and put an end to the anarchy. Diocletian (A.D. 284–305) initiated a series of reforms that ensured the Empire's survival for another century. The continual pressure of the barbarians on the borders led Diocletian to consider defense as a priority. First of all, he decided that the emperor should no longer live in Rome, but as close as possible to the border; secondly, he considered that one person was no longer enough to deal with all the complex political problems. He thus instituted the Tetrarchy, a system of government whereby power was shared between two Augustuses aided by two

Caesars, who would later come to power and appoint two Caesars to replace them. Jurisdiction was divided on a territorial basis. The aim was to prevent the disintegration caused by the gradual diversification of problems in the various areas of the Empire. The benefits of the Tetrarchy were felt immediately; the defense of the borders became easier and more effective, and various attempts at rebellion were stifled at birth. In practice, however, this situation already heralded the division of the Empire into East and West. The succession system proved excessively complicated and did not work when Diocletian retired to private life in A.D. 305 and persuaded his colleague Maximian to do the same. The two Caesars, Galerius and Constantius, came to power and a fierce battle arose between the two aspiring Caesars excluded from that office, Maxentius and Constantine. Constantine, who declared that the Christian god was on his side, confronted Maxentius in Italy. This was a turning point in the history of both the Empire and Christianity, which had suffered greatly from the persecutions ordered by Valerian and Diocletian.

Maxentius's troops were defeated in A.D. 312 in an epic battle at the gates of Rome near the Milvian Bridge, and Constantine proclaimed his devotion to the cross, the symbol of Christianity. This was undoubtedly a political gesture, which allowed the victor to pursue the unity of the Empire with the support of the new religion. The next year, Constantine and Licinius, the legitimate Augustus of the East, shared

power. However, Constantine defeated his colleague in A.D. 324 and reunited the Empire. His political action, which proved to have far-reaching consequences, in many respects followed the route initiated by Diocletian. Constantine passed some laws of major

importance. The Edict of Milan, promulgated in A.D. 313, forever put an end to the tragic persecutions of the Christians and gave full freedom to the Church, now considered an element of unity of the Empire. In A.D. 330 the capital was transferred from Rome to Byzantium, renamed Constantinople, in the knowledge that the seat of power should be close to the threatened borders. In practice, however, this act led to the decline of the western part of the Empire.

Finally, wishing the Church to maintain its unity, Constantine (who was not only the emperor but also effectively head of the Christian Church) presided over the Ecumenical Council of Nicea in A.D. 325. This council produced the Nicene Creed, which was to heal the split between Catholics and Arians, thus reuniting the Christian world.

THE LATE EMPIRE

The move to the East of the capital of the Empire marked the beginning of the historical period called the Late Empire. At this political stage the decadence of the western world was evident, although Rome still maintained its dignity and it was a flourishing period for architecture. The Eastern and Western parts of the Empire were by now two different worlds, with little communication between them, while on the edges of the Empire there was increasing pressure from barbarian populations that confronted an ever-weakening army. On Constantine's death the Empire was again divided between squabbling heirs, then reunited in A.D. 353 under Constantius. In A.D. 361, Julian was proclaimed emperor by the troops in Gaul. Julian, nicknamed the Apostate by the Christians, pursued his aim of restoring the greatness of the Empire by means of a return to the ancient cultural values of paganism. He died fighting the Parthians in A.D. 363 while trying to conquer the East, following in the footsteps of Alexander the Great. Thus ended his hopeless attempt to restore the greatness of Constantine's dynasty. In A.D. 364 the Empire was divided between Valentinian and Valens, who defended it bravely until the disastrous defeat of Adrianople in A.D. 378, in which Valens died. After this defeat the Goths invaded the Balkans, from which they never withdrew. Under Valentinian, the western capital of the Empire, the Gaul city of Trier (Trèves), reached its greatest splendor. In A.D. 375 Valentinian was succeeded in the West by his son Gratian, who called on a man of great value, Theodosius, to replace Valens in the Eastern part of the Empire. Under this emperor the last great move towards the Church took place, when Catholicism was declared the State religion. The Empire was reunited for a short period under Theodosius; he died in A.D. 394, leaving as heirs his sons Honorius for the West and Arcadius for the East. Thereafter, however, the two Empires moved rapidly towards separate destinies.

DECLINE AND FALL OF THE WESTERN EMPIRE

The emperor of the West had a hard time governing his realms. In practice, power was held by the military leaders, often barbarians, and the large landowners; the Church asserted its political power, the economy was undergoing a serious recession and there was a sharp decline in the population. Under these circumstances, invasion by the barbarian populations became increasingly easy, and as the Empire disintegrated, the emperor's sovereignty became effectively limited to Italy alone. In the East, however, the emperor had no difficulty in ruling; among other things he could rely on an efficient bureaucracy, more controllable military commanders and a Church that submitted to the Imperial will. The economy and trade were flourishing and, save for rare exceptions, the barbarians were unable to make lasting breaches in the unity of the Empire. The separation from the West was emphasized when Greek became the official language in A.D. 440 and Latin disappeared from the administration. In the West, the barbarian general

Stilicho, loyal to Honorius, strenuously defended Italy against the barbarian hordes. However, after his death the Visigoths under Alaric attacked and sacked Rome in A.D. 410, to the horror of the entire civilized world.
Barbarian kingdoms were now forming on Roman soil, and though they declared themselves subjects of the emperor, in practice they did not recognize his authority. Roman general Aetius was the last bulwark against the mounting tide of barbarians. He reunited the inhabitants of the Empire, old and new, in the campaign against Attila and the Huns, who were beaten in the epic Battle of Châlons in A.D. 451. Just a few years later, however, Genseric's Vandals again sacked Rome. This event, together with the death of Emperor Valentinian III, in practice marked the end of the Roman Empire in the West. Formally, its demise is dated at A.D. 476, when the barbarian Odoacer, chief of the Heruli, deposed the last emperor, Romulus Augustulus, seized power and sent the Imperial insignia to the Eastern emperor.

56-57 Theodosius (A.D 379–395), Augustus of the East from A.D. 379, reunited the Empire, but only for a short period. His policy of religious intransigence, which culminated in A.D. 392 with a ban on private worship of the pagan gods, led to an uprising in the West, which was still attached to the traditional deities. Although Theodosius won the day, he was forced just before his death to divide the Empire again between his sons Arcadius and Honorius.
This picture reproduces one of the four great reliefs decorating the base of the obelisk erected by Theodosius in the Constantinople Hippodrome, which depict the Imperial family and some court dignitaries watching the games. The rigidly frontal composition and static poses herald the basic characteristics of Byzantine art.

ASPECTS OF THE ROMAN CIVILIZATION

58 Women were not usually allowed to act at the theater; masks with women's features were therefore worn by male actors when the action required the appearance of female characters. Designs similar to this Pompeiian mosaic decoration also appear on ivory or stone theater "tickets" found in numerous archaeological excavations.

58-59 This famous mosaic, discovered in Rome, portrays a circus charioteer with his steed. His head is covered by a kind of rigid leather helmet, and his chest is protected by interwoven leather strips. The Romans were so fond of circus contests that these events became an integral part of society during the Empire.

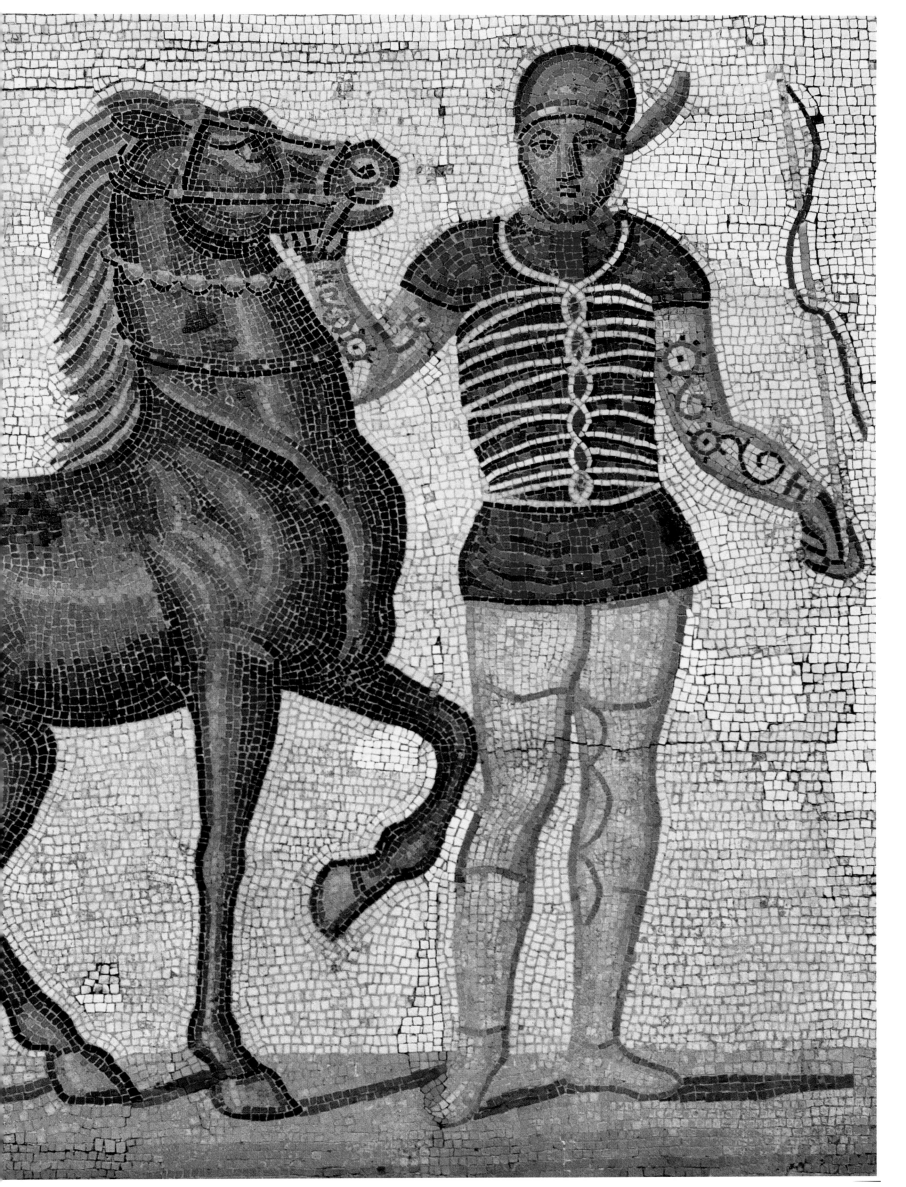

EVERYDAY LIFE IN ROME

We know that at the time of Cicero, Rome looked as though it was hanging in the air because of its superimposed buildings. Under Augustus the city was built even higher and, as Vitruvius wrote, "The majesty of the Urbs and the considerable growth of its population necessitated an exceptional extension of its homes. The result of this situation was that a remedy was sought in the height of the buildings."

The government occasionally intervened in the tricky subject of town planning, but usually with poor results. Augustus himself, though he boasted that he had found a city of brick and left a city of marble, was unable to solve the general situation of overcrowding, unhealthiness and congestion in the lower-class districts. Fire and collapse were the most common disasters. The addition of upper stories allowed many people to crowd into a small space, but they were built of wooden materials supporting light

60 top left This marble relief dating from the 1st century B.C., found in the area of Lake Fucino, shows a Roman town surrounded by walls; note that the insulae appear to be arranged in a strictly perpendicular layout. Roman surveyors used quite advanced technical instruments for town planning purposes.

60 bottom left. Traffic in Roman towns was very busy. Four-wheeled passenger coaches (raedae) similar to the one illustrated in this bas-relief jostled with the much heavier four-wheeled goods carts (sarraca) and the only slightly smaller carts with two solid wheels (plaustra) used mainly by farmers to take their produce to market.
A kind of light raeda was used for the cursus publicus velox, *the rapid state-run transport service. The most suitable vehicle for long journeys was the* carruca dormitoria, *in which passengers could sleep under cover.*

masonry; they were thus very quick to build, extremely cheap and highly profitable, but proved very fragile and easily caught fire.

Paradoxically, the person responsible for limiting this catastrophic state of affairs and partly renovating the appearance of the city was Nero.

The terrible fire of A.D. 64, which destroyed three Augustan regions and seriously damaged many others, led to the passing of regulations that prohibited unauthorized and makeshift constructions. The height of private properties had to equal twice the width of the street; porticoes were built, wooden ceilings were prohibited, and the separation of buildings from one another was made compulsory.

In the Imperial age Rome became a true metropolis of the ancient world. However, despite the magnificent setting provided by its monuments, the city was chaotic and spread out like tentacles. As no real town plan had ever been introduced, its inhabitants were crowded into the small space left over by the Imperial palaces, markets, gardens and numerous public buildings.

In the 4th century A.D. the city contained some 44,000 tenement blocks (insulae) and 1,800 houses (domus). The population amounted to almost a million inhabitants, not counting slaves and the huge, variegated, cosmopolitan mass of immigrants of every kind and color. All of these people huddled inside the city walls in the most amazing muddle and the untidy layout of the town was accentuated by a rather poor road network. There were no rigid territorial divisions between the various districts of the city; uncomfortable, fragile buildings connected by narrow, dark alleys, often coexisted with splendid noblemen's mansions.

Only a few fortunate citizens lived in comfortable houses. The majority of the population lived in small domus and above all in large rented apartments of varying degrees of decency; those into which the plebs crowded were barely fit for human habitation. There were attics, inhabited not only by slaves but also by ordinary people, cellars, in one of which a poet friend of Martial's lived, rooms under staircases and shops with garrets used as dwellings for the humbler people. The large number of shops (tabernae) made the city look like a huge bazaar. Its lively appearance was accentuated by the presence of numerous peddlers who mingled with the crowd looking for potential customers. All sorts of things were sold in the tabernae, from foodstuffs, fabrics and crockery to jewelry and books. There were also premises used for other businesses, such as laundries, purple-cloth dyeing, tanneries, bakeries, blacksmithing, shoemaking, pottery-making, carpentry, glaziery and stone-dressing. The tabernae argentariae

60-61 This relief shows a view of the monuments of ancient Rome.
Although the splendor of its buildings made it a unique metropolis, Rome faced many of the problems that have become common nowadays. In order to cope with the enormous traffic problems, for example, carts were not allowed on the streets during the day, with the sole exception of those transporting refuse or building materials for public works. It thus became necessary to provide large parking areas for vehicles and horses (areae carruces), and vehicle park attendants were employed. Refuse disposal and road cleaning posed considerable problems for the city's administrators and fire prevention was also a difficult task. It was handled by a corps of vigiles organized along military lines who were equipped with ladders, buckets, fireproof blankets and pumps that could be connected to the public fountains.

62 top This relief shows a butcher's tools. Trade in ancient Rome was structured in accordance with very similar methods and conventions to those of the present day; there were wholesalers, retailers and even salesmen who traveled all year round to sell and advertise the goods of the major firms.

62 bottom left This relief illustrates the interior of a butcher's shop, with great attention to detail. Note the steelyard behind the shopkeeper, the various cuts of hung meat and the basin to catch the blood. Eating meat, especially lamb and pork, became more frequent among the Romans during the 2nd century B.C.

62 bottom right This relief, dating from the 1st century A.D., shows a knife-maker's shop. The first tradesmen's guilds, which played an important part in the development and management of the Roman economy, were founded in the Royal age. There were already over 150 of them in the time of Augustus, when they were subjected to government regulation and required to hold Imperial authorization.

were "banks," which mainly dealt in currency exchange. The business of all these traders was mainly conducted outdoors and their stalls obstructed the streets and porticoes, increasing the traffic problem.

There was also a busy traffic of litters, sedan chairs and vehicles of all kinds, as well as flocks of sheep and herds of cattle. By night the streets were dark and dangerous, as there was no public street lighting except for the central area, and anyone obliged to venture out had to go in groups, or at least be preceded by slaves bearing torches or lanterns. Life was mainly carried on outdoors and there was a continual hum of noise both by day and by night when carts carrying heavy goods and materials were allowed to circulate freely in the city streets which were finally empty.

There was an incessant babble of voices and, as Martial wrote: "The schoolmasters won't leave you in peace in the morning or the bakers by night, and at all hours of the day the coppersmiths are beating with their hammers. Here, there's a moneychanger who, having nothing else to do, overturns a pile of coins on his filthy table; over there is a workman with a gleaming hammer beating gold ore from Spain, already smashed into pieces, while the fanatical rabble of initiates of the cult of Bellona never ceases to bawl. The shipwrecked sailor, all bandaged up, will insist on repeating his story, the little Jew, trained by his mother, will insist on whining for alms, the rheumy-eyed match-seller will insist on barking his wares…and who can tell how many hands beat copper receptacles in the city when, during an eclipse of the moon, spells are cast and magic rites practised?"

Despite this apparently gloomy picture that evokes striking contrasts, in many respects Rome and Roman towns in general gave their inhabitants a quality of life that was unimaginable thereafter,

63 top Roman doctors were able to diagnose numerous illnesses, performed surgical operations, gave dental treatment and prescribed medicines. This relief shows the interior of a pharmacy.

at least until the end of the Age of Enlightenment. A good example is provided by the complex problem of the water supply. It has been calculated that between the 3rd and 4th centuries A.D. the city of Rome, supplied by 11 aqueducts, was provided with over three million cubic feet of water a day to meet the needs of a population of around

63 center Fabric merchants display their goods to customers. Note the three fringed cushions hanging from the ceiling in the left-hand relief.
The Romans were always very fond of these luxury items, preferably brightly colored, which played quite an important part in home furnishings.

63 bottom This marble bas-relief shows an argentarius (banker) in his office. The tabernae argentariae were the equivalent of the modern banks; the operations performed included deposits, loans subject to payment of interest, investments in production operations and exchange of foreign currency. Each operation was recorded in books of account.

a million. This capacity allowed per capita daily consumption twice as high as at the present day. However, the baths, fountains and other public installations absorbed a high percentage of the total supply. Rome, at the height of its glory, boasted 11 large thermae, 856 public baths, 15 nymphaea, (a sort of monumental fountains), two naumachiae, (the places where battles between war vessels were held) and 1,352 fountains and basins. The amount of water used every day in Pompeii was also high; only the houses of the less well-off citizens were not connected to the town water supply, but numerous fountains, usually situated at crossroads, provided for their needs. Finally, in most towns, waste water was efficiently removed by complex sewage systems.

DWELLINGS
AND FURNISHINGS

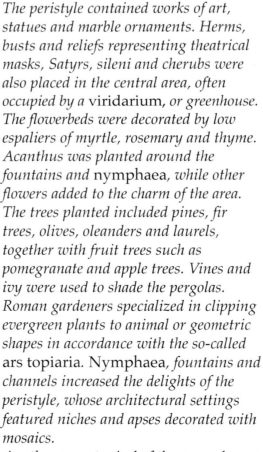

A great deal of time separated the prehistoric huts of Latium from the complex, well-organized homes of Pompeii, during which the primitive layout was transformed into that of the well-known Roman type. The oldest layout of the Roman house can be traced to the Etruscan-Italic environment and the older types of Pompeiian homes, such as the Surgeon's House. This consisted of an entrance (fauces) leading to the central courtyard (atrium), which was equipped with an impluvium, the tank used to collect rainwater. The cubicula, or small rooms, were situated along the parallel sides of the atrium and on the third side, opposite the main entrance, was the tablinum (dining room). Nearby were the minor rooms (alae). The tablinum led through a corridor to the garden (hortus). This layout obviously varied, but was found in the homes of the Etruscans, Romans and Campanians, at least until the end of the 3rd century B.C. In the 2nd century B.C., this model changed to the Greek-Roman type, with the result that houses became larger and more luxurious. One of the most characteristic examples of these residences is Pansa's House in Pompeii; in addition to the traditional Roman layout, a second one was added, whereby the existing rooms were extended to increase the size and potential use of the house. This is an example of the "peristyle house," so called because its specific feature is a large garden surrounded by a colonnaded portico. This type of house, mainly found in Pompeii, reached the height of its popularity during the later Republican age; such houses sometimes featured double peristyles, bathrooms, libraries, cryptoporticuses (porches or galleries), triclinia and other rooms whose names revealed their Greek origin.

The peristyle contained works of art, statues and marble ornaments. Herms, busts and reliefs representing theatrical masks, Satyrs, sileni and cherubs were also placed in the central area, often occupied by a viridarium, or greenhouse. The flowerbeds were decorated by low espaliers of myrtle, rosemary and thyme. Acanthus was planted around the fountains and nymphaea, while other flowers added to the charm of the area. The trees planted included pines, fir trees, olives, oleanders and laurels, together with fruit trees such as pomegranate and apple trees. Vines and ivy were used to shade the pergolas. Roman gardeners specialized in clipping evergreen plants to animal or geometric shapes in accordance with the so-called ars topiaria. Nymphaea, fountains and channels increased the delights of the peristyle, whose architectural settings featured niches and apses decorated with mosaics.
Another room typical of these new homes was the triclinium. Situated near the

peristyle, it was used only as a dining room, and came into use when the practice of eating in a reclining position was introduced in Rome. The triclinia of the Pompeiian domus only give a rough idea of those to be found in the mansions of Rome, which could seat a multitude of guests. There were also many open-air triclinia with attractive water effects situated in the garden, under the pergola, for use in the warm weather.
The true Roman home, however, was not the rich domus but the insula, the large, intensively occupied tenement block. These were built of masonry with a brick curtain wall; there were often shops on the ground floor, and the most comfortable, luxurious apartments were situated near the inner courtyard. On the upper stories were the other dwellings, whose structure became less and less stable towards the top.
The insulae of Rome have nearly all disappeared, but many specimens still exist in Ostia, like the House of the Charioteers, the House of the Serapis and

64 This relief shows two servants performing household tasks. Roman society was rigidly divided into freemen and slaves (prisoners of war, debtors and offenders whose crimes involved loss of liberty), whose masters had the right of life and death over them. They were sold in slave markets and used for a wide variety of tasks (from farm-work to teaching mathematics), depending on their abilities; some fetched exorbitant prices. Sometimes, for special merits, slaves were granted the status of freemen; many freemen were able to accumulate large fortunes as a result of their skills, and bought other slaves in turn.

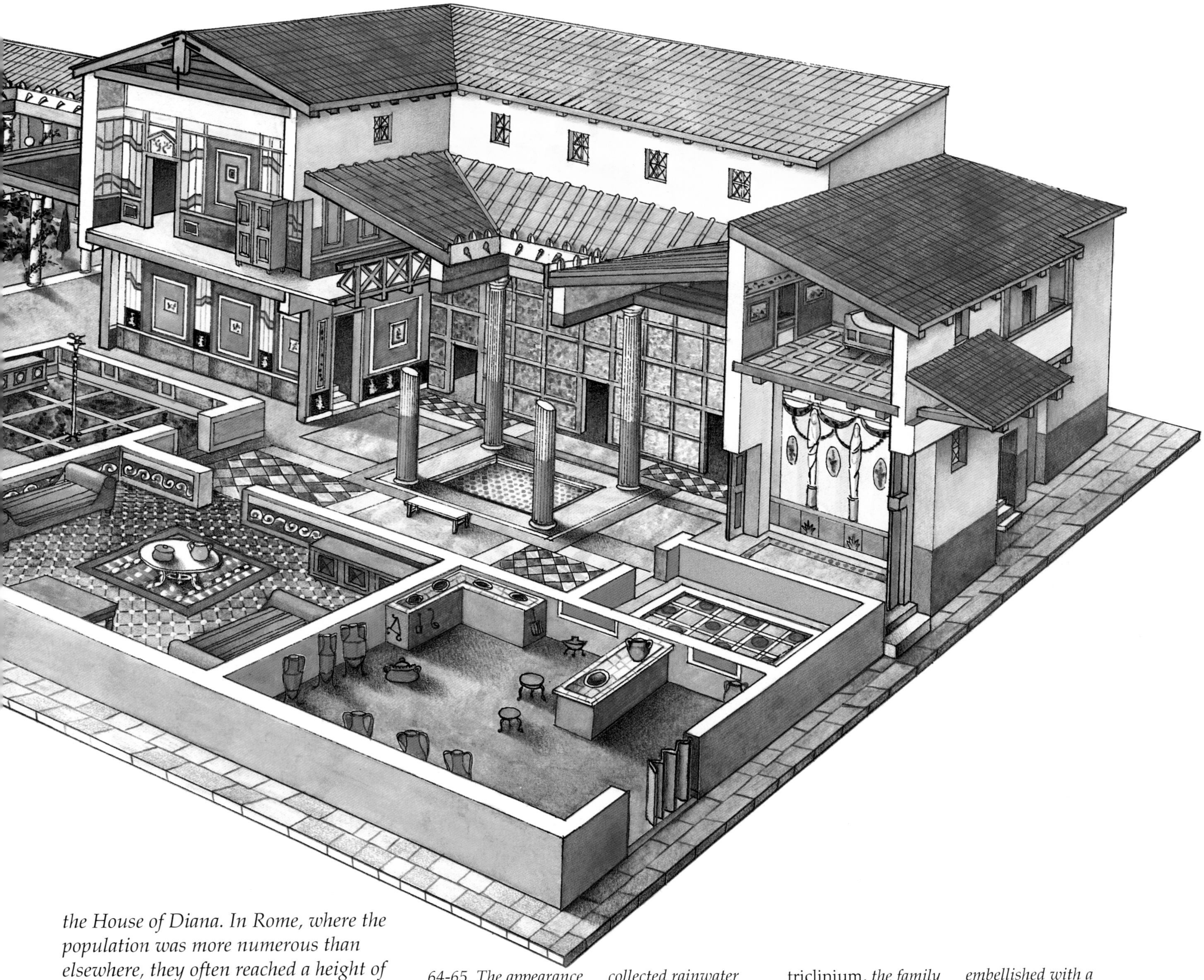

the House of Diana. In Rome, where the population was more numerous than elsewhere, they often reached a height of 100 feet. Rents were very high, often impossibly so in Rome, where they amounted to four times the rates paid in other towns. Rent amnesty often had to be granted to the poorer citizens. The greed of the owners often forced tenants to sublet their homes. Property speculation was rife, and some buyers of these buildings deliberately caused collapses and started fires.

64-65 The appearance of a typical Pompeiian domus is reconstructed in this explanatory drawing. The door opened onto a passageway (fauces), which led to an unroofed courtyard (atrium), partly shown here without plaster to reveal the structure of the masonry. In the center was a basin (impluvium), which collected rainwater and conveyed it to a cistern below. The atrium was surrounded by bedrooms (cubicula); at the end there were sometimes two open rooms, the alae, used for various purposes. The room situated in front of the entrance was the tablinum, where the owner received guests; next to it was the triclinium, the family dining room.
The kitchen, near which the toilet was generally located, was a small room overlooking the atrium. The upstairs rooms were used for various purposes (study, library) and as servants' quarters. At the rear was the peristylium, a garden surrounded by porticoes, often embellished with a fountain.
One of the rooms overlooking the main road was often used as a shop.
Unlike modern homes, the Roman domus was almost entirely inward-facing; light and air entered through the atrium and peristyle, and there were very few windows in the walls on the street side.

There were also other discomforts to put up with in the insulae. In the apartments of the poorer people who lived on the upper floors there were few essential services. As the remains of these buildings go no further than the second floor, we have no archaeological evidence of the presence of running water; in any event, there were financial difficulties involved in using the city water supply. Toilets were equally reduced to the bare minimum and dangerous braziers had to be used for heating. The common people

66 Especially after the conquest of the Hellenistic kingdoms, from which luxury goods continually arrived, Rome went through a period of great elegance. This was reflected in the furniture, numerous specimens of which have survived almost intact. These three pictures show a magnificent bronze bed dating from the late 1st century B.C., found at Amiterno in Abruzzo. The wooden parts have been entirely reconstructed.

did not cook much at home; most people ate in the streets at no particular time, as in many Asian countries today. Hawkers offered roasted meats, sausages, fried fish, olives and sweetmeats. There were also the inns. The ones in Ostia were famous; in addition to a food counter, they had sunken pitchers for food storage, an oven, fireplaces and braziers. These places, also called popinae, had a bad reputation as they were frequented by people of all kinds and gambling was common.

The culinary habits of the rich, who enjoyed organizing magnificent banquets, must have been very different: the main dish was usually based on meat; its cooking was nearly always elaborate, requiring complicated stuffings and strong flavorings.

While it may seem odd that only a small space was devoted to the kitchen in Roman homes, it is even more surprising that furnishings in general were few and far between. Numerous niches and built-in cupboards were hollowed out in the walls to hold objects and household

goods. Beds and tables were often made of masonry. In the insulae, because of the small amount of space available, there was little more than a pallet, a table and a few chairs. In the domus, near the entrance, in the atrium or near the kitchen of the domus was the lararium, the shrine dedicated to the Lares (the household gods who protected the family). Food and libations were placed in front of their images. Next to them were kept the imagines maiorum, wax portraits representing the ancestors. The most characteristic items of furniture in the dining rooms of wealthy homes were the triclinium couches, usually arranged in a horseshoe shape. There was room for three people on each couch, the most attractive specimens of which were made of high-quality wood with bronze ornaments. The turned legs and headrests (fulcra) were also made of bronze. The food was placed on a round three-legged table. An abacus (a sideboard of Etruscan origin) was used to display the best crockery.

There were numerous varieties of tables and chairs. The former were distinguished by the number of legs and the elegance of the top. Particularly exquisite were the monopodia, single-legged and made of highly prized types of wood such as cedar and Mauritanian maple, which were introduced after the conquest of Asia Minor. The different types of chairs included the solium, used by the paterfamilias, and the cathedra, the typical woman's chair, with no arms and a high, curved back. Cupboards and chests containing a variety of objects completed the furniture of the home. The furnishings included candlesticks of different shapes and sizes, carpets and curtains. Mosaics and paintings were also very important in the wealthier homes. The latter, in particular, embellished the rooms, using clever perspective effects to expand the space. The wealthier citizens might collect statues, objets d'art and sometimes rare books.

67 top The wealthier families owned entire dinner services made of finely worked silver, comprising jugs, plates, drinking horns and cutlery; the less wealthy used bronze or pottery articles.

67 center The Romans called everything used to furnish the home (from crockery to wall frescoes) suppellex. Glassware was very popular and its manufacture reached levels of true perfection.

67 bottom Braziers of various shapes and sizes were used to heat the rooms of the home. The one illustrated, with legs shaped like young Satyrs, was found in Herculaneum, and is of a particularly elegant design. The ithyphallic representation, which was by no means considered vulgar, had an auspicious and apotropaic function in Roman times. That is why painted or carved phalluses intended to ward off the evil eye appear on the walls of many homes in Pompeii.

LEISURE PURSUITS

68 In the bath complexes, the women entered the palaestra *and bathed wearing a brassiere (fascia pectoralis)* and briefs (subligar), *similar to the modern bikini. In this detail of the famous mosaic decorating the* Ten Girls Room *in the Piazza Armerina villa, two young women are engaged in gymnastic exercises to warm up before the various stages of bathing. The baths, which were patronized by all classes of society and constituted the hub of the city's social life, not only contained the structures required for personal hygiene, but also served as a meeting place and reading room and were used for conferences and sports contests.*

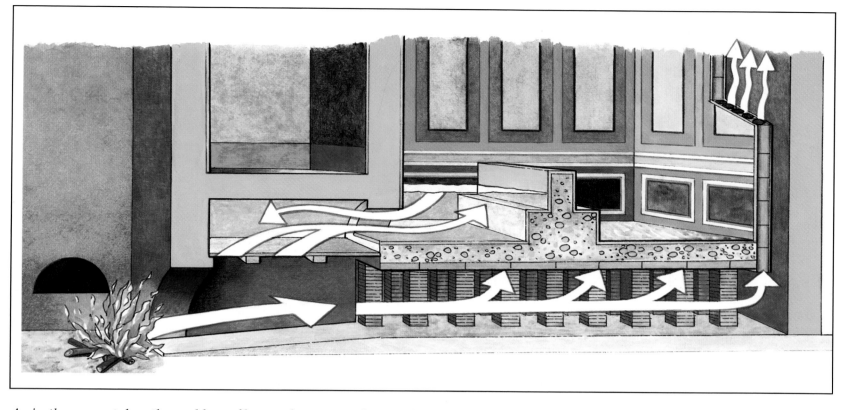

As in the present day, the problem of how to occupy one's free time also arose in ancient Rome. For the mass of loafers, unemployed, immigrants and adventurers there was an endless choice; they could roam around among the forums, basilicas and porticoes, drink and gamble in the inns. For ordinary citizens, the working day ended quite early and it was necessary to find something to do until suppertime. It was impossible to go out at night because the city became dangerous.

A good solution for all was going to the baths. They were a daily habit with rich and poor, young and old, men and women alike. In the Imperial age they were open to the public free of charge; at most, entrance might cost a quadrans, far less than a liter of wine or a loaf of bread. The various rooms were structured in accordance with a sequence of operations.

The first room was the changing room (apodyterium), followed by the hot bath room (caldarium), then a moderately heated intermediate room (tepidarium), and finally the cold bath room (frigidarium), completed by the swimming pool (natatio), usually situated in the open air. All around were rooms for saunas, anointments, massages and depilation. There were also gymnasiums, libraries, reading rooms, lounges and even places to eat a snack. The baths thus constituted not only a place that met the need for physical fitness, but also an opportunity for social contact, where people met for the pleasure of the encounter as well as to talk about politics, sports and business.

One of the most popular games at the baths were ball games. Depending on the game played, outdoors or in special closed rooms called sphaeristeria, the ball would be filled with feathers, sand or air. The most common game was trigon, played by three people. There was also harpastum, similar to the modern rugby, in which a player had to obtain control of the ball and keep it, withstanding pushes and shoves by a crowd of opponents.

Another great attraction were the places of entertainment, mainly the circus and the amphitheater. Public performances had always been used as a means of political and electoral propaganda in Rome and in the Imperial age constituted the method on which absolute Imperial rule was based. Together with periodic corn doles they served to keep the population under control; satiated and occupied, the people had little desire to think. Having acquired this special role, entertainments, generically called ludi (games), multiplied over the years and the feast days with which they were

69 The water for the baths, provided by the aqueduct, was collected in large cisterns and conveyed through pipes regulated by valves and taps to the cold bathing pools. The water that was to be heated was diverted to the boilers, then mixed with more cold water if necessary and conveyed to the hot bathing pools. Another method, shown in the drawing, provided both water and space heating in the caldarium. From the oven, hot air passed under a section of the pool (testudo alvei), maintaining it at a constant temperature as a result of the convective flow typical of fluids, which means that cold water tends to fall and warm water to rise. The hot air was conveyed to the hypocaust (the cavity under the floor, which was supported by pillars) and then rose to the vents on the roof of the building, flowing through the brick pipes that entirely covered the walls of the caldarium. Although the floor was formed by a thick insulating suspensura, it was often too hot, and bathers, therefore, wore wooden-soled clogs. Similar heating systems were also used in private villas.

originally associated were increased, amounting to the record number of 182 a year by the Imperial age.

The games were generally held by day, but sometimes they were also held at night, by torchlight. They could last for hours and, including intervals and interruptions, even a whole day, as in the case of the amphitheater. The ludi constituted a social event; people went there "to see and be seen," wearing elegant clothes, hairstyles and jewelry and attended by maids, even at the price of getting into debt or squandering their fortunes. The circus games (ludi circenses), which were the oldest of all, were held in the Circus Maximus. This huge building could hold over 250,000 spectators due to its special structure, which allowed wooden stands to be erected in addition to the stone terraces. The main feature of the circus was the spina, a low longitudinal wall 1,122 feet long, with a wealth of architectural and decorative elements such as the gigantic obelisk of Rameses II, brought to Rome to commemorate the conquest of Egypt. At each end there was a group of seven large gilded bronze eggs and another group of seven bronze dolphins; an egg or a dolphin was removed from each group alternately to indicate the number of laps run by the chariots during races.

Light, fast chariots drawn by two, three or four horses competed in the chariot races, held in the circus. Charioteers had to drive seven laps of the circuit at the highest possible speed counterclockwise, drawing alongside the spina and rounding it at the metae (sets of three conical pillars situated at either end). During the race, all kinds of dirty tricks were not only acceptable but positively enjoyed by the crowd, including the one in which the right-hand chariots crowded the left-hand ones as far as possible with the aim of making them crash into the spina.

The horses and charioteers were divided into factions, each with their own color. There were originally two, but the number was later increased to four: Russata (red), Albata (white), Veneta (blue) and Prasina (green). Russata usually raced with Veneta, and Albata with Prasina. The clothing worn by the charioteers during the races bore the color of the faction. It consisted of a tunic with a band of leather straps tightly swathing the chest to prevent fractures of the ribs, leggings to protect shins and thighs, and a helmet to protect the head.

The charioteers were very popular, and often accumulated huge fortunes. The horses also had their fans, who gave them impressive names like Victor or Incitatus, or jokey names like Piripinus.

The spectacles put on in the amphitheater were another craze. The Flavian Amphitheater, a building truly worthy of a city like Rome, which combined grandiosity with ultra-modern functionality, was inaugurated in A.D. 80 It had an elliptical plan, a circumference of 1,772 feet and a height of 165 feet. Below the arena, the floor of which consisted of wooden boards covered with sand, was the basement used for the numerous amphitheater services,

70 top Circus scenes are very common among the wealth of mosaics produced in the late Imperial period, confirming the great popularity of this type of entertainment. The actual races alternated between contests of skill and comedy shows, but the audience really went wild when the charioteers of the four official teams appeared.

70 bottom This lively terra-cotta bas-relief shows a charioteer about to drive around one of the metae. The contestants most popular with the public were those who demonstrated their courage and skill by performing reckless stunts; these feats were generously rewarded by their managers.

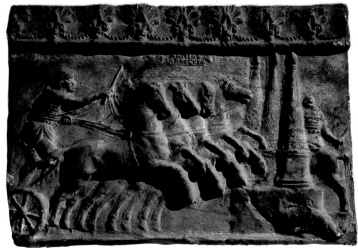

71 The charioteers were very popular and usually accumulated huge fortunes. The horses also had their fans, who gave them impressive names like Victor or Adorandus, or jokey names like Piripinus. Furious disputes often broke out between the supporters of the various teams.

72-73 This mosaic, showing a scene in the amphitheater, dates from the 4th century A.D. Gladiatorial combat originated among the Etruscans; slaves or prisoners were forced to fight on the occasion of funerals of famous men to satisfy the blood-lust of the gods. The custom was then adopted in ancient Rome, where its significance gradually changed, and the combats became increasingly grandiose public entertainments. The munera were held in purpose-built structures and financed by emperors and politicians seeking to win the people's favor, and successfully spread to every province of the Empire.

73 right The gladiators were classed according to their weapons and equipment. The performances required considerable organization, and there were special schools where all the tricks of the trade where taught. The most famous school for gladiators, called Ludus Magnus, was in Rome, near the Coliseum.

including the machinery to lift the scenery and the wild beasts to the arena level. A large sectional tarpaulin that could be operated from the outside by special naval squads served to protect spectators from the heat. The inaugural celebrations went on nonstop for 100 days, during which hundreds of gladiators and 5,000 animals died. Gladiatorial combat took place in the amphitheater. This consisted of a series of duels between specially trained pairs of opponents who specialized in various types of combat for which special weapons and techniques were used. After various preambles, to the sound of a kind of orchestra that highlighted the most important moments with music, the show began. Duels between several pairs of gladiators took place simultaneously; those who were not killed but were unable to continue laid down their weapons, and could ask for mercy by raising an arm. The decision rested with the emperor, who usually complied with the demand shouted by the crowd: "mitte!" (send him back) or "iugula!" (cut his throat). The gladiators were divided into various categories: secutores, oplomachi, provocatores, retiarii, murmillones and thraces. The retiarius was an interesting figure. His only defense was a kind of "sleeve" of metal strips protecting his left arm to above the shoulder. He was armed with a long trident and a net, with which he tried to immobilize his opponent. He usually fought against the murmillon, heavily armed and wearing a helmet on which appeared a fish (murma). The combat thus symbolized the battle between fish and fisherman. The gladiators had various origins; they were usually slaves, prisoners of war or prisoners condemned to death, but there were some freemen attracted, perhaps by

74-75 The
construction of the
Flavian Amphitheater,
better known as the
Coliseum, took just
five years, from
A.D. 75–80, when it
was inaugurated with
100 days of munera
and venationes
(games and wild beast
hunts).
It is a marvel of
design, especially if
the dimensions of this
architectural wonder
are considered; it is
165 feet high and 617
feet long on the major
axis, and held
50,000–70,000
spectators. It is
estimated that its
construction required
130,000 cubic yards of
travertine, 6,000 tons
of concrete and 300
tons of iron for the
brackets that held the
blocks together.
To accelerate the
work, the site was
divided into four
sectors, each
commissioned from a
different contractor.
Each sector was
organized according
to the materials and
the height reached, in
accordance with a
detailed plan aimed at
optimizing costs.
The Coliseum consists

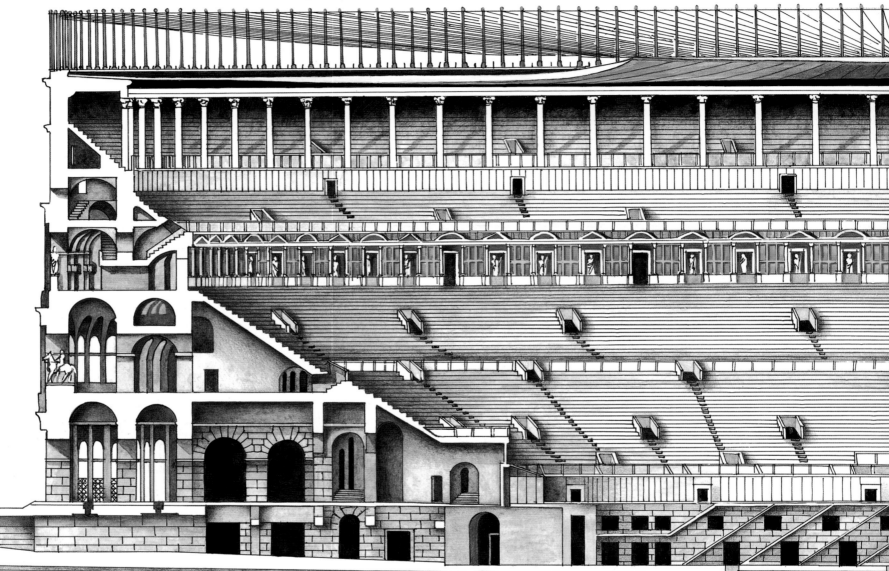

hunger, to this terrible career.
Wild beast hunts (venationes) were also typical of the amphitheater. The animals were flung into the arena after a long period in the dark without food. Their death had to be spectacular, so a kind of bullfight was held with bulls or rhinoceroses, battles between animals, and animals chasing totally unarmed men, who were inevitably torn to pieces in the end. The scenery was carefully designed to reproduce the original environment of the wild beasts.
There were also other minor kinds of entertainment. These ranged from exhibitions of tamed animals and parodies of venationes, with hares chased by dwarfs, to turns by jugglers,

acrobats and illusionists. Some very popular shows recounted mythical and historical episodes and folk sagas, like that of the brigand who is captured and crucified or torn to pieces by a bear. All this was taken very seriously. The crowds held an unbridled enthusiasm for bloody spectacles, and in particularly permissive periods, even some ladies of good society performed in the arena. As one account describes: "Mervia, bare-breasted and brandishing a skewer, chases a Tuscan wild boar around the arena." Inured to such excitement, the populace was less interested in more decorous entertainment. Athletic contests and gymnastic exhibitions were actually considered immoral, despite the fact that

Domitian had built a magnificent stadium on the Parade Ground with the intention of reviving the sporting contests of ancient Greece. Domitian also built an odeon next to the stadium for performances by musicians and singers. The naumachiae, miniature naval battles fought in the artificial lakes of the same name, in which the combatants actually died, were more popular. The naumachia of Augustus in Trastevere, 1,769 feet long and 1,178 feet wide, was famous; it was supplied with water by a special aqueduct and inaugurated with a performance in which 3,000 fighting men took part, not counting the crews of the ships.

of 80 radial walls, converging from the outer to the inner ring that supported the great auditorium made of travertine blocks, and the complex system of tunnels and staircases that allowed the audience to leave the huge building in a few minutes.

The load-bearing structure is made of hewn stone blocks, while the vaults between one wall and the next were cast in concrete. The outer ring consists of four stories: the first three each contained 80 arches that supported one another, distributing the weight of the building on the foundations in a perfectly balanced way. The 240 poles that supported the ropes of the great canopy used to shade the auditorium were driven into the perimeter of the fourth story, with its square windows. The canopy, which consisted of numerous strips of canvas, was operated by a hundred sailors from the Misenum fleet.

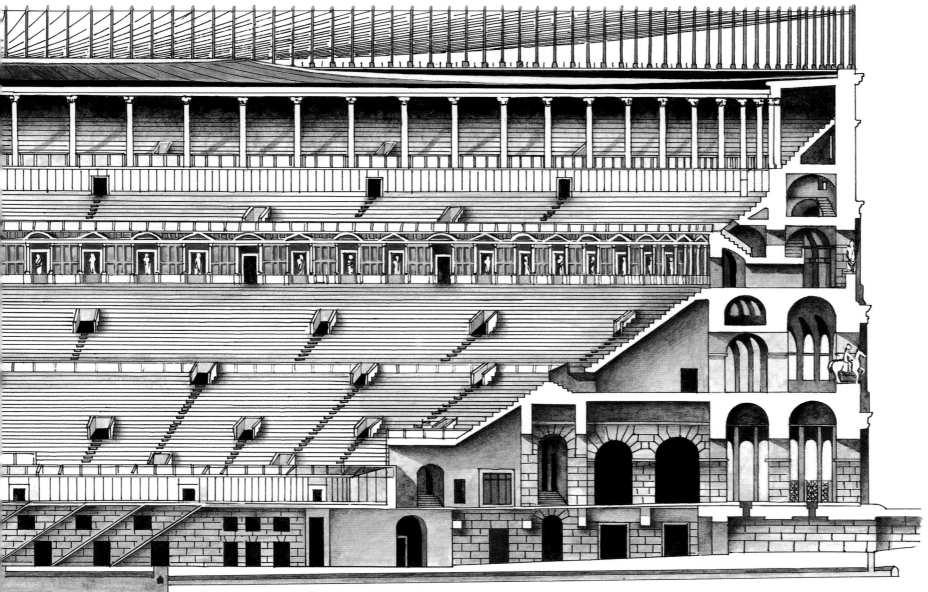

75 bottom These terra-cotta statuettes portray two gladiators engaged in combat. Gladiators were usually criminals condemned to death or forced labor or slaves who had committed serious offenses; sometimes, however, they were freemen attracted by the chance of becoming famous and earning large sums of money. Incredible as it may seem, numerous gladiators who were freed after winning their latest battle continued to fight, tempted by the great profits to be made; many of them were known and loved by the crowds, and concluded their long careers as wealthy men. It is believed that the most famous gladiators minimized the risks when they fought, making the crowd wild with their consummate skill, as in present-day wrestling.

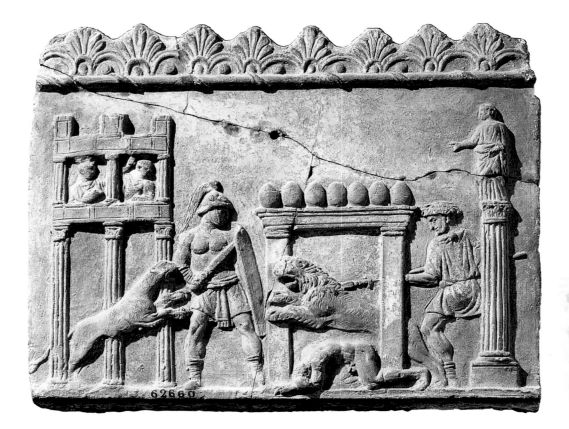

76 Gladiators were owned by a "manager" (lanista), who trained and equipped them at his own expense. Weapons and breastplates, like the helmet and shin-guard found in Pompeii, were often magnificently decorated. The gladiators, who were grouped into organizations called familiae, lived in special barracks as if in prison, but this did not prevent them from receiving visits from fans, or perhaps a matron attracted by their rippling muscles. Only the most skilled veterans, after a long career, could regain their freedom, symbolized by a wooden sword, but they usually stayed in the business as trainers.

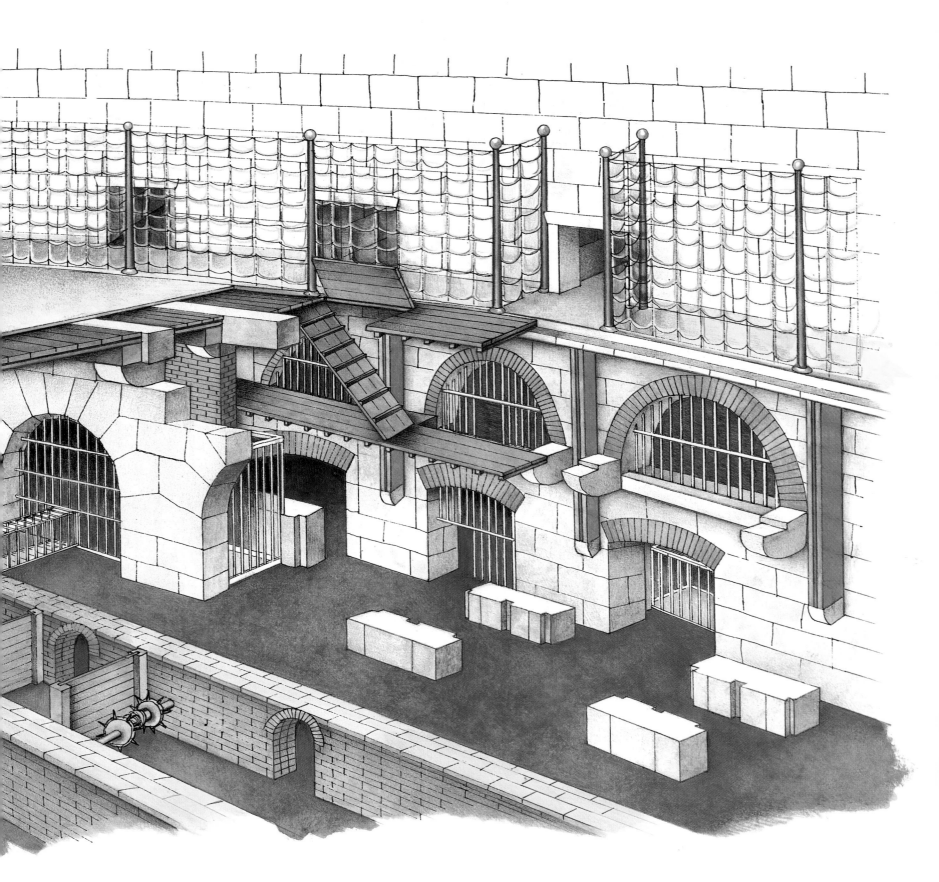

76-77 The construction of the Coliseum basements was ordered by Domitian, who decided to use other purpose-built structures for the naumachia (miniature naval battles for which the arena was flooded). With the aid of this maze of tunnels, cells and service corridors, the amphitheater reached the peak of its functionality; wild beasts and groups of gladiators could be made to appear suddenly in the middle of the arena with the use of ramps and elevators operated by winches and counterweights, together with sets portraying temples, woods or mountains. The passages between cages could be closed with partitions to reduce the risk of escape. The basement was roofed with wooden boards covered with fine sand in which the various trapdoors were concealed. A strong net surrounded the entire perimeter of the arena to protect the spectators in the front rows from the wild beasts.

78 top This bas-relief, portraying a comic scene, dates from the 1st century A.D. After the successful season of the great names in Roman theater (Livius Andronicus, Ennius, Plautus and Terence), the public lost interest in this kind of performance. They preferred simple performances based on extempore gags and dirty jokes to the traditional Greek style of theater; in the Imperial age dramas were no longer staged, but read in private drawing rooms before an elite audience.

78 bottom Staging a theatrical performance was quite an expensive business, and although the government paid a generous grant, the most famous theatrical companies could command very high fees and impose their own terms on impresarios, who also had to pay the wages of stagehands, dressmakers and set designers. In this mosaic, found in Pompeii, actors are preparing for a play; one of them is playing the tibia, a wind instrument similar to the flute.

78-79 In Rome, theatrical performances were far less popular than circus races and gladiatorial contests. This state of affairs was at least partly due to the ostracism of the theater decreed in the 2nd century B.C. by the aristocracy, which prevented the construction of permanent theaters until the time of Pompey.

This hostility was due to the risk involved in concentrating a large number of people in a place where an author might rouse the rabble with excessively libertarian or otherwise dangerous subjects. Even in the Imperial age the plays staged were very carefully controlled.

The glorious old tragedies were not very popular either with the Romans in the Imperial age, who preferred mime shows to traditional theatrical performances. These were episodes taken from the theatrical repertoire, and adapted to highlight their macabre, mysterious or grosser aspects. The mimic alone portrayed all the action, accompanied by musicians and dancers. Some of these actors became true idols and made a fortune.

80-81 Until 55 B.C. Rome had no permanent masonry theater, only temporary wooden structures. A century earlier, a proposal to build a permanent structure had met with strong opposition from the Senate, which was convinced that such a project would lead to moral corruption. The construction of the Pompeii theater and the extension of the range of leisure activities offered to the plebs by Caesar changed the situation, and theatrical buildings were soon erected in many parts of Italy and the provinces of the Empire.

In Roman theaters (see the above Theater of Marcellus in Rome), unlike Greek ones, the auditorium was not usually built onto a natural hillside but supported by special masonry structures. The stage front was much higher and more elaborate, so that it had the appearance of a two- or three-story set of monumental wings containing the three entrances for the actors. The central entrance (regia) was used by the leading actors, and the two side entrances (hospitalia) by the supporting cast; the side of the stage from which they entered (right or left) indicated the origin of the character (town or country). Sets and stage machinery added to the interest of the performance, which was accompanied by an orchestra seated in the orchestra pit at the foot of the stage.

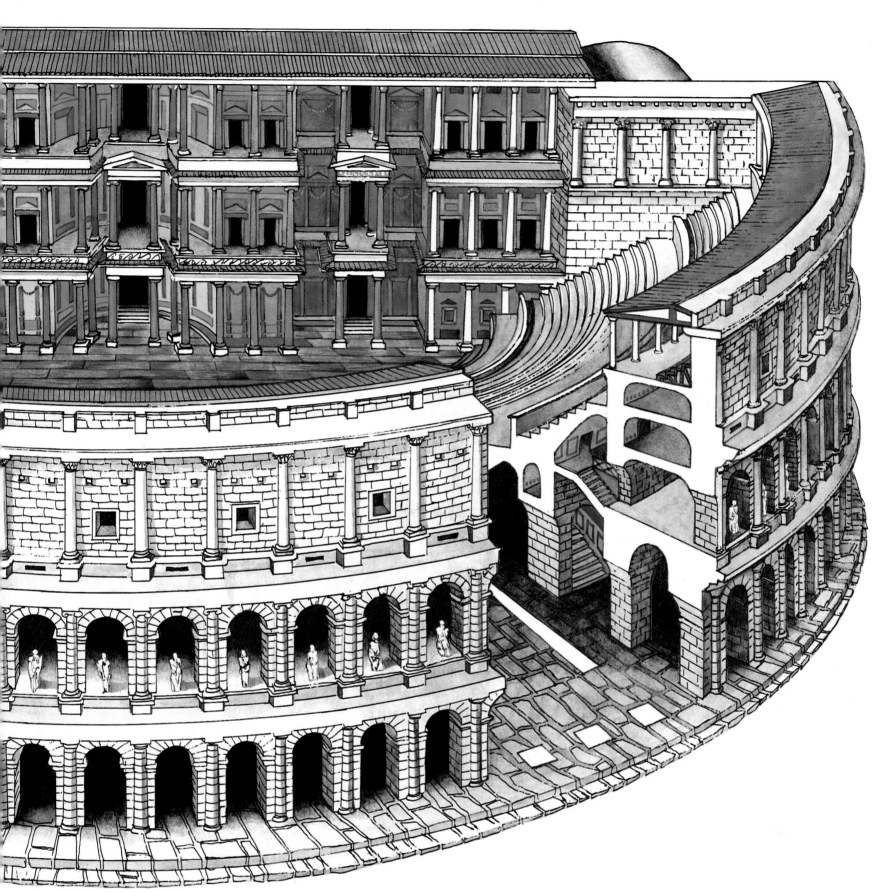

82-83 This famous mosaic dating from the 1st century B.C., signed by an artist of Greek descent, Dioskourides of Samos, was found in what is known as Cicero's Villa in Pompeii; it portrays some New Comedy characters, strolling players who belonged to the cult of Cybele. The success of the two genres destined to supplant Greek tragedy – mime and pantomime – began in the 1st century B.C. In the former, which featured comic and erotic subjects and were sometimes tinged with political satire, acting alternated with dancing, and masks were not used. Women also took part in these performances, usually scantily clad, and were sometimes called on to perform a veritable striptease; in view of their profession they were considered little better than prostitutes. Pantomime, which featured tragic subjects, was inspired by mythology and history; the actors were dancers whose gestures were emphasized by the voice of a narrator and background music.

CLOTHING AND HAIRSTYLES

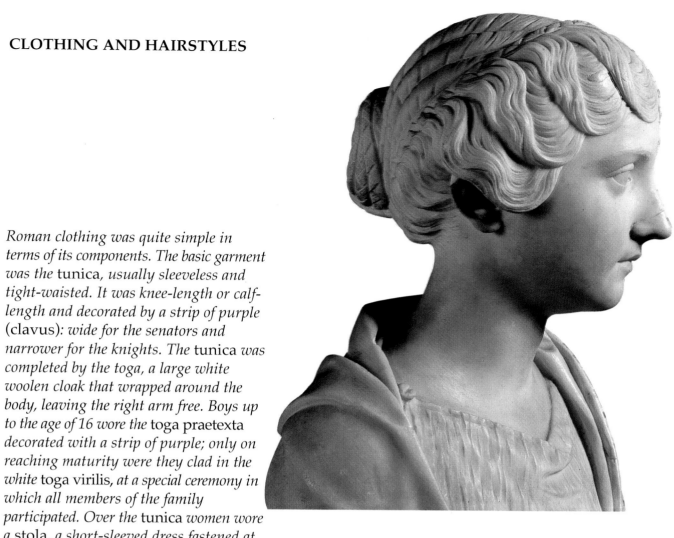

Roman clothing was quite simple in terms of its components. The basic garment was the tunica, usually sleeveless and tight-waisted. It was knee-length or calf-length and decorated by a strip of purple (clavus): wide for the senators and narrower for the knights. The tunica was completed by the toga, a large white woolen cloak that wrapped around the body, leaving the right arm free. Boys up to the age of 16 wore the toga praetexta decorated with a strip of purple; only on reaching maturity were they clad in the white toga virilis, at a special ceremony in which all members of the family participated. Over the tunica women wore a stola, a short-sleeved dress fastened at the waist by a belt and cleverly draped to form elegant pleats. Outdoors they wore a cloak (palla), which could be used to cover the head. The most common type of footwear were calcei, similar to ankle boots. The fashion in ladies' hairstyles varied from period to period, thus constituting a very useful dating element. In the more ancient times, hairstyles were simple. The hair, worn with a central parting, was gathered in a bun at the back of a neck or in a ponytail, sometimes decorated with a thin fringe of curls on the forehead. Hairstyles began to grow more elaborate in the Augustan period, and reached the peak of sophistication in the Flavian era, when they became monumental constructions of curls. The indispensable tools were the comb, made of bronze, bone or ivory, and the calamistrum, hollow curling tongs heated on a brazier. Women also used hairpins, ribbons, nets, wigs and hairpieces that increased the bulk and volume of their hairstyles. Dyes and bleaches were also used. Spuma batava was often employed to dye the hair a copper-blonde color.

85 top In this bust Faustina the Younger, daughter of Antoninus Pius, wears a hairstyle that frames the face with broad waves; the hair was gathered on the head in what was known as the "melon" style, then formed into a chignon of rolled plaits.

85 bottom Hairpieces were widely used to add volume to the more complex creations; at the nape of the neck the hair was gathered into complicated "doughnut" style buns. The wealthier matrons had their hair and makeup done by the ornatrix, a slave who specialized in beauty treatments.

84 In Trajan's time women's hairstyles became very elaborate. A pile of curls like this was produced by the calamistrum, metal curling tongs that were heated before application to the wet hair.

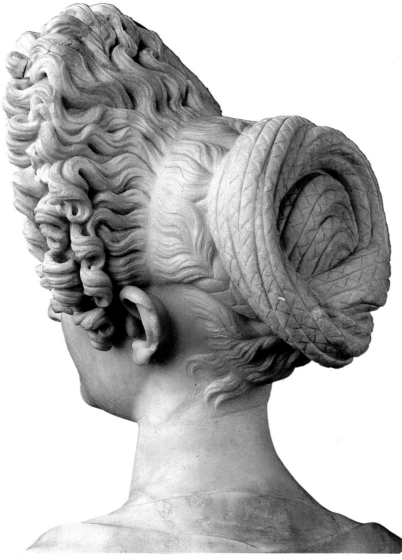

JEWELRY AND PERFUMES

86 top A collet with bas-relief decoration, surrounded by a knurled edge, ornaments this gold bracelet.
A naked cherub holds a mirror in front of a female figure wearing a long chiton; the subject, known as the Venus of Pompeii, also appears in some wall paintings found in the buried town.

86 center This kind of ring, formed by a knurled strand of solid gold in which a pearl is set, became very common in Roman jewelry from the 1st century A.D.; the pearl might be replaced by a semi-precious stone.

86 bottom The small collets composing this unusual pair of earrings contain quartz fragments. The two jewels are among the numerous valuable specimens of Roman jewelry found at Oplontis, near Pompeii.

True Roman jewelry was first made in the 1st century B.C. The spoils of war had brought to Rome not only works of art, but also pearls and precious gems. The personal ornaments found in Pompeii, Stabia, Herculaneum and Oplontis give some idea of the jewelry that was most common in the early Imperial age. There was a preference for highly colorful, though not very elaborate compositions; pearls, gems and glass paste contrasted with the bright yellow of the gold to produce jewels of great effect and ostentation, beloved of the nouveaux riches like Fortunata, the wife of Trimalchio. Earrings (inaures) of all shapes and sizes were very popular. According to Pliny, "People nowadays go to buy clothes in China, look for pearls in the depths of the Red Sea, and emeralds in the bowels of the earth. Moreover, the practice of piercing the ears has been invented: it evidently did not suffice to wear jewels round the neck, in the hair and on the hands; they also have to be stuck in the body." Cosmetics were also important, and formed the subject of a flourishing trade. Ointments and perfumes were contained in small, elegant china or alabaster jars or glass bottles. All Romans made immoderate use of them, and women in particular devoted a great deal of time to make up and to concocting highly elaborate facial masks containing all sorts of ingredients, including plants and various organic compounds, some of which are quite unspeakable.

87 This ribbon necklace decorated with oval mother-of-pearl collets alternating with emerald prisms dates from the 1st century A.D., and was found in Pompeii. The necklace of the same date in which gold spindles alternate with emeralds was found in Oplontis. Emeralds were very popular with the Romans, partly because they are found in nature in the form of regular crystals.

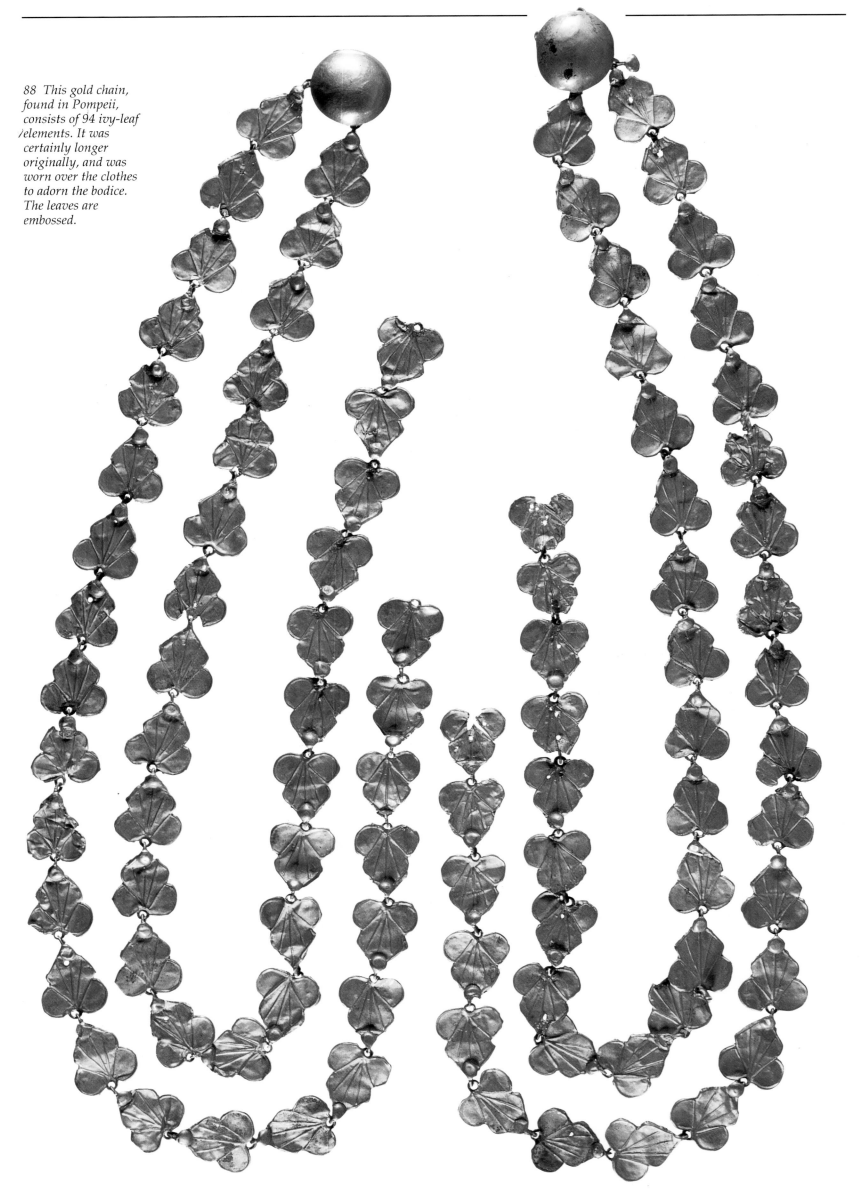

88 This gold chain, found in Pompeii, consists of 94 ivy-leaf elements. It was certainly longer originally, and was worn over the clothes to adorn the bodice. The leaves are embossed.

The various cosmetics were mixed in saucers and bowls. As foundation, women used a layer of white lead or ceruse mixed with honey and fatty substances. To produce a pinker complexion, the white lead was mixed with dyes such as red ocher, saltpeter foam, or the cheaper wine dregs. To make the skin shine, the face was sprinkled with spangles made by grinding blue-gray hematite. The eyelashes and eyebrows were highlighted with soot, and the eyelids with green or blue eyeshadow. A final touch of elegance was given by a small beauty spot on the cheek, and a touch of rouge brushed onto the sides of the face. The following are some of Pliny the Elder's cosmetic tips.

Against wrinkles: "Asses' milk is believed to remove wrinkles from the skin of the face and make it soft and white; certain women are known to treat their cheeks exactly seven times a day. It was Poppea, the wife of the Emperor Nero, who started this fashion; she also used it to bath in, which is why she took herds of asses with her on journeys."

Against acne, "Acne spots on the face are removed by spreading butter over them, especially if it is mixed with white lead." Against facial ulcers, "Ulcers on the face are treated with cow's placenta, still warm." Against facial lichens, "Glue made from calf genitals, dissolved in vinegar with quick sulphur and mixed with a fig branch; apply fresh twice a day."

89 top and 89 center
In contrast to the elegant detail of Hellenistic jewelry, Roman jewelry was much simpler; it abandoned complex types of manufacture like granulation and filigree work in favor of a more solid, intentionally striking effect. Cameos, made of different materials such as rock crystal, sardonyx, agate or the more modest glass paste, were very popular. The use of cameos in pendants or as settings for rings gradually became more common from the early Imperial age, and was widespread by the 1st century A.D. The subjects ranged from portraits to portrayals of deities and mythological episodes.

89 bottom left
Drop-earrings consisting of two or more pearls were called crotalia, by analogy with the tinkling sound of the simple percussion instruments called crotali. Pearls were highly prized; the most valuable, usually imported from the Red Sea, could fetch exorbitant prices. The less well-to-do had to be content with glass or mother-of-pearl imitations.

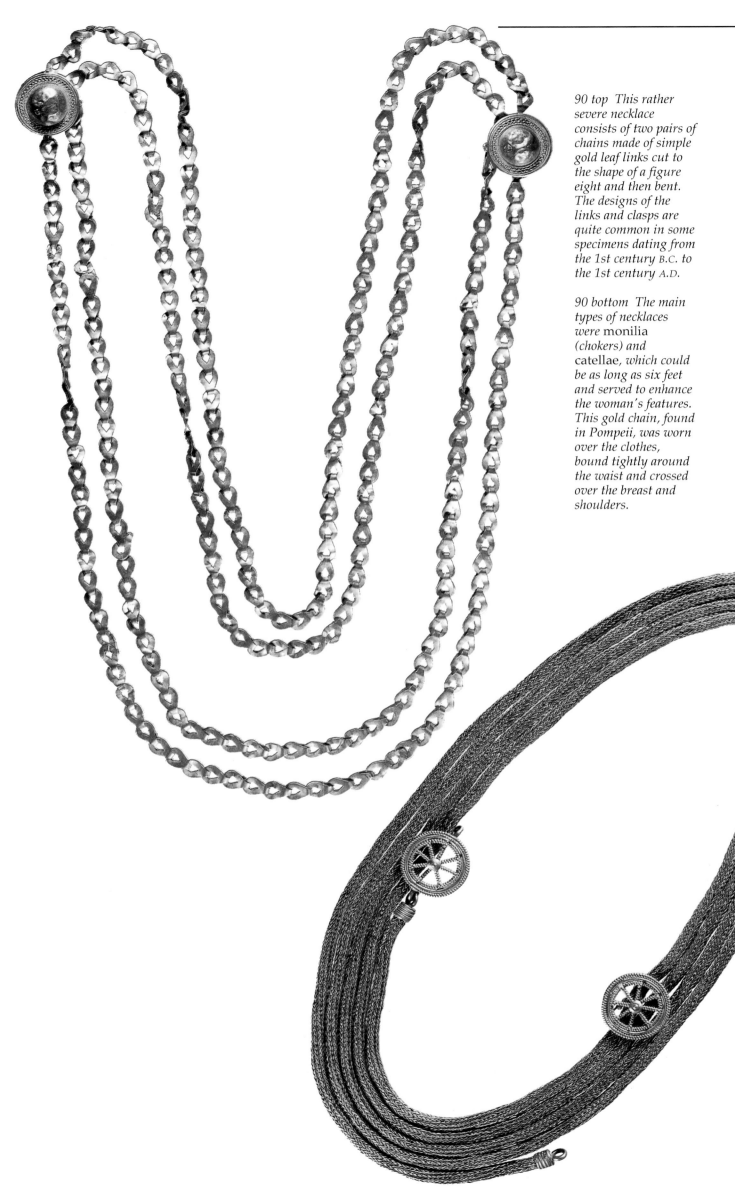

90 top This rather
severe necklace
consists of two pairs of
chains made of simple
gold leaf links cut to
the shape of a figure
eight and then bent.
The designs of the
links and clasps are
quite common in some
specimens dating from
the 1st century B.C. to
the 1st century A.D.

90 bottom The main
types of necklaces
were monilia
(chokers) and
catellae, *which could
be as long as six feet
and served to enhance
the woman's features.
This gold chain, found
in Pompeii, was worn
over the clothes,
bound tightly around
the waist and crossed
over the breast and
shoulders.*

91 top left This magnificent gold snake bracelet belonged to a wealthy matron from Pompeii. The same subject, which also had an apotropaic purpose, was very common throughout the Imperial age.

91 top right The type of ring with two facing snake heads, like this one found in Pompeii, never went out of fashion, even when the use of gems was at its height.

91 bottom This gold leaf bulla decorated with filigree work was found in Pompeii. The Romans called any object with a rounded shape that looked as though it were full of water a bulla. The same name was originally given to a pendant made of leather or other material designed to be worn around the neck. In time it became a jewel rather than a lucky charm, although it still contained amulets to ward off the evil eye. Bullae were worn by freeborn citizens.

THE ROMAN ARMY

92 top Numerous
sarcophagi dating
from the Imperial age
were decorated with
battle scenes. From
the time of its origins,
Roman society was
strongly permeated
with a military spirit,
which influenced its
entire development.

92 bottom The
legionnaires were
professionals able to
fight in any situation
and deal with the
various logistical
necessities. In this
relief on Trajan's
Column, soldiers are
engaged in building a
fort.

The economic and cultural power of
Rome, first conquered by force of arms,
was strenuously defended by force of
arms until the final collapse of the
Empire. In many respects it is therefore
true to say that the power of Rome
depended on the strength of its legions.
When they were overcome by waves of
barbarian attacks, Roman society, which
was already facing a serious crisis, was
no longer able to muster the material or
spiritual resources to oppose the pace of
events.

Until the fall of the Empire, the Roman
army had constituted the best-organized,
most efficient military apparatus in the
ancient world. The excellent training and
specialization of its troops, an extensive
network of logistical support and
technologically advanced weaponry made
it a perfect mechanism, whose lethal
efficacy was placed at the service of able
strategists for over eight centuries.
Although information about the first
Royal age is somewhat fragmentary, it is
known that society was divided between
free citizens and those who did not enjoy
full rights, and were therefore not called
up for military service. The contingents
that formed the original Roman army
were drawn from three tribes, which
provided 1,000 infantrymen and 100
horsemen each in case of need. Their
equipment consisted of a leather
breastplate, helmet and greaves, a
wooden shield, a pike and a sword. As the
soldiers were equipped at their own
expense, weapons and equipment were
not standard, and varied according to
income.

The first reform of the army, which took
place in the Servian age, had major
military, and especially political
repercussions. The entire population was
divided, according to income, into five

93 The Praetorian
Guard was founded by
Augustus as a
personal bodyguard,
and constituted the
main military system
of controlling the
capital for his
successors.
Quartered in barracks
on the outskirts of the
city, the Praetorians
wore special uniforms,
received more pay
than the legionnaires,
and served for a
shorter period.
For over two centuries
they were the only
troops stationed in
Italy, and their
influence brought
several emperors to
power.

classes, and each class was subdivided into "centuries," which amounted to a total of 193. In practice, those belonging to the highest income brackets (census) had to pay more taxes and perform more important military functions. The cavalry contingents were therefore drawn from the wealthier citizens, while the mass of the infantry was supplied by the working population; those without possessions were excluded from this obligation.

Differences in financial status were obviously reflected in the equipment. The frontline infantry were fully equipped, while the other troops were gradually less equipped, and the velites in the rear were armed only with catapults and short

javelins. The tribunes were in command, while every cavalry turma (a troop consisting of 30 horsemen) was placed under the orders of one of the decurions of the turma.

Thus structured in phalanx legions (infantry regiments deployed in a number of very compact lines), the Roman army suffered from limited maneuverability. This problem was solved by Furius Camillus, who instituted the manipular legion, a subdivided, flexible formation that effectively fought the enemies Rome was gradually having to confront. This new formation was based on the maniple (manipulus), a company consisting of 120 men in the first two lines, and 60 in the third. On the battlefield, the maniples in the three lines were generally drawn up in a chessboard formation. The soldiers in the first two lines had a new weapon, the javelin (pilum), while the others were probably still armed with pikes. The velites and cavalry remained unchanged.

The strength of the legions varied, depending on the extent of the war front; the original two legions were increased to four in the Second Samnite War, and to 25 during the Second Punic War. The

minimum income required for eligibility for army service was gradually reduced, and auxiliary units supplied by subjugated populations began to be used. However, this military organization became increasingly inadequate to the real needs of Rome, which pursued ambitious expansionist plans. In the second half of the 2nd century B.C. military service was increased to six years, but this caused serious problems, especially for those who constituted the base of the legions, like the small rural landowners. This factor suggested the great reform attributed to Caius Marius, which led to the transformation of the soldier into a professional warrior. Recruitment based on financial status

disappeared, eligibility was based merely on Roman citizenship, and legionnaires remained on permanent active service for many years.

Major changes in tactics also took place with the introduction of the cohort, formed by a combination of three maniples, which had a strength of 500–600 men. All the legionnaires were equipped and armed in the same way, while the cavalry's numbers were further reduced. The cohorts thus became flexible, easily commanded basic units that, when deployed in two or three lines in a chessboard pattern, were also able to fight individual actions.

Under Augustus a wide-ranging reorganization of the armed forces began, which involved not only the legions but the entire military apparatus; in its basic forms, this renovation remained almost unchanged until the reign of Diocletian. The legions, consisting of 5,000–6,000 men and commanded by a legatus, were never as numerous as might be expected; there were rarely as many as 30 on active service at the same time. The legionary infantry were enlisted between 17 and 25 years of age. The duration of military service was established under Augustus at 16 years, and later at 20 years. However, some men apparently continued to serve even after that period had expired, remaining on active service for 40 years.

The training of recruits, placed under the authority of a centurion instructor, lasted four very tough months. During this period the young soldiers learned to march in close ranks, covering up to 24 miles in five hours, laden with weapons and armor, clothing, food rations and miscellaneous equipment weighing over 60 pounds. The exceptional mobility of the Roman army often proved to be a

94 top This precious scabbard, dating from the early 1st century A.D., was found in the Rhine near Magonza. It was decorated with a portrait of Tiberius, and must have belonged to one of his senior officers. The gladius (sword) was the hand-to-hand combat weapon typical of the Roman army for centuries.

94 bottom In this relief found in Magonza, two legionnaires are shown in battle. Note the position of the first, who is protecting his left shoulder with his shield and holding his sword in a horizontal position, ready to lunge rather than slash. This blow was considered the most effective and lethal.

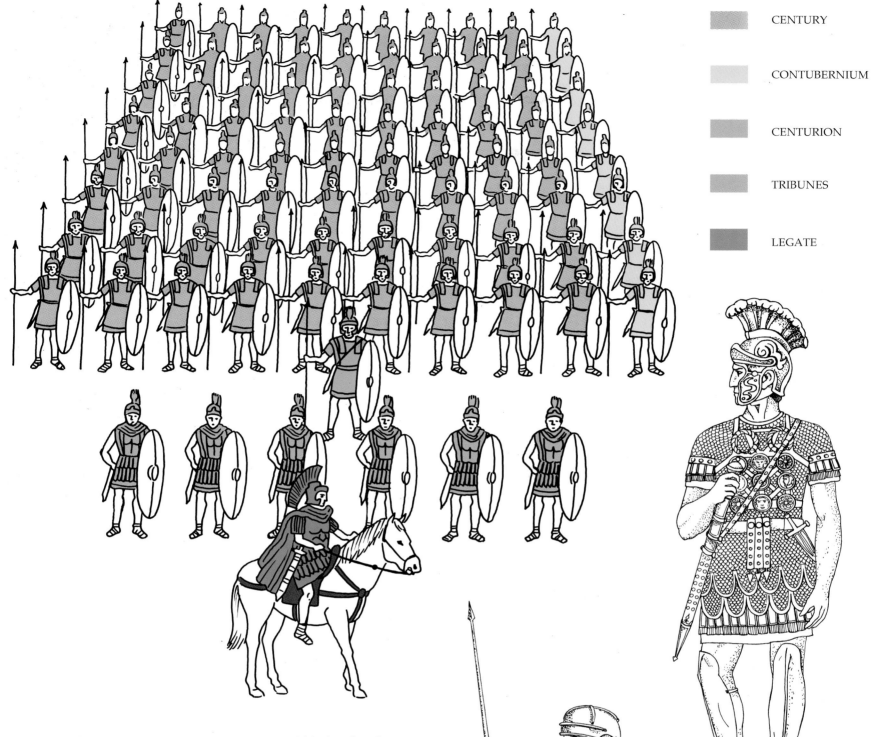

95 top The legion constituted the basic unit of the Roman army. Although its deployment varied considerably over the ages, each legion consisted of 10 cohorts that were sub-divided into six "centuries," containing around 80 men each. This drawing shows a typical century; it consisted of 10 contubernia, groups of eight legionnaires who shared the same tent. Each century was commanded by a centurion, who received his orders from the tribunes. Each legion, which also included four turmae of cavalry (120 men), was commanded by a legate, who usually belonged to the senatorial class.

95 right Centurions were legionnaires who had distinguished themselves by their valor and were given command by the tribunes. Their tasks included training the troops and maintaining discipline.

This drawing shows a centurion wearing his numerous decorations, in the form of armillae and falere (the former were similar to bracelets, and the latter to embossed metal disks), on the breastplate.

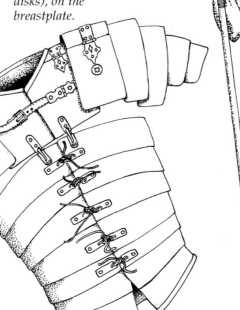

95 bottom left This drawing reproduces a lorica segmentata, a breastplate allowing great agility of movement, which was worn by legionnaires from the 1st century A.D.

95 bottom right
This is what a Roman legionnaire looked like in the 2nd century A.D. His shoulders and chest were covered by the lorica, and his head and neck were covered by a helmet. His armor consisted of a broad shield, a gladium and a javelin.

95

96 top The triumph was the greatest honor paid to a general who won a decisive victory over the enemy. He was entitled to ride through the streets of Rome on a quadriga, his head crowned by a laurel wreath, between two rows of applauding crowds, followed by the war booty, including enemy weapons and chained prisoners, as shown in this bas-relief.

decisive factor in taking the enemy by surprise. At the end of the march, the legionnaires also had to be able to set up camp for the night if necessary. The recruits then underwent an intensive course of physical activities and training with different kinds of weapons. They were also taught the most effective combat techniques in attack and defense; in particular, they learned how to form the testudo, the best-known Roman military formation. This "tortoise," formed by the soldiers' own shields, perfectly protected the unit from above and on the two most exposed flanks, so that they could advance even

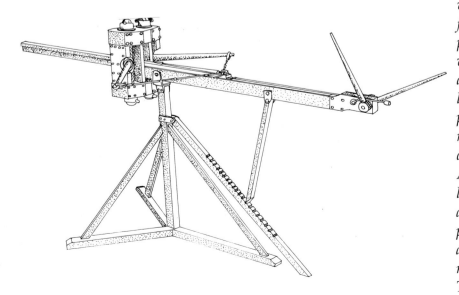

under a violent hail of enemy fire. When the training period was over, the soldiers embarked on regular military life. Although marches and simulated combats were far less frequent, leisure time was still a luxury, as the legionnaires were called on to perform numerous tasks such as maintenance work on their quarters, guard duty and, if they were stationed in recently conquered territory, building roads, bridges, aqueducts and even new towns. Some reliefs on Trajan's Column show squads of sappers assembling pontoon bridges over the Danube and legionnaires erecting the fortifications of a new camp. Roads, above all, played an essential part in achieving rapid pacification, control and Romanization of recently subjugated territories; the extent and efficiency of the road network, even in the remotest areas, was one of the distinguishing features of Roman civilization. Sometimes soldiers were required to perform policing tasks or patrol duties; in any event, being professionals, they underwent continual training throughout their military careers. The historian Flavius Josephus praised the Roman military organization on several occasions, highlighting its outstanding discipline and the speed with which the men obeyed orders. Large-scale military maneuvers were regularly held, especially when the territorial expansion of the Empire began to slow down, so that troops stationed along the borders maintained their high level of training. Often, if time allowed, the commanders performed a rapid check on their men's abilities before going into battle. In combat, especially during sieges, the Roman army used a wide variety of heavy equipment, ranging from vineae (strong mobile sheds used to protect soldiers approaching the city walls) to the various types of catapults and ballistae; the latter, which resembled large crossbows, were long-range precision weapons. Some horse-drawn mobile types could fire a projectile for a distance of around 550 yards. As already mentioned, the Roman legionnaires were usually supported by auxiliary troops that were not required to perform the same duties as the legions, and could carry out specific tasks requiring great flexibility and versatility. Their numbers were always large, equaling and perhaps exceeding those of

96 center Roman naval power began during the First Punic War, when the Romans realized they needed a fleet to defeat the Carthaginians, who were excellent sailors. Taking a captured enemy ship as their model, they soon managed to build a large number, and won their first naval battle at Mylae in 260 B.C. A typical feature of Roman warships was the rostrum, a pointed beam usually covered with thick bronze plates that projected from the prow of the hull at water level; this lethal weapon served to ram enemy ships, opening great breaches in their planking. The rostra of ships captured in battle were prized military trophies; they were displayed in the Forum, on a dais called the Rostra, named after these beams.

96 bottom The Roman army had various long-range artillery weapons that were particularly effective during sieges. In addition to the missile launcher illustrated here, called the scorpio, which could hurl a javelin, there were various kinds of catapults; the most powerful, called the onager, could hurl a 110-pound projectile for a distance of over 400 yards with devastating effects.

the legionary infantry. The auxilia units might be infantry units (coortes) or cavalry units (alae), with a strength of 500 or 1,000 men. After entering the service of the state, auxiliaries served for 25 years. Their pay was lower than that of Roman soldiers, but they were given Roman citizenship on their discharge. The auxiliary units were distinguished from the others by special names or nicknames, and their weapons and equipment were often characteristic of the units to which they belonged. Some famous contingents of auxilia were the Numidian cavalry, the slingsmen of the Balearics, and the Cretan archers.

Paradoxically, until the time of the Punic Wars the Romans were not expert mariners, and even after the reform of the navy introduced by Pompey in 67 B.C., their ships still basically followed the Greek pattern. However, the invention of the corvus (a drawbridge fitted with an iron grappling-hook that could be lowered onto the deck of enemy galleys to allow boarding) was entirely original.

The corvus, which proved highly effective in the wars against Carthage, was later abandoned because it made ships difficult to maneuver.

However, by that time Rome had gained total supremacy on the seas as well as on land.

97 Roman strategy was outstandingly effective on the occasion of sieges. Julius Caesar finally conquered Gaul by besieging Alesia, a fortified city in which Vercingetorix, leader of the Gauls, had taken refuge with some 80,000 men. Caesar, with 10 legions, surrounded the stronghold first with a long palisade preceded by a ditch and sharpened stakes, and then with an outer defensive ring designed to protect the besiegers against the 250,000-strong army of warriors led by Vercassivellaunus. Though they found themselves fighting on two fronts, the Romans repulsed the attacks and decimated the enemy, forcing Vercingetorix to surrender from hunger.

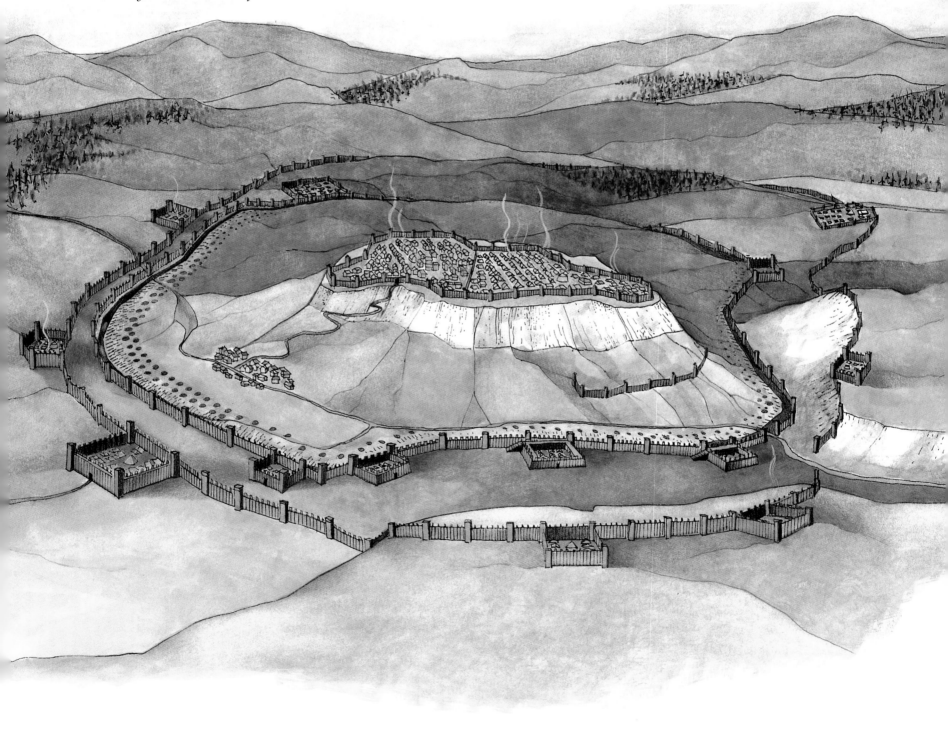

ROMA, CAPUT MUNDI:
THE CAPITAL OF THE WORLD AND ITS SPLENDORS

98 This silver denarius dating from the 1st century B.C. shows a quadriga driven by Jupiter; the denarius was the base of the Roman monetary system from the Republican age.

98-99 The Flavian Amphitheater, better known as the Coliseum, was built by the Flavians in the depression between the Palatine, Caelian and Esquiline hills, on the former site of the lake of Domus Aurea, Nero's magnificent Golden House.

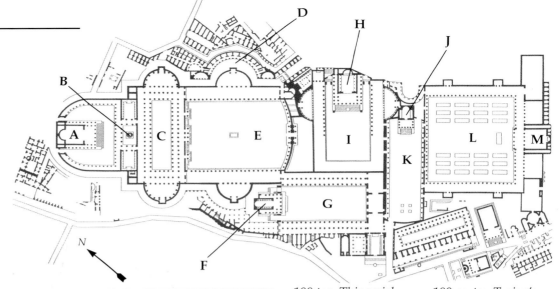

THE IMPERIAL FORUMS

A Temple of the Divine Trajan
B Trajan's Column
C Basilica Ulpia
D Trajan's Markets
E Trajan's Forum (A.D. 113)
F Temple of Venus Genetrix
G Caesar's Forum (42 B.C.)
H Temple of Mars the Avenger
I Augustus's Forum (2 B.C.)
J Temple of Minerva
K Nerva's Forum or Forum Transitorium (A.D. 97)
L Vespasian's Forum or Forum of Peace (75 B.C.)
M Temple of Peace

In ancient times, Rome had quite a different appearance from the present day; its features included high, steep hills surrounded by deep ravines and impassable valleys. Lush vegetation, including centuries-old woods, covered the hillsides and the outskirts of the city, together with forage and cereal fields, vegetable gardens and vineyards. The streams that flowed through the valleys often turned to marshland, forming ponds and small lakes. Villages stood on the hilltops, thus distinguishing the various communities that lived in the area. In the Royal age Rome was densely populated; even then it was one of the largest cities in the western Mediterranean. Alongside the many clay and straw huts dating from earlier periods, masonry houses with tiled roofs and inner courtyards, similar to the contemporary Etruscan houses, began to be built. The patrician houses, built on the hilltops, were often surmounted by high towers. This is what the royal mansions of which evidence survives must have been like, including those of Ancus Martius, Tarquinius Priscus and Tarquin the Proud (all built on the Velia) and that of Servius Tullius, built on the Oppian Hill. At this period, the monumental part of the city was obviously very limited. Its outskirts presented vast open areas which included the necropolises, the Parade Ground (designed for assemblies of men bearing arms and military exercises), brick kilns, and large areas from which clay was extracted near which the fortified town of Janiculum stood. A massive fortified wall bordered the ridges of the hills, descending along a continuous route of almost seven miles and enclosing an area of almost 1,000 acres. From the ancient time a suitable layout had been given to the square in the town center, the Forum, where the first public buildings were gradually erected. The city was dominated by the huge Temple of Capitoline Jupiter, built by Tarquin the Proud who, among

100 top This aerial view shows the remains of Augustus's Forum and Nerva's Forum, both of which are part of the huge Imperial Forum complex. They were built next to the Roman Forum with the intention of creating larger and more rational monumental spaces destined not only for the emperors' personal ceremonies, but above all for the public life of Rome. They were used for business and political discussions, religious ceremonies and markets.

100 center Trajan's Forum, erected with the booty from the Dacian wars, was the last to be built in Rome. It was also the most grandiose in terms of architectural design and the use of valuable materials. It was designed by Apollodorus of Damascus, who introduced numerous innovative features, such as the transverse position of the Basilica Ulpia in relation to the rest of the complex, and the semicircular Trajan's Markets, a set of tabernae *occupying six floors.*

100 bottom The construction of Trajan's Forum required the leveling of the Quirinal Hill, which was equal in height to the spiral column. Apollodorus of Damascus exploited the excavated area to construct the markets, which also acted as a retaining wall for the hillside behind. The best-preserved part of the complex is the section known as Via Biberatica.

101 This aerial view shows the area of Augustus's Forum and the foundations of the Temple of Mars the Avenger in the foreground and, in the background, the remains of Trajan's Forum and the adjacent markets, into which dozens of shops selling foodstuffs were crowded. The occasional free handouts of food to the plebs were also held here.

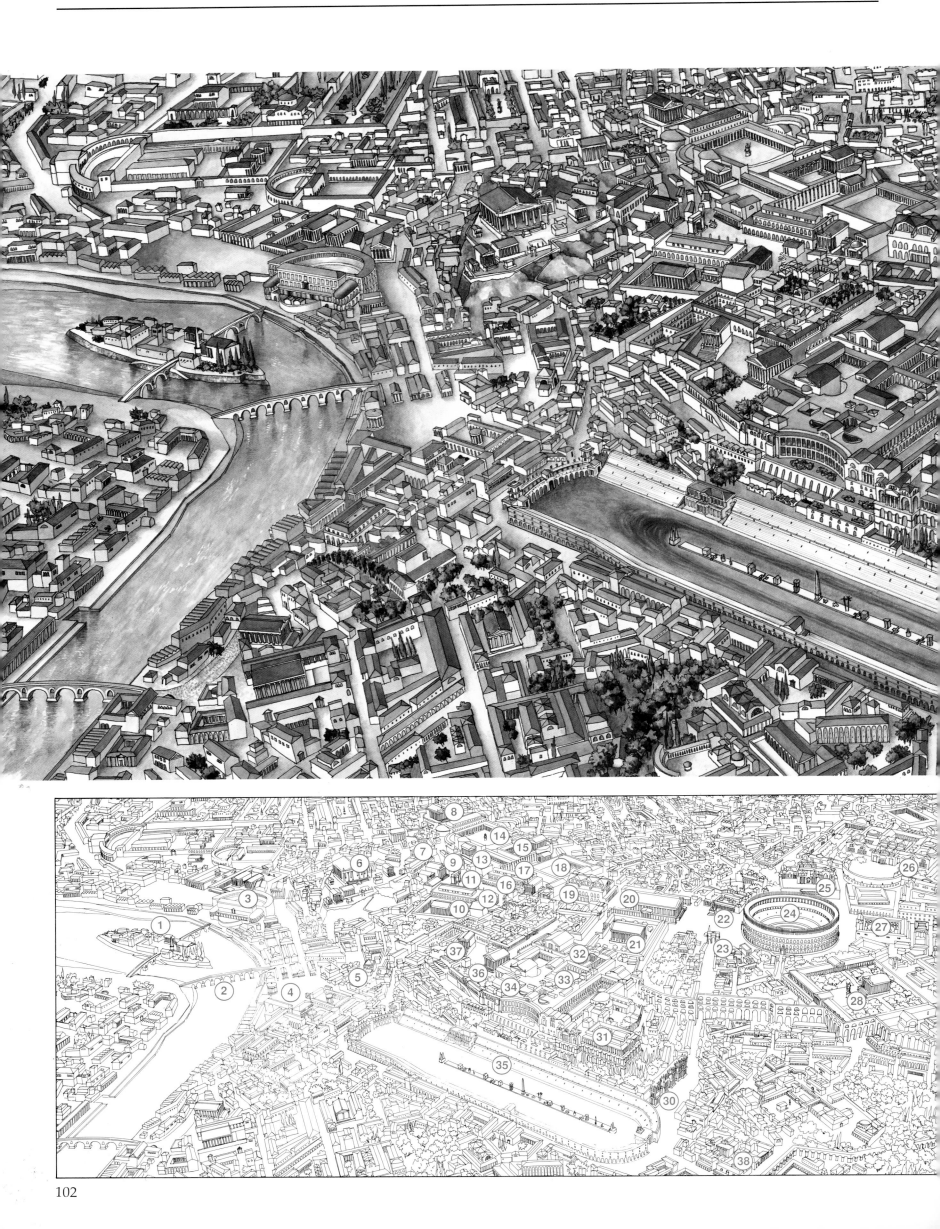

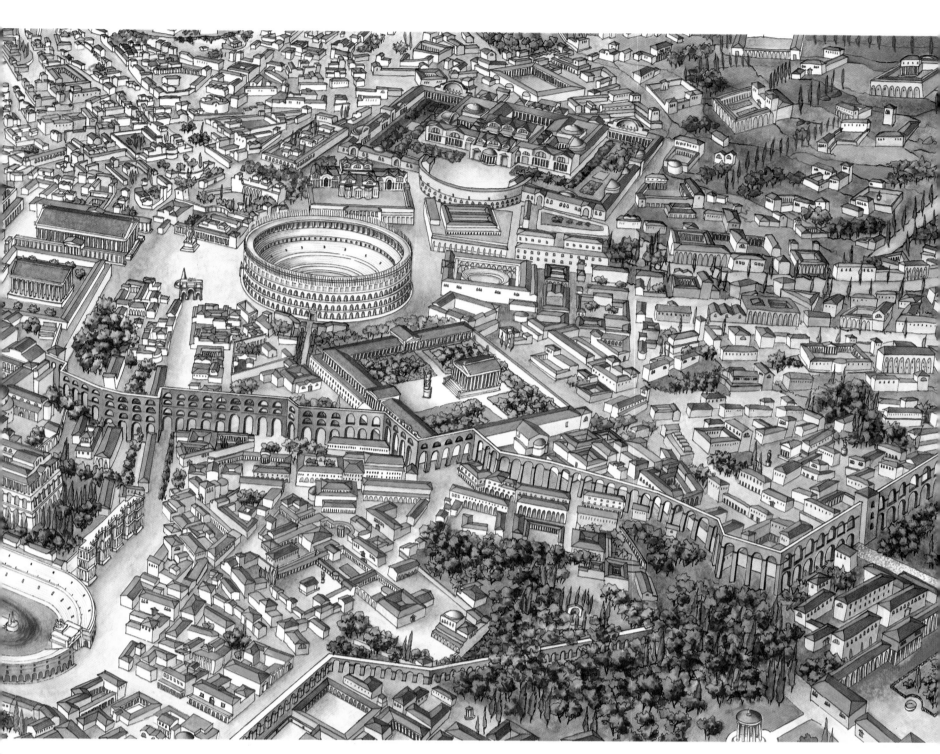

1	Tiberine Island	20	Temple of Venus and Rome
2	Aemilian Bridge	21	Temple of the Caesars
3	Theater of Marcellus	22	Colossus of Nero
4	Cattle Market	23	Arch of Constantine
5	Arch of Janus	24	Flavian Amphitheater or Coliseum
6	Temple of Capitoline Jupiter	25	Baths of Titus
7	Tabularium	26	Trajan's Baths
8	Temple of the Divine Trajan	27	Ludus Magnus
9	Arch of Septimius Severus	28	Temple of the Divine Claudius
10	Julian Basilica	29	Acqua Claudia aqueduct
11	Curia	30	Septizodium
12	Roman Forum	31	Palace of Septimius Severus
13	Caesar's Forum	32	Domus Flavia
14	Trajan's Forum	33	Domus Augustana
15	Augustus's Forum	34	Palatine Hill
16	Basilica Aemilia	35	Circus Maximus
17	Nerva's Forum or Forum Transitorium	36	Temple of Apollo
18	Vespasian's Forum or Forum of Peace	37	Temple of Cybele
19	Basilica Nova or Basilica of Maxentius	38	Acqua Marcia aqueduct

102-103 A city of over a million inhabitants, which grew up without a precise town plan, its crowded urban fabric dominated by the great Imperial palaces on the Palatine Hill, large public buildings and huge aqueducts; this is how Rome looked in the mid-4th century, a few years after Constantine's victory at the Milvian Bridge, before the long period of decadence that was to lead to the ruin of the proud monuments of the greatest city in the ancient world.

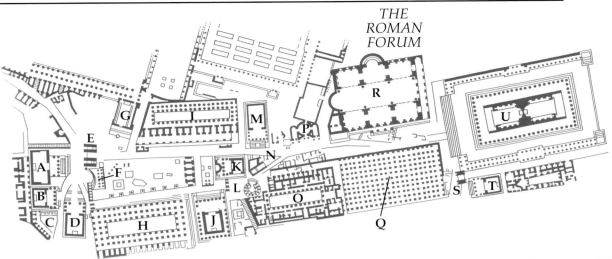

other things, promoted the first reorganization of the Circus Maximus, designed for chariot races. However, it was Servius Tullius who was responsible for much of the monumental layout of the city. It was divided for administrative purposes into four regions, and its trade was boosted by the construction of the Tiber Port in the Cattle Market. The Temples of Fortune and Mater Matuta were built close by.

The construction of the Temple of Diana on the Aventine Hill, the headquarters of the Latin federal religion, is also attributed to Servius Tullius; earlier, Ancus Martius had built the first stable bridge over the Tiber (the Sublicio). Tarquinius Priscus

reclaimed the entire valley bottom by cleverly channeling the water into the Cloaca Maxima.

During the Republican age the work previously begun was completed, and new buildings were constructed. Some examples are the Temple of Capitoline Jupiter on the Capitol, the Temples of Saturn and Castor and Pollux in the Forum, the Temples of Ceres, Liber and Libera on the slopes of the Aventine Hill, the Temple of Semus Sancus on the Quirinal Hill, and many other minor temples. At the beginning of the 5th century B.C. and for long after, this building work was greatly reduced because of the continual wars fought against the Latins, Etruscans and Volsci. In 390 B.C. the Gauls defeated the Romans on the River Allia, entered Rome and put it to fire and sword. Though devastated, the city was rebuilt but, as reported by historian Livy, the work was done in such haste that no town plan was introduced, and everyone occupied whatever area he thought fit. The already complicated urban situation thus became very difficult, and Rome, unlike its colonies and the newly built towns, which had wide streets and a regular layout, increasingly resembled an agglomeration of houses rather than a properly built city. A few years later, in 378 B.C., the old city walls were strengthened and their defensive capacity improved. New temples were erected, like the Temple of Juno the Admonisher on the Arx, the Salus Temple on the Quirinal Hill, the Temple consecrated to Jupiter the Victor on the Palatine Hill, the Temple of Quirinus on the Quirinal Hill, and others. The first aqueduct was built in 312 B.C. by the censor Appius Claudius, and in 291 B.C. the Temple of Aesculapius, god of healing, was founded on the Isola Tiberina. After the disappearance of the Carthaginian threat a new construction boom began in the city, which was already divided into

A Temple of Concord
B Temple of Vespasian
C Dei Consenti portico
D Temple of Saturn
E Arch of Septimius Severus
F Rostra
G Curia
H Julian Basilica
I Basilica Aemilia
J Temple of Castor and Pollux
K Temple of the Divine Julius
L Temple of Vesta
M Temple of Antoninus and Faustina
N Regia
O House of the Vestal Virgins
P Temple of the Divine Romulus
Q Porticus Margaritaria
R Basilica Nova or Basilica of Maxentius
S Arch of Titus
T Temple of Jupiter the Messenger
U Temple of Venus and Rome

104 top The Arch of Septimius Severus was erected in the Roman Forum to commemorate the emperor's victories in the East. The various episodes of the war are described in great detail in the numerous reliefs decorating the monument.

104 bottom Behind the three surviving columns of the Temple of Castor and Pollux (dating from the age of Tiberius) stands the white bulk of the Arch of Titus, erected in 81 B.C. to commemorate the victories of Vespasian and his son over the Judaeans.

104-105 The Roman Forum was the center of the city's public life for centuries. The columns of the Temple of Saturn can be seen on the left, the Temple of Antoninus and Faustina in the center, and the Temple of Castor and Pollux on the right.

105 top left Among
the most interesting
monuments in the
Roman Forum is the
House of the Vestal
Virgins, the residence
of the priestesses who
tended the sacred fire
of Vesta, goddess of
the household, which
burned in the nearby
circular temple.

105 top right
The last and most
grandiose basilica
built in Rome was
begun by Maxentius
in 308 B.C. and
completed by
Constantine, who
added a colossal
acrolith statue of
himself in the apse on
the north side.

105 bottom
This graph shows the
huge proportions of
Maxentius's Basilica:
the building, which
was 320 feet long and
200 feet wide, was 175
feet high at the apex of
the nave and just
under 82 feet in the
two aisles.

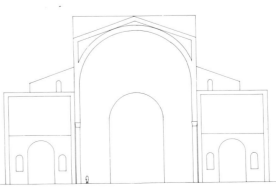

106-107 This is how
Maxentius's Basilica
must have looked in
the 4th century.
Covered in red and
green porphyry with
inlays of precious
marble, it had superb
box vaults decorated
with multicolored
plaster. The statue of
Constantine stands in
the apse.

*four regions (*Collina, Esquilina, Suburana *and* Palatina*). The commercial structures on the Tiber were improved; new buildings included the Emporium at the cargo wharf, the huge Porticus Aemilia, the impressive ruins of which can still be seen on the Testaccio plain, and the first* horrea *(food storage warehouses) made of masonry. The Flaminian Circus was founded on the Parade Ground, and the two oldest temples in the Largo Argentina complex were erected nearby. Between 184 and 170 B.C., Porcius Cato, Aemilius Lepidus and Sempronius Gracchus erected large buildings called basilicas on the Hellenistic pattern (named Porcia, Aemilia and Sempronia after them) to give the city suitable premises for discussing legal proceedings and business deals, which until then had*

108-109 According to Roman historian Pliny the Elder, the famous marble group of Laocoon decorated Titus's palace. This was an original Hellenistic Greek work, attributed to the sculptors Agesandrus, Polydorus and Athanadorus of Rhodes. It perhaps originally stood in a monumental building at Pergamum, and was imported to Rome after the kingdom of Attalus became a Roman province. Hailed by Pliny as a masterpiece, the great figured complex, which illustrates the myth of the Trojan priest punished by Athene, demonstrates the great success that Greek statuary encountered in the Roman world during the 2nd century B.C. Copies of Greek originals were very popular in the Imperial age, and many Hellenic sculptors moved to Rome.

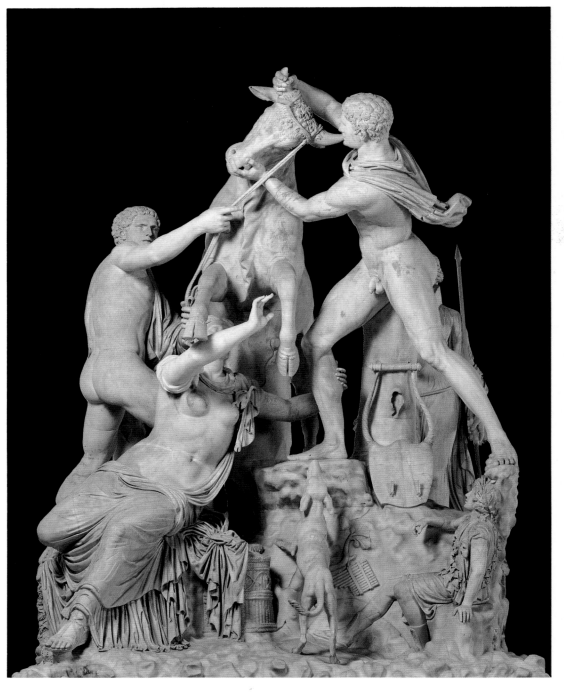

been done in the open air at the Forum. For the same reason numerous porticoes were built in various parts of the city. Aemilius laid the piers of the first masonry bridge over the Tiber, downstream of Isola Tiberina; a few years later, the piers were connected with supporting arches, thus introducing a type of construction that was later used to built aqueducts and suburban streets after the invention of opus incertum, a mixture of stones and grout that allowed increasingly bold architectural designs. During this period, contact with the Greek colonies led to the import of sculptures, and this started the fashion for reproducing Greek originals, which later became very widespread. However, even the homes of the wealthiest Romans remained fairly modest, while those of the poorer classes, which were small and crowded together, were mere trelliswork structures of wood and brick. Lifestyles were generally austere; there were few slaves, and domestic life was very simple. In the religious sphere, sacrifices were offered to the Lares (the tutelary divinities that protected the family and the house) on the household altar. Wax images of the Penates (the spirits of the ancestors) were jealously preserved, and displayed at funerals and the more solemn family ceremonies. Little by little, many gods such as Ceres, goddess of agriculture, Castor and Pollux (the twin sons of Jupiter who, according to legend, fought at Lake Regillus alongside the Romans), Heracles, Aesculapius and others were introduced into public worship. The Greek and Roman gods gradually came to correspond to one another, although the Romans continued to worship their traditional deities, and were somewhat suspicious of religions that might undermine their power system. The most important ceremonies included the triumph, an honor reserved to those who had made a major contribution to

extending the borders of the state, destined to take on increasing importance over the centuries. The victorious general rode on a chariot drawn by four white horses along a long route to the Temple of Capitoline Jupiter: as the living image of the god, he was dressed in purple, crowned with a laurel wreath, and held a scepter surmounted by an eagle in his right hand. The procession was opened by magistrates and senators. Then followed the booty, often consisting not only of weapons and insignia, but also of works of art, precious objects and exotic animals. Next came the sacrificial victim, the lictors with the fasces, and the veterans of the successful campaign, who sang songs and directed salacious jokes at their commander. An important part in the pageant was played by processions of prisoners and enemy chieftains, chained and wearing national costume, who followed the triumphal chariot. The most important episodes of the war were often illustrated on large boards carried in the procession, as was a

110 One of the most outstanding of the many works of art that adorned the Baths of Caracalla was the famous marble Farnese Bull group, a copy, dating from the Antonine age, of a Greek original by Apollonius of Tralles. The sculpture portrays the myth of the punishment of Dirce, who was tied to the bull by Zethus and Amphion to revenge their mother, Antiope.

111 The statue known as The Dying Galatea is a Roman copy of a bronze original belonging to a votive group dedicated to Attalus I, King of Pergamum. The encounter with Hellenism was crucial to the birth of Roman art; however, at the beginning of the long creative process many ethical prejudices were expressed in conservative patrician circles.

list of the towns and populations subjugated, the numbers of the enemy killed, and the number of prisoners. Literary production, though still modest, was partly associated with military glories, and convivial songs celebrating the feats of the ancestors were usually sung at banquets. Theatrical performances, which had a popular tone, were mostly of rural origin. The ruling class tended to cultivate the art of oratory for eminently practical reasons, as politicians had to be

skilled orators, able to address their peers in the Senate and to win over the masses. The age of the Punic Wars brought about radical transformations in social and cultural life. The annexation of the Greek towns of southern Italy and numerous contacts made in the Mediterranean provided new stimuli. Hellenism (the literary and artistic civilization that the Greeks had developed during the reign of Alexander the Great) proved particularly suited for export to Rome. Everything congenial to the ideology of the ruling class was accepted without delay. Thus oral literature and the sacred and popular forms of earlier periods were abandoned, and gradually replaced by the epic poem, the tragedy, the comedy and the history. Livius Andronicus, a Greek from Tarentum taken to Rome as a slave, gave the Romans, who had now begun their Mediterranean ventures, the Latin translation of the Odyssey, while the Campanian Gnaeus Naevius composed a poem about the events of the First Punic War in which he had fought as a soldier. Fabius Pictor and Cincius Alimentus actually wrote historical works in Greek, a language that was now known by many Romans. By imitating the forms developed by the Greeks, poets and historians began to create a Latin literature suitable to illustrate the main stages of Roman expansionism. From the religious standpoint, the attitude of tolerance and acceptance of different faiths was similar to that demonstrated towards literature. In 204 B.C., for example, the cult of Cybele, a Phrygian divinity, was accepted in Rome, whereas the rites in honor of Bacchus, called the Bacchanalia, encountered open hostility. Adepts belonging to different classes met in secret associations, and the fact that this religion crossed social barriers, although it had no political aims, was interpreted by the Senate as a threat to the existing order. In 186 B.C., a decree therefore banned attendance at these meetings. In the political sphere,

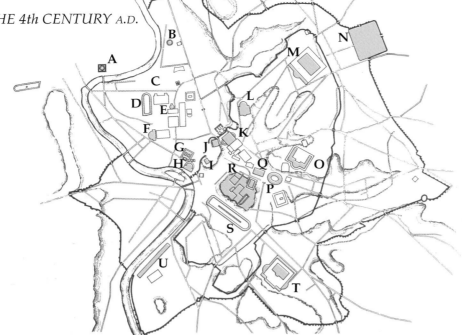

the history of Rome at this period was dominated by the powerful Scipio gens (family). After the battle of Zama, seven Scipios were appointed consuls in 10 years, while other magistratures were given to their friends and relations. Both Scipio Africanus and Scipio Aemilianus were distinguished by a special attitude to the society of the period, having chosen classical culture to enhance their prestige by instituting a literary circle. Its members included the historian Polybius, the philosopher Panezius, and the poet Ennius, the author of works that exalted the military glories of Rome with the result that he was considered the Latin Homer. The African Terence, who came to Rome as a slave when still a boy, and was later freed and adopted by the Scipios, brought the world of the middle classes into the limelight, replacing the realism of his predecessor, Plautus (a playwright and manager of a theater company), with a less obvious, more elegant style of comedy. At the same time, the faction of the nobility jealous of the Scipios's leadership, represented by Marcus Porcius Cato, was advocating a more rigid form of imperialism that was to triumph a few years later. Cato, who strongly defended

Roman tradition against Greek influence, was also an orator and author; after accusing Scipio Africanus of illicit dealings, he forced him to retire to his villa at Liternus in Campania, where he died in 183 B.C., the very year in which Hannibal committed suicide rather than being handed over to the Romans by the king of Bithynia. Towards the second half of the 2nd century B.C., Rome began to acquire a monumental appearance. Its architecture was being transformed by the introduction of colonnades, trabeations and mezzanine floors made airier by the addition of galleries. Flat ceilings were replaced by round arches, which also began to be used alone as triumphal monuments. Numerous craftsmen from the Greek world were working in Rome, and copies of famous statues were commissioned from them to decorate private homes and public buildings. In the meantime portrait painting was introduced. It was very original right from the outset; the subjects were not idealized but portrayed realistically, their features sometimes being depicted quite unmercifully. During the same period a new literary genre became popular, namely the satire, symptomatic of a

1 Hadrian's Mausoleum	11 Trajan's Forum
2 Augustus's Mausoleum	12 Constantine's Baths
3 Parade Ground	13 Diocletian's Baths
4 Domitian's stadium	14 Castra Praetoria
5 Pantheon	15 Trajan's Baths
6 Pompey's Theater	16 Coliseum
7 Portico of Octavia	17 Temple of Venus and Rome
8 Theater of Marcellus	18 Palatine Hill
9 Temple of Capitoline Jupiter	19 Circus Maximus
	20 Baths of Caracalla
10 Arx	21 Porticus Aemilia

116 bottom The eight statues of Dacian barbarians that crown the attic story definitely date from the age of Trajan, while eight of the ten tondi were plundered from a monument erected by Trajan. Despite its varied origins, the Arch of Constantine is outstanding for its architectural harmony and pure proportions.

116-117 The Arch of Constantine was inaugurated in 315 B.C. to commemorate the emperor's victory over Maxentius at the Battle of the Milvian Bridge. The 82-foot-high arch, with its three archways, stands alone near the Coliseum. Many of its friezes, statues and medallions were taken from buildings dating from the periods of Trajan, Hadrian and Marcus Aurelius. In particular, in the attic story the Emperor Hadrian's head was replaced with Constantine's. The few reliefs made specifically for the monument are recognizable by their hasty workmanship, decline in plasticity and lack of perspective.

118-119 According to tradition, Romulus founded Rome on the Palatine Hill, where the emperors later built their palaces. In the foreground are the remains of the Domus Augustana, built by Augustus; the elongated structure visible in the center is Domitian's stadium, destined for competitions and festivals.

120 top The frieze encircling Trajan's column consists of some 2,500 figures, and Trajan himself appears around 60 times. Battle scenes alternate with peaceful activities and sacrifices to the gods to ensure the success of the military campaign.

120 bottom Originally surmounted by a statue of Trajan, the column now features that of St. Peter, placed there in 1587; the cubic podium, 33 feet tall and covered in friezes, contained the emperor's funeral cella.

121 The sequence of the various episodes along the frieze, with its wealth of technical and geographical details, had a clearly educational and commemorative function. The monument was definitely multicolored.

developing society in which the contrasts between the old world and the new were evident. The creator of the genre was Lucilius who, in the surviving fragments, appears to have been a faithful chronicler of his time. The great construction boom that began around the middle of the 2nd century B.C. continued with even greater vigor in the age of Sulla. For the first time marble was used in the construction of temples, and was also employed, though to a lesser extent, in patrician residences, whose walls were decorated with colored paints. A typical example of the architecture of this period is the Tabularium, the state archives built in 78 B.C. in the valley between the Arx and the Capitol. The political antagonism between Caesar and Pompey, which influenced the political life of the period, also affected the construction industry. The desire to associate his name with major public works to gain the favor of the populace led Pompey to erect the first masonry theater on the Parade Ground in 55 B.C., surrounded with imposing porticoes and decorated with Greek works of art. Near the scene of the theater was a room used as a curia for meetings of the Senate; it was here that Caesar was assassinated by conspirators on the Ides of March in the year 44 B.C. This violent death put an end to the intensive building activities of the great military leader, who had demonstrated his gift for town planning by building a second Forum, designed according to Hellenistic canons, in the middle of which stood the Temple of Venus Genetrix, the tutelary divinity of the Julian gens. At the same time he began extensive improvement and renovation work on the Republican Forum; among other things he began the construction of the new Basilica Julia, which was to replace the now obsolete Basilica

Sempronia. The projects he was unable to complete included a masonry theater, which was terminated by Augustus and dedicated by him to his son-in-law Marcellus. Caesar is also believed to have drafted a general town plan, whose main aim was to divert the course of the Tiber so that it ran alongside the Vatican hills, in order to connect Trastevere to the Parade Ground, the area of which was to be allocated for private building. An outstanding personality, Caesar was not only a shrewd politician but also a brilliant writer who recorded his military exploits in a clear, precise style, thus leaving important evidence not only of his conquests, but also of a period that was crucial to the social and political life of Rome. At this time of great transformations and contrasts, Roman society endeavored to achieve a stable organization that would offer citizens greater harmony and tranquility. While Latin spread throughout the West, Greek was studied by the sons of the ruling class.

Oratory reached the height of its glory thanks to Cicero, and historiography thanks to Sallust and Caesar. Poetry reflected the spiritual aspirations of the time; previously, it had mainly exalted the Roman state, but now it focused on the search for truth and inner peace (as in the verses of Lucretius) or was inspired by the sphere of friendship and feminine love, described by Catullus.

The social gap was very evident, however; the aristocracy lived in comfortable houses on the Palatine Hill or in other residential areas, while the common people were crowded into unhealthy districts cluttered with tall, narrow houses. The wealthy owned villas in the country and by the sea, along the Tyrrhenian coast as far as Naples. Women of high birth enjoyed a freedom and prestige unknown in ancient times, and marriages of convenience between wealthy families became increasingly frequent. The proletariat consoled itself by attending public entertainments, especially gladiatorial combats and the venationes, in which wild beasts fought one another or the gladiators. The town plan devised by Caesar was not implemented by his successor, probably because it was too radical and expensive. The more conservative Augustus preferred not to make any great changes, only carrying out improvements and restoration work, but reorganized the public services. Augustus also abolished the old division of the city into four regions, which had become obsolete in view of the huge increase in its size. The reform, introduced in A.D. 7, involved the division of Rome into 14 regions, each of which comprised a suitable number of vici (districts). Eight regions were situated inside the old city walls, six on the outside, and one of the six, namely the 14th, was on the right

122 bottom The
construction of the
Pantheon, a temple
dedicated to all the
tutelary deities of the
Julia family, was
generously financed
by Agrippa,
Augustus's son-in-
law, in 27 B.C. After
being destroyed by
fire, it was rebuilt in
its present form by
order of Hadrian.

122-123
The Pantheon is the
best-preserved Roman
building and one of
the greatest
achievements in world
architecture. Its dome,
with a diameter of 143
feet, is still the largest
ever made without
reinforced concrete.

123 bottom
The huge dome of the
Pantheon,
representing a starry
sky, is illuminated by
the great central
oculus 30 feet wide,
which symbolizes the
Sun. The minimum
thickness of this
exceptional structure
is five feet.

bank of the Tiber. This division lasted
until the late Empire.

At the time of Augustus, there were
approximately 263 districts. Each one was
placed under the protection of a divinity
whose statue was erected at the main
crossroads, and was governed by 24 citizens
(the vicomagistri) elected from among
the residents and two senior magistrates.
The different types of dwellings were the
high-class domus and the multistoried
insulae (tenement blocks) for the lower
classes. In order to improve the quality of
life, Augustus inaugurated numerous
fountains and markets, installed night
lighting in the central area and instituted
the corps of the Vigiles and Urbaniciani
to perform public services. He also gave
particular attention to works of public
utility; he had the bed of the Tiber cleaned,
restored the old Appia, Marcia, Old Anio
and Tepula aqueducts, and supplied Rome
with three new ones (the Julia, Virgin and
Alsietine aqueducts).

In the Roman Forum he completed the
Curia, the Basilica Julia and the Rostri.
He renovated various temples, including
the Temple of Castor and Pollux and the
Temple of Vesta, the House of the Vestals
and the Regia. He erected the Temple of
the Divine Julius and built his home on
the Palatine Hill. Nearby, he erected one
temple consecrated to Vesta and one to
Palatine Apollo, which he furnished with
two libraries. A new forum dedicated to
him, grandiose in terms of its luxury and
decorations, stood opposite Caesar's; at
the center was the huge Temple of Mars
the Avenger. Equally noteworthy was the
activity of Augustus at the Parade
Ground, where he reclaimed a large area of
land. In this area he built his mausoleum,
the Ara Pacis (Altar of Peace) and a
sundial.

In the same area Agrippa, his son-in-law
and loyal assistant, founded the Pantheon,
the Baths, the Basilica of Neptune and the
Saepta, designed for meetings of the

populace during the comitia centuriata.
Finally, the Theater of Marcellus was
completed, and a new bridge built over the
Tiber. At the same time many patrician
villas were built on the Pincian, Palatine
and Esquiline hills, and in Trastevere.
Under Augustus, literature reached its
apogee. Maecenas, a rich, cultivated man,
introduced writers like Virgil, Horace and
Propertius into the emperor's circle. In the
Aeneid, which became the national poem,
Virgil celebrated the legendary origins of
Rome, exalting the greatness of the city
and of Augustus. Horace, in his Carmen
Saeculare, lauded the eternity of Imperial
Rome, while Propertius and Tibullus
dedicated their elegies to more private,
personal themes. Other men of culture
were Ovid, who described love in the
worldly setting of the capital; Livy who,
with his 142-volume History of Rome,
testified to the exceptional historical role of
Roman rule; and Vitruvius, who wrote a
detailed, valuable treatise on architecture.
During the reign of Tiberius, Augustus's
successor, no great public works were
undertaken. The only major constructions

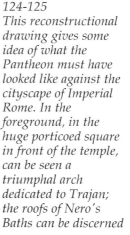

124-125
This reconstructional
drawing gives some
idea of what the
Pantheon must have
looked like against the
cityscape of Imperial
Rome. In the
foreground, in the
huge porticoed square
in front of the temple,
can be seen a
triumphal arch
dedicated to Trajan;
the roofs of Nero's
Baths can be discerned
in the right-hand
corner. Behind the
temple, a wing of
Neptune's Basilica,
also rebuilt by
Hadrian, can be seen
in partial cross-
section. At the top left
is the Temple of
Minerva, standing in
the center of the
Saepta Julia, a great
porticoed square
originally destined for
elections that later
became an art market.

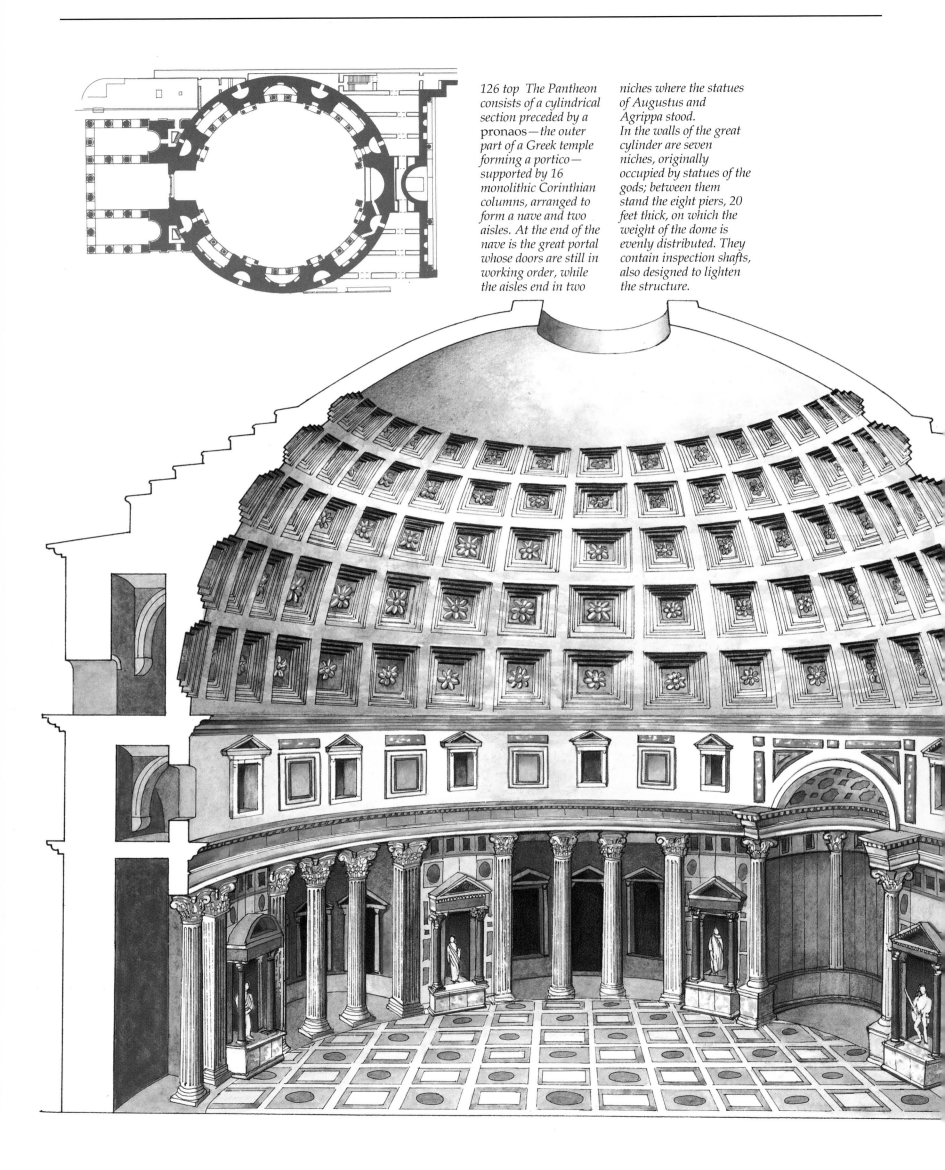

126 top The Pantheon consists of a cylindrical section preceded by a pronaos—the outer part of a Greek temple forming a portico— supported by 16 monolithic Corinthian columns, arranged to form a nave and two aisles. At the end of the nave is the great portal whose doors are still in working order, while the aisles end in two niches where the statues of Augustus and Agrippa stood. In the walls of the great cylinder are seven niches, originally occupied by statues of the gods; between them stand the eight piers, 20 feet thick, on which the weight of the dome is evenly distributed. They contain inspection shafts, also designed to lighten the structure.

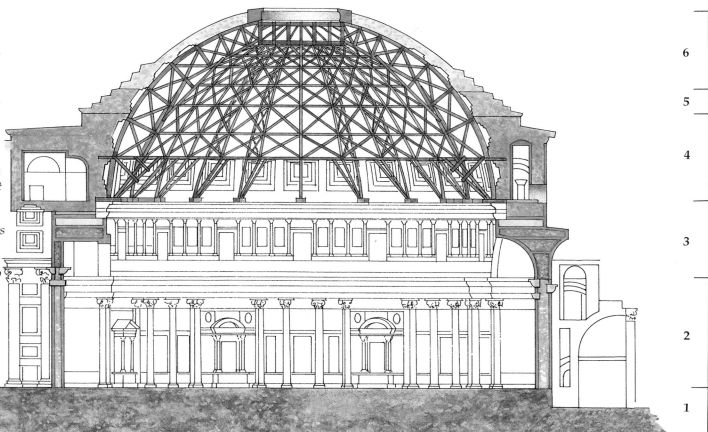

126-127 *Inside, the height of the rotunda is equal to the diameter (143 feet), so that the dome is a perfect hemisphere. The dome, lightened by five rows of coffering, has a volume of over 69,000 cubic yards. The structure is made with cast Pozzuolana cement faced with brick, alternating with horizontal rows of bricks and blocks of tufa. The materials become lighter towards the top*

6

5

4

3

2

1

127 top *This drawing illustrates the six types of concrete used in the structure. The foundations, 15 feet thick, are made of travertine chip concrete (1); the walls of the rotunda, from the floor to the first cornice, are made of concrete with tufa and travertine chippings (2); a second casting of opus incertum with tufa and bricks continues to the springing line (3); the first ring of the dome is made of concrete with brick fragments (5); the second ring is made of concrete lightened with tufa and brick fragments (6); and the calotte is made of concrete bonded with pumice stone and blocks of tufa. The dome was cast on an extraordinary self-supporting wooden frame onto which the forms of the coffers, anchored in the masonry of the cylindrical section, were fitted.*

127 right *This cross-section shows the construction technique used for the large round temple. The walls are internally faced with horizontal rows of bricks, used as forms for casting the concrete that constituted the core. Above the niches, large relieving arches and flat arches resting on stone quoins direct the weight of the masonry onto the columns, preserving the trabeations from fracture. The first ring of the dome, from the impost of the vault up to a height of some 40 feet, presents great arches of brick embedded in concrete, which limit the thrusts and aid distribution of the weight of the calotte between the eight piers. Similar arches are visible in the outer masonry of the drum. In the dome, the only bricks used are those of the oculus ring.*

128-129 The great mausoleum that Hadrian erected for himself and his successors was transformed over the centuries into what is now known as Castel Sant'Angelo. Its great cylindrical bulk, crowned by a mound of earth on which cypresses are planted, was surmounted by a high podium on which a statuary group or a bronze quadriga stood.

128 bottom The great Mausoleum of Augustus, which later became the sepulcher for the Julio-Claudian and Flavian dynasties, now appears as a circular building with a diameter of 287 feet. On the top there was a hillock decorated with cypresses, at the center of which there was probably a cylindrical structure crowned by the gilded statue of the emperor.

were his house on the Palatine Hill, the Domus Tiberiana, which was completed by Caligula, and the Castra Praetoria, the great camp for the praetorian cohorts built on the advice of Sejanus, his praetorian praefectus. Caligula founded a circus in the Gardens of Agrippina in the Vatican; an obelisk, specially made in Egypt for the circus, was later placed by Nero on the spina. Claudius built two new aqueducts, the Claudius and the New Anio, and built the Port of Ostia at the mouth of the Tiber, which guaranteed all the supplies needed by the city for over a century.

The reign of Nero is tragically famous for the terrible fire that devastated Rome for nine days; three of the 14 Augustan regions were reduced to a heap of rubble, and seven more were seriously damaged. The Esquiline Hill, the Oppian Hill, and part of the Aventine Hill, the Caelian Hill and the Velia were devastated, including the Regia and the House of the Vestals, and several other monuments were badly damaged. Many precious relics of ancient Rome were irretrievably lost, and thousands of inhabitants were made homeless. Nero drew up a complex, ambitious plan for the reconstruction of the city. The houses, whose height was to be limited, could no longer have party walls, and the front had to be protected by huge porticoes. These rules were not followed up by any real practical interest on the part of Nero (under Trajan large areas were still uninhabited), who gave all his attention to the building of the Domus Aurea, the new Imperial residence, in which unrivaled luxury and splendor ran riot. This "House of Gold" occupied all the Palatine Hill, much of the Caelian and Oppian Hills, the Fagutal, Carine and Velia and part of the Republican Forum. The only public building erected by the emperor was the Nero's Baths complex on the Parade Ground near the Pantheon. In the literary field, the patriotic and celebratory subjects that had characterized the Augustan era were abandoned. His successors had not succeeded in obtaining the wide consensus on which the Empire was founded; moreover, Caligula and Nero had demonstrated a clear inclination to introduce the worship of their own persons. Intellectuals therefore preferred to

neglect political subjects and take refuge in introspection, exalting freedom of the spirit far from the conditioning of public life. Outstanding writers of the period were Seneca, who investigated the values of the human soul in a search for wise serenity, and C. Petronius Arbiter who, in his novel Satyricon, gives us a realistic picture of the society of the day, poking fun at the nouveaux riches, namely the freedmen, who enjoyed brazen, vulgar luxury. Portrait painting, which was idealized under Augustus, once again became highly realistic, as demonstrated by the portraits of Tiberius, Claudius and Nero. The life of the people also changed; their favorite entertainments were still gladiatorial combat and chariot racing at the circus, but the custom of attending the baths, increasing numbers of which were built, also became popular.

The three Flavian emperors (Vespasian, Titus and Domitian) had the difficult task of reconstructing a city that, as the historian Suetonius said, "had lost its appearance because of ancient fires and ruins." Many districts were entirely rebuilt, and numerous new buildings were

129 top right
The Circus Maximus, which dates from the time of the Tarquins and was rebuilt on several occasions, was the largest entertainment building in Rome. In Trajan's time it was 1,980 feet long. Although estimates differ, it is believed to have housed 250,000 spectators and, in exceptional cases, up to 320,000.

129 bottom right
All that now remains of the magnificent Aemilian Bridge is a single span, known as Ponte Rotto (broken bridge). A small arch, clearly visible in the massive left-hand pier, was designed, like other similar ones, to reduce the pressure of the water against the structure when the Tiber was in full spate.

erected in various areas. The most radical work was undertaken in the valley between the Oppian and Palatine hills; the lake that was part of the Domus Aurea was drained, and the monument that was to become the symbol of Rome was built there: the Flavian Amphitheater, also called the Coliseum. The huge structure was inaugurated by Titus in A.D. 80, before its completion. Under Domitian the restoration of many old buildings continued, and new ones were built. The Temple of Capitoline Jupiter was rebuilt for the fifth time, and another temple, dedicated to Jupiter the Custodian, was erected. Work on the new Imperial palace

on the Palatine Hill was completed; for this purpose the two peaks of Cermalus and Palatium were leveled, and the saddle between them was filled in. The Domus Tiberiana and the Temple of Apollo were restored. In the forum a temple was consecrated to the memory of Vespasian and Titus, and the Arch of Titus, commemorating the conquest of Jerusalem, was built over the Via Sacra. On the Parade Ground, the emperor built the Stadium, with an odeum next to it, stables for the four circus factions, the Naumachia (a large lake designed for miniature naval battles), and a portico in the place where Vespasian and Titus stood as they waited to celebrate the triumph of the Jewish War. Domitian also completed the forum area; the mountain saddle joining the Capitol to the Quirinal Hill had been removed, the transitional forum was built, and a new baths complex was constructed on the Oppian Hill. For the first time, Rome thus had a large-scale and above all rapidly implemented town plan. The Flavians ruled during a period of order and prosperity, except for the terrible catastrophe caused by the eruption of Vesuvius in A.D. 79, which destroyed Pompeii, Stabia and Herculaneum, and also killed the famous scientist and naturalist Pliny the Elder.

The economic and social development of the provinces led to the spread of Roman traditions throughout the Empire; as a result, although it continued to attract intellectuals of all backgrounds, Rome was no longer the only center of cultural life. Many writers used languages other than Latin, including Arrian, Plutarch of Chaeronea, Appian and Flavius Josephus, who wrote about the Jewish War. A vivid portrait of the life of the period is given by Spanish poet Martial in his Epigrams. With Quintilian, the art of oratory regained vigor, though it was now far removed from the splendors of the Republican age. Trajan completed the work begun by Domitian, especially in the forum and the baths, which were named after him. He finished restructuring the slopes of the Capitol and the Quirinal Hill and built the grandiose Basilica Ulpia, behind which a Latin and a Greek library were erected opposite one another, in the

130 top The 1,690-foot-long Circus of Maxentius, erected outside the city walls in 309 B.C., is one of the best-preserved circuses from the Roman world.

130 top right St. Sebastian's Gate, with its single span flanked by crenelated towers, forms part of the Aurelian walls, 11.8 miles long, that surrounded the city.

130 right center Ordered by Censor Appius Claudius in 312 B.C., the 335-mile-long Appian Way connected Rome to Brundisium. Some sections near the capital are lined with funeral monuments.

130 bottom The tomb of Cecilia Metella, daughter-in-law of Triumvir Crassus, is the most famous monument on the Appian Way; the sepulcher, dating from the last decades of the Republican age, was converted into a fortress in the Middle Ages.

131 Next to St. Paul's Gate is the marble pyramid of Caius Cestius, the highly original sepulcer of the Praetor and Tribune of the Plebs who died in 12 B.C. The building is inspired by styles that became fashionable after the conquest of Egypt.

Consul   Augustus   Consul   ⌞————— The four Flaminian priests —————⌟   Lictor

new forum. In the space between the two buildings stood the famous Trajan's Column, on which episodes from the Dacian Wars are carved. This monument is of great interest in artistic terms, because it represents the best of Roman figurative art, and in historical and documentary terms. It is also original in terms of type, and is one of the few ancient monuments that came through the Dark Ages unscathed. Near one of the large exedrae of the forum he built Trajan's Markets, a trading district with a novel layout. Trajan also gave the city a new and more efficient port, consisting of a magnificent hexagonal basin to replace that of Claudius, which was now silted up, and built the last great aqueduct to supply Rome with water. His successor, Hadrian, gave the city two temples that soon came to symbolize Roman civilization, the Pantheon (founded by Agrippa but now dilapidated) and the Temple of Venus and Rome. On the right bank of the Tiber he built his mausoleum, connected to the opposite bank by a new

bridge, the Aelius, still used today. On the Parade Ground he erected a portico and a temple in honor of Marciana and Matidia, Trajan's sister and niece; Matidia was the mother of Hadrian's wife Vibia Sabina. Apart from the column erected on the Parade Ground to commemorate the victories won by Marcus Aurelius against the Germans and Sarmatians, the Antonine emperors did not construct any major buildings, merely completing those created by their predecessors. The city was now full of public works of all kinds, and the only buildings erected in the later centuries were baths and porticoes. During this period the state showed particular interest in education; among other things many libraries were opened, and state schools and professorships were financed. The ability to read and write became more common than in the past, and many people were bilingual in Greek and Latin.
The most vivid poetic voice during the reign of Trajan was that of D. Junius Juvenalis (Juvenal), who in his Satires

gives an unrelentingly realistic picture of the society of the day. The greatest historian was Tacitus, mainly known for his biographies of the emperors, from Tiberius to Nero. Suetonius, who among other things narrated the lives of the emperors from Caesar to Domitian, was also a leading biographer, but demonstrated a greater tendency to erudition. Other outstanding figures belonging to the Antonine age were the great doctor Galen, the erudite Gellius, the famous rhetorician, Cornelius Fronto, and the African, Apuleius, author of the novel The Golden Ass, which came to symbolize the intellectual restlessness of the time, and the search for inner serenity that neither philosophy nor traditional religion could any longer provide. The next period, dominated by the Severus dynasty, began with Septimius Severus, who mainly devoted his time to restoring and completing existing buildings. His name is only associated with the construction of the Settizodio, built at the foot of the Palatine Hill. This imposing

Agrippa   Caius   Julia   Tiberius   Antonia   Germanicus Drusus   Domitius Antonia Domitia Domitius Ahenobarbus
           Caesar   the Younger   the Elder

132-133 The Ara Pacis Augustae, a monument of outstanding historical and artistic value, was totally reconstructed in the late thirties on the basis of fragments discovered in 1568. This altar of peace was commissioned by the Senate in 13 B.C. to give thanks for Augustus's gift of peace to the entire Roman world after the victories in Spain and Gaul. It was consecrated on the Parade Ground in 9 B.C. with a solemn ceremony. It consists of a rectangular marble outer wall on a podium containing two doors, each reached by a staircase. Inside, at the top of three steps, is the richly decorated altar. The outer wall has magnificent sculptural decorations both inside (consisting of a plant festoon motif with paterae, or drinking saucers, and bucrania, ox-skull ornaments) and on the outside, where it is divided into two sections. In the lower strip is an elegant repeating frieze pattern of acanthus volutes with swans and other animals, while the upper strip portrays four mythological scenes (one on each side of the doors) and the procession to mark the consecration of the altar, divided between the two shorter sides. While the one to the north is badly damaged and less important, the group of characters on the south side is of great interest because it includes Augustus with priests, magistrates and members of the Imperial family. The illustration shows the procession on the south side, with the exception of the first sector in which the reliefs are lost. The procession is headed by two of the lictors, followed by Augustus between two consuls; then come the four Flaminian priests and the Flaminian lictor; Agrippa, his son, Caius Caesar, and the former's wife, Julia, Augustus's daughter; Tiberius; Antonia the Younger (Augustus's niece) and her husband, Drusus, Tiberius's brother, with his son, Germanicus; Antonia the Elder (Augustus's niece) with her children, Domitius and Domitia, and finally her husband, Domitius Ahenobarbus.

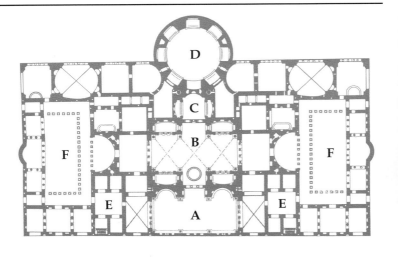

scenic structure (probably a nymphaeum adorned with statues and exquisite marbles) acted as a grandiose backdrop to the urban part of the Appian Way, providing a very attractive sight for strangers arriving in Rome. Although he also began the construction of the magnificent baths later completed by his son Caracalla, after whom they were named, Septimius Severus preferred to devote his attention not so much to the capital of the Empire as to his birthplace, Leptis Magna, which he embellished with magnificent buildings. The subsequent emperors are not associated with any monument in particular, except for Severus Alexander, who built the baths on the Parade Ground; they were supplied by the new Alexandrine Aqueduct, the last to be brought to Rome. Finally, at the end of the century, Aurelian started work on a mighty city wall that, though extensively rebuilt, still surrounds the city, with a perimeter of nearly 12 miles. There was quite a wealth of cultural life at this period, due to the sponsorship of Julia Domna, wife of Septimius Severus, who gathered at court leading personalities such as the historian Cassius Dio and the jurists Papinian and Ulpian. However, the absolute Imperial rule that had eliminated all free and spontaneous inspiration did not give rise to original literary production, but rather favored the study and imitation of existing works. A profusion of Christian writings, which, in view of the religious tolerance of the period were allowed to circulate freely, was characteristic of this century. In this respect, the works of apologists defending the new faith are important, especially those of the Carthaginian Tertullian, who supported the Christian doctrine with great religious zeal and passionate moral rigor. The last period of extensive construction work in Rome took place under Diocletian and Constantine. The grandiose baths at either end of the Quirinal Hill and Helena's Baths on the Esquiline Hill were built under these emperors. Maxentius erected a new basilica in the forum, and a large circus at his residence on the Appian Way. Constantine, who governed the Empire alone after the battle of the Milvian Bridge, strengthened and restored many dilapidated public buildings, and also promoted the erection of new Christian basilicas. The Arch of Constantine near the Coliseum, which symbolized the end of the pagan world, was built in his honor. In the latter part of the 4th century A.D., the old temples were gradually abandoned or converted into Christian churches. Only the walls and bridges were kept in efficient order for obvious safety reasons. Despite the major restoration work on the city walls ordered by Arcadius and Honorius, they were unable to withstand the barbarian hordes led by Alaric, and in 410 A.D. the city suffered serious damage when it was sacked and stripped of its greatest works of art. This event marked the beginning of the decline that was accentuated in the second half of the 5th century, leading to the end of the Roman Empire of the West. Art also underwent a radical transformation in the last period of the Empire's life. In depicting the human figure they passed from realism to increasingly marked stylization, in line with the new image of power and its holders. The major sculptures are represented by sarcophagi; also some important mosaics belong to this period, in which the new Christian themes were featured more and more often.

By contrast with this development, the lifestyle of the Roman populace remained almost unchanged. The great public

134-135 Begun circa A.D. 212 by Septimius Severus and inaugurated four years later by his son, after whom they were named, the Baths of Caracalla were considered the most magnificent in Rome. Covering an area of 156,000 square yards, they could hold up to 1,600 people engaged in various activities.

135 bottom The surviving mosaics do not do justice to the magnificence that led to the fame of the Baths of Caracalla, originally ornamented with priceless marbles, multicolored plaster and statuary groups. In addition to the bathing rooms, the huge complex included palaestrae for physical exercise, saunas, libraries and lounges.

136-137
This reconstruction shows what the Baths of Caracalla must have looked like. The central area, shown in cross-section, features the swimming pool, the frigidarium, the tepidarium, and the caldarium, a circular room with a diameter of 115 feet, now destroyed. Magnificent gardens surrounded the complex.

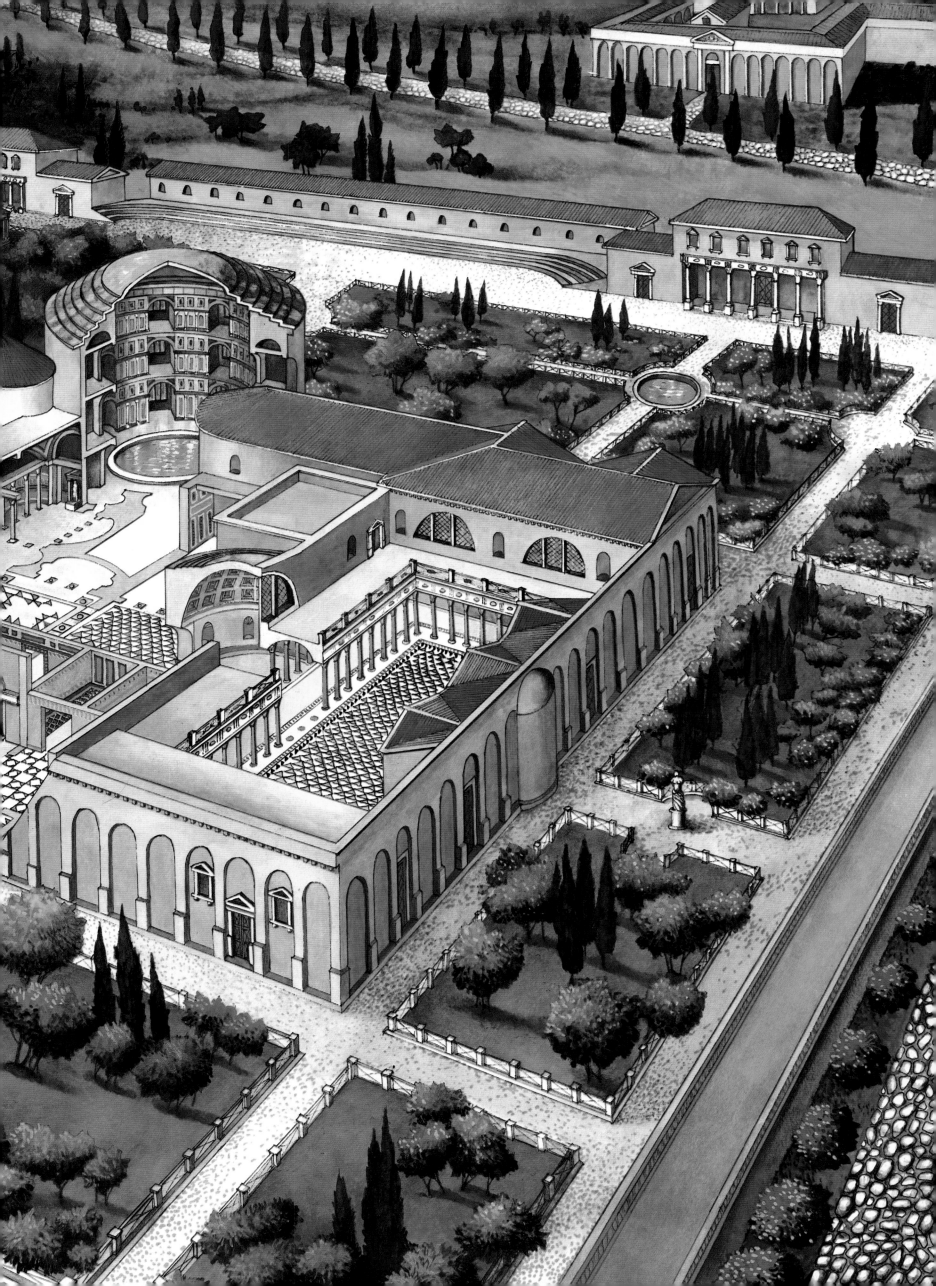

138 top The Basilica of Santa Maria degli Angeli was built in 1566 by Michelangelo, who adapted to this new purpose the huge tepidarium *of the Baths of Diocletian, the largest ever built in Rome. The façade of the sacred building, shown in the picture, was actually one of the two exedrae of the* caldarium, *nothing else of which survives.*

138-139 This aerial photo shows the impressive size of the ruins of Diocletian's Baths. The tepidarium, *later converted to the transept of the church modified by Vanvitelli in 1749, is 300 feet long and 92 feet high. The entire complex, made wholly of brick between* A.D. *298–306, could be used by some 3,000 people at once.*

A Natatio
B Frigidarium
C Tepidarium
D Caldarium
E Palaestra

entertainments continued to be held whenever the Imperial purse could afford it. However, the financial crisis that was inexorably advancing forced everyone, including the court, to adopt a more austere way of life. Under the influence of emperors like Diocletian and Constantine, support for literature continued. The main works produced during this period were studies of grammar and rhetoric, while the last followers of the pagan tradition vainly attempted to defend what was now a declining world. There were many mediocre epitomists and biographers who, following in the footsteps of Suetonius, wrote biographies of emperors. The only voice really worthy of the historiographic tradition of the past was that of Ammianus Marcellinus. The Christian culture led to the development of a new kind of intellectual who, while acknowledging the validity of the past philosophical and literary tradition, only accepted those elements he considered useful to the interpretation of Christianity. The greatest personality of the time was Saint Augustine, whose philosophy expressed the drama of the human soul in the highest tones. The last, grieving witness of the declining Empire was Gallic poet Rutilius Namazianus who, in De reditu suo, narrates his return to his country, describing the sea voyage undertaken because the old consular roads had become impassable. When he takes his leave, he addresses Rome in highly poetic accents: "Hear, O beautiful queen of the world which is thine, O Rome now received among the celestial spheres! Hear, O mother of men and mother of gods, thou who, through thy temples, make us feel less distant from the heavens! We sing of thee and always of thee – as long as the fates allow, we sing: no one who has

139 bottom right The Roman National Museum, the entrance of which is shown here, is housed in a wing of the Baths of Diocletian.
The plan of the building repeated the distribution system already used for the Baths of Caracalla in a more grandiose but basically unchanged form. Thermal baths were one of the most characteristic signs of Roman civilization, and buildings of this kind have been found in every province of the Empire. There is definite evidence that there were 10 monumental bath complexes in Rome alone, but written sources refer to at least six more, whose location is uncertain. The huge amount of water required by these structures was usually supplied by specially built branches of the main city aqueducts.

survived in the world can be unmindful of thee…Just as nature, the bringer of life, has reached out to the furthermost confines of the world, so has the earth been accessible to thy value. Thou hast created for people of every country a single fatherland; for lawless peoples it was great fortune to be subjugated by thee. In offering the vanquished the equality of thy rights, thou hast made a city of what once was the world…" (urbem fecisti quod prius orbis erat).

140-141
Roman art, in its principal manifestation, was a tool that served the purposes of Imperial political propaganda. However, as demonstrated by these two portraits of youths, which are delicate but slightly academic, the more affected and elegant themes of Hellenistic art were very popular with cultivated, wealthy individuals who sometimes spent ridiculous sums on decorating their villas with marbles and bronzes. This enthusiasm was due more to snobbishness than to any real interest in artistic values, however. In fact, the practice of art was never considered really worthy of a Roman citizen, and was willingly left to the Greek and Asian masters who emigrated to Rome, or to plebeians and freemen.

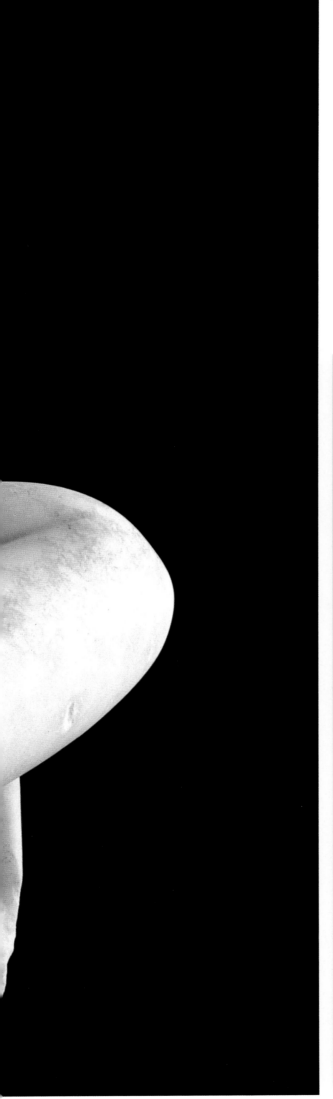

142 *Both the Capitoline Venus (right) and the Hermaphroditus (left) are excellent Roman copies of Greek originals. The encounter between the Roman world and Greek-Hellenistic art took place at a time when the former (which until then had concentrated on the more pressing needs of the initial stage of expansionism) was beginning to show enthusiastic interest in beauty as an end in itself (as the result of the arrival of great riches), while the latter (which had reached a stage of full maturity after centuries of development) was returning to certain archaic forms popular during its former political and cultural supremacy. Rome therefore willingly imported similar models, with the result that Roman figurative art was strongly influenced by them; however, official art continued to be associated with the utilitarian and celebratory function it had performed since the origins of the Republic. In practice, the Romans considered sculpture as having a decorative and scenic function, which explains its success with wealthy citizens and in public architecture, whereas triumphal portraits continued to follow the lifelike models of historical tradition, sometimes interpreted in a virtuoso manner drawn from Hellenism. The field in which the Roman creative spirit was expressed with the greatest originality was architecture.*

144-145 This relief, part of the outer decoration of the Ara Pacis, shows Tellus, a buxom female figure who personifies the fertility of the earth, surrounded by two nymphs symbolizing air and water. The scene represents the three elements of the world subjected to Roman power, and is at the same time an allegory of the peace of Augustus, who brought prosperity to Italy. The monument (about which valuable information is provided by Ovid and by Augustus himself, who referred to it in his autobiography, Res Gestae Divi Augusti), is essential to the understanding of public art under Augustus. In the Ara Pacis influences of Hellenism can be seen in the outer volute decoration and the Tellus relief, while Neoattic taste is evident in the spatial composition of the two processions. At the same time, the evident propagandistic intention and the attention given to the historical value of the work are typically Roman. This basic eclecticism, together with themes from Italic tradition, is characteristic of the late Republic and particularly of the early Imperial age.

EVIDENCE OF ROMAN CIVILIZATION IN ITALY

THE POLITICAL ORGANIZATION OF ITALY

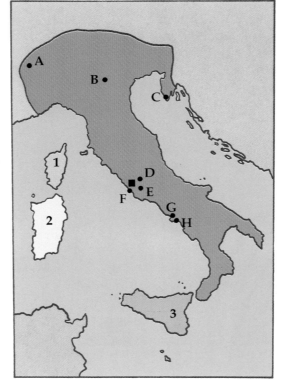

The fact that Rome is located in the center of Italy nearly always enabled the Romans to confront their enemies separately. However, the gradual increase in conquered territories necessitated the introduction of a suitable defensive system, which took the form of the typically Italic institution of the colony. Citizens were sent with their families to strategically crucial points, mainly existing towns, not only to defend the new conquests but also to cultivate the land allotted to them. This land consisted of a third of the enemy territory, divided into small plots and redistributed in the form of private property. These citizens were called coloni (colonists), and the new communities were called coloniae (colonies). The colonists might be Latin or Italic allies or, far more often, Roman citizens who were equated with Latin allies or maintained their rights of citizenship. This originated the distinction between coloniae Latinae, coloniae Latinorum and coloniae civium Romanorum (Latin colonies, colonies of Latins and colonies of Roman citizens). The oldest colonies were the Latin colonies, i.e., those situated on land conquered by the Latin League, some of which dated back to the age of the monarchy. The foundation (deductio) of those towns, to which 1,500–6,000 colonists were usually sent, continued even after the dissolution of the League in 338 B.C.; the last Latin colony in Italy was Lucca, founded in 180 B.C.

These colonies, allied to Rome by a special treaty, had their own constitution, their own laws and their own magistrates. They paid no taxes to Rome, but had to supply military contingents in wartime. Founded to consolidate the territorial advantages obtained during the Latin War, they were mainly formed by Roman plebeians who gave up their citizenship in return for ownership of a plot of arable land. Latin colonies were mainly used to defend the land borders, whereas in the case of the coastal borders, Rome founded smaller colonies formed by Roman citizens. According to tradition, the first Roman colony was Ostia, founded by Ancus Martius. The inhabitants of these colonies, usually 300, retained the rights guaranteed by Roman citizenship, and had their own magistrates. In 183 B.C., Roman colonies began to replace Latin colonies in defending the territory. The foundation of Modena and Parma in Cisalpine Gaul and Saturnia in Etruria dates back to this period. On that occasion, the number of colonists was increased to 2,000.

Sometimes Rome was unable to send colonists to the conquered territories, in which case the inhabitants of the subjugated towns were allowed to enjoy Roman citizenship to a greater or lesser extent, and continued to live in their own homes. Thus the municipium (municipality) was introduced. The first municipium is believed to have been the Latin Tusculum, whose inhabitants were granted Roman citizenship in 381 B.C. The municipal system was applied on a large scale to the Latin towns after the dissolution of the Latin League and, at the same period, to the towns of

147 bottom left On the cliff that dominates the valley of the Aniene Falls at Tivoli stand the ruins of a round temple dating from the late Republican period; it is called the Temple of Vesta or of the Sibyl, but was probably consecrated to Hercules. This Corinthian-style building exerted great influence over 19th-century European monumental architecture.

147 bottom right Verona, founded in a loop of the River Adige, was one of the largest Roman towns in northern Italy. The amphitheater, commonly called the Arena, dates from the first half of the 1st century A.D. Though much restored, it is one of the best preserved in the world, and is still used for a famous opera season.

146-147 *Pula, now a town in Croatia, on the Istrian peninsula, was a Roman colony from the mid-1st century B.C. Its amphitheater presents the unusual feature of four massive towers along the outer perimeter, containing the staircases leading to the upper floors.*

147 top *One of the most interesting of the numerous surviving Roman monuments in Pula is the funeral arch of the Sergia family, with a single archway between pairs of Corinthian columns. It dates from the 3rd decade B.C., and is one of the oldest specimens to survive intact.*

Campania. The inhabitants of the Latin towns obtained either citizenship carrying full political rights or citizenship not carrying the right to vote (civitas sine suffragio). This kind of town belonged to an inferior category of municipality which, as jurisdiction was exercised by praefecti sent from Rome, were known as praefecturae. There were also civitates foederatae, towns allied with Rome by a treaty that maintained the title of sovereign state provided that they did not dispute Roman supremacy. Almost all the towns in Etruria and Italy south of Vesuvius had this legal status.

The institution of colonies, which had lost much of its defensive role in the meantime, was restored in 123 B.C. by Caius Gracchus in order to give land to the Roman proletariat; his attempt, violently opposed by the nobility, ended in bloody riots, during which he was assassinated. The growing dissatisfaction of the Latin colonists and all the allies in the Italic confederation, who had long made an active contribution to the rise of Rome but were denied the status of Roman citizens, led to a full-scale armed conflict. In 89 B.C. the Allies' War led to the conversion of the remaining Latin

colonies, which retained a solely legal function, and the grant of the highly prized ius civitatis to the towns below the Rubicon.

From then on, the municipal system was extended throughout Italy. The municipium had greater administrative independence, and was long considered a perfect example of town organization. Primacy was only regained by the colonies in the second half of the 1st century A.D.

At the beginning of the 1st century B.C., first under Marius and then under Sulla, the types of colony founded were extended in order to reward army veterans with grants of land. This practice was later consolidated by Caesar and Augustus. On these occasions, the land required for the new colonists was confiscated, as in the case of the 18 towns that had supported the conspirators against Caesar, or was purchased. The title of Roman colony became highly sought-after, and many emperors granted this status to numerous Italian towns.

As regards the organization of all the towns described so far, despite the numerous transformations that took place over the years, their constitutions were generally patterned on that of Rome, and increasingly came to resemble it. Rome adopted systems of government that varied according to the period, the nationality of the new citizens and the treatment granted to them. The supreme magistrates of the colonies and municipalities in the Imperial age were the duoviri or quattuorviri iure dicundo. Within certain limits they exercised civil and criminal jurisdiction, convened and chaired sessions of the council and people's assemblies, handled the interests of the town, organized public works and ensured that religious duties were observed. All the magistrates were elected by the people in comitia, as demonstrated by the electoral "posters" that can still be seen on the walls of Pompeii.

Every town had its own budget to manage. Its income consisted of miscellaneous receipts with which the

town had to cover a range of expenses: corn supplies, postal services, billeting of troops, entertainments, and the construction and maintenance of city walls, roads, aqueducts and public buildings. It was by no means unusual for wealthy private citizens to erect buildings of public utility or pay for entertainments out of their own pockets. As in the organization of the political and social life of the colonies, in terms of town planning the Romans demonstrated a strong propensity for strictly classifying the spaces under their jurisdiction beginning with the Republican age. When a colony was founded, the selected site, measuring around 28 square miles, was measured from the town center at the intersection of two roads, called the cardo, which ran north-south, and the decumanus,

which ran east-west. On the basis of these coordinates the land was divided into plots of 200 iugeri (approximately 125 acres), which constituted the basic cadastral unit. These plots were called centuries (centuriae, i.e., areas comprising 100 units of two iugeri), and the operation of division into centuries was called centuriatione. Apart from centuries, the land could be divided per strigas et scamna, i.e., into rectangular strips, one running north-south, and the other east-west. Each plot belonged to a single owner, with the result that a century was divided equally between a number of owners. In wooded areas or those crossed by streams, the necessary adjustments had to be made when the plots were distributed to ensure that some of the

colonists were not discriminated against. The main tool used to divide the land was the groma, used by surveyors, who were therefore called gromatici. The groma was a cross-shaped instrument with arms of equal length, fixed horizontally to a rod that was driven into the ground. Four plumb lines were secured to the ends of the arms so that perpendicular alignments could be established. When the groma had been placed in the center of the land to be divided, two basic right-angled axes could be drawn. The lines parallel to them were then defined at a distance of 20 actus apart, to obtain a regular lattice. The actus, equal to 117.08 feet was the unit of flat measurement, calculated on the basis of the area of land along which oxen could draw the plough

148-149 The oracular sanctuary of Fortuna Primigenia in Preneste (now Palestrina) is one of the most important religious complexes of the Roman period in Italy. The group of buildings was extended further and further up the hillside from the 2nd century B.C. to the age of Sulla. The main section of the lower part consisted of a colonnaded room; to the left was the cave of the oracle, and on the right was another smaller room, the floor of which was decorated with a magnificent mosaic portraying the Nile in flood, shown in

the left-hand picture. In the upper part of the sanctuary the architects' imagination ran riot; they invented a highly scenic distribution pattern organized around three terraces, culminating in a large semicircle surmounted by a tholos, a type of circular building. With its extraordinary anticipation of later architectural forms, Preneste influenced the monumental buildings of the Imperial age (including the design of Trajan's column) and the religious buildings of the colonies.

in a single draft. A plan of the land thus divided and allocated was then drawn up, and a copy was sent to Rome. The division of the land into regular areas in accordance with a system of right-angled axes had pre-Roman origins, and was widely practiced in Magna Grecia and Etruria, where it was associated with religious factors. In much of the Italian countryside, aerial photographs clearly show signs of division into centuries, the layout of which can still be identified by observing local roads, canals and boundaries.

A similar method of land division was used in the foundation of new towns. The town center presented the same layout as a military camp, with a rectangular or square shape and a chessboard pattern of roads aligned parallel to the cardo and decumanus. Inside the city walls, along which guard towers were built at regular intervals, were the forum, the basilica, the curia, the temples, the baths, the market, the theater and, in the most recently founded towns such as Aosta, the amphitheater.

Despite some variations due to the topography, this pattern was always followed. It had wide-ranging effects on the development of many towns of Roman foundation, even after the fall of the Empire. Especially in northern Italy, where Roman architects were free to plan, in accordance with rational, unitary patterns, the construction of new colonies founded to control conquered lands, the regularity of the road networks of numerous town centers reveals their ancient origins.

In Turin, Aosta, Como, Pavia and Piacenza, as well as Verona, Bologna and Lucca, the right-angled lattice of the Roman town remained at the basis of medieval town planning, and even influenced more recent building; in many cases, even the roads that crossed the surrounding countryside followed the ancient routes, with few modifications. The imposing monumental remains still visible in these provincial capitals also demonstrate their flourishing economies and quality of life, which have only been equaled and surpassed in modern times, over 13 centuries later.

150 The statue known as the Aphrodite of the Esquiline *is an eclectic product (however superb the result) of the last period of Hellenistic art, in which the archaic trend is cleverly blended with a naturalistic portrayal of the nude. Copies of Greek originals have been found in many parts of the peninsula, demonstrating their great popularity. In official portraits the craftsmen, often Greek immigrants, sometimes only sculpted the client's face in marble, and then fixed the head to mass-produced bodies inspired by famous works of the past. Wealthy Romans were enthusiastic collectors of art and antiques.*

151 This famous fresco fragment from Pompeii, which dates back to the 1st century A.D., shows a newly-wed couple; the woman is holding a wax tablet, while the man holds a roll of parchment. He is considered by some to be the baker Pacuius Proculus, and by others to be an unknown city magistrate. Whatever the correct interpretation, the important thing is the evident wealth acquired in the early Imperial age by the middle classes who, enriched by trade or public office, had become the true ruling class. The portrait also demonstrates the emancipation of Roman women, exceptional in the ancient world.

AOSTA, STANDING SENTRY OVER THE PENNINE ALPS

Map legend:
- **A** Tourneuve
- **B** Decumanus Gate
- **C** Leper's Tower
- **D** North Gate
- **E** Sacred area
- **F** Forum
- **G** South Gate (Bramafam Tower)
- **H** Baths
- **I** Pailleron Tower
- **J** Knight Commanders' Tower
- **K** Amphitheater
- **L** Theater
- **M** Praetorian Gate

Aosta, a Roman colony founded by Augustus in around 24 B.C. with the name of Augusta Praetoria Salassorum, stands at the foot of the Pennine Alps, at the confluence of the Dora Baltea and the Buthier Stream, at the point where the roads leading to Helvetia and Gaul started. The city was built by 3,000 discharged praetors on the site of the military camp of the praetor Aulus Terentius Varro, who had quartered his troops near a major cultural center of the Salassi, the Celtic tribe he was ordered to subjugate. Ancient Aosta presented a highly regular layout, and is widely considered to be the model of a Roman city that comes closest to the ideal canons. Even now the city walls, just over 1.5 miles long, appear complete, and feature various quite well-preserved towers, such as the Pailleron Tower and the Leper's Tower. The famous Praetorian Gate on the east side of the walls is one of the loveliest to have survived from ancient times. Consisting of two sections enclosing a huge intermediate courtyard, it has two mighty square towers at the sides of a triple passage consisting of a large central supporting arch and two minor side arches. The height of the right-hand tower, now used as an exhibition area, was considerably increased during the 12th century. The remains of a temple are to be found in the city center in the area corresponding to the forum, surrounded by a large quadrangular cryptoporticus. This kind of underground structure, common to many forums built in Gaul, was probably used as a processional route. The remains of the theater and amphitheater are situated not far from the gate, in the northeastern sector of the city. The grandiose straight back wall of the theater auditorium, with its three tiers of arches intersected by an intermediate row of rectangular openings, is very attractive. Excavations have brought to light various elements of the scene, but only the lower part of the tier of steps has survived. Numerous construction features suggest that the Aosta theater was one of the few roofed theaters in the Roman world.

Little remains of the amphitheater, which was situated inside the city walls; this is quite unusual, as this kind of building was usually erected outside the town. The Aostan amphitheater, now partly incorporated in a convent, was

152 bottom Among the most interesting relics housed in the Aosta Archaeological Museum is a silver bust of Jupiter Poeninus found at the Little St. Bernard Pass, and a superb bronze baldric dating from the 2nd century A.D.

152-153 Numerous construction features suggest that the Aosta theater, of which part of the end wall of the auditorium still survives, was one of the few entirely roofed theaters in the Roman world.

one of the first to be built in stone, a century before the Coliseum; it held around 15,000 spectators. The triumphal arch of Augustus, which stands alone a few hundred yards from the Praetorian Gate, straddling the suburban road that crossed the Buthier Stream on a bridge with a 56-foot span, has survived almost intact. The arch is in a good state of repair, except for the attic story, now lost, which contained the dedicatory inscription. It was

probably erected to commemorate the victories won by the emperor over the Alpine populations, especially the Salassi. It has a single supporting arch with a tall plinth on which stand semi-columns built onto the pillars; rectangular niches are inserted in the intercolumniation of the frontages. Aosta is now a flourishing regional capital that, because of the monumental remains that perfectly fit into the life of the town, constitutes an area of international historical and town planning research.

153 bottom The Arch of Augustus, made of hewn pudding-stone blocks, is the oldest surviving arch. The construction of such an impressive building in a place that was still relatively distant from the capital of the Empire was intended to intimidate the recently subjugated population, and to stir the pride of the new colonists.

154-155 Aosta, surrounded by countryside accurately divided into "centuries," took the form of a rectangle measuring 2,390 by 1,890 feet. The mighty city walls guaranteed its defense, while the great public buildings met the rapidly growing population's desire for monumental constructions.

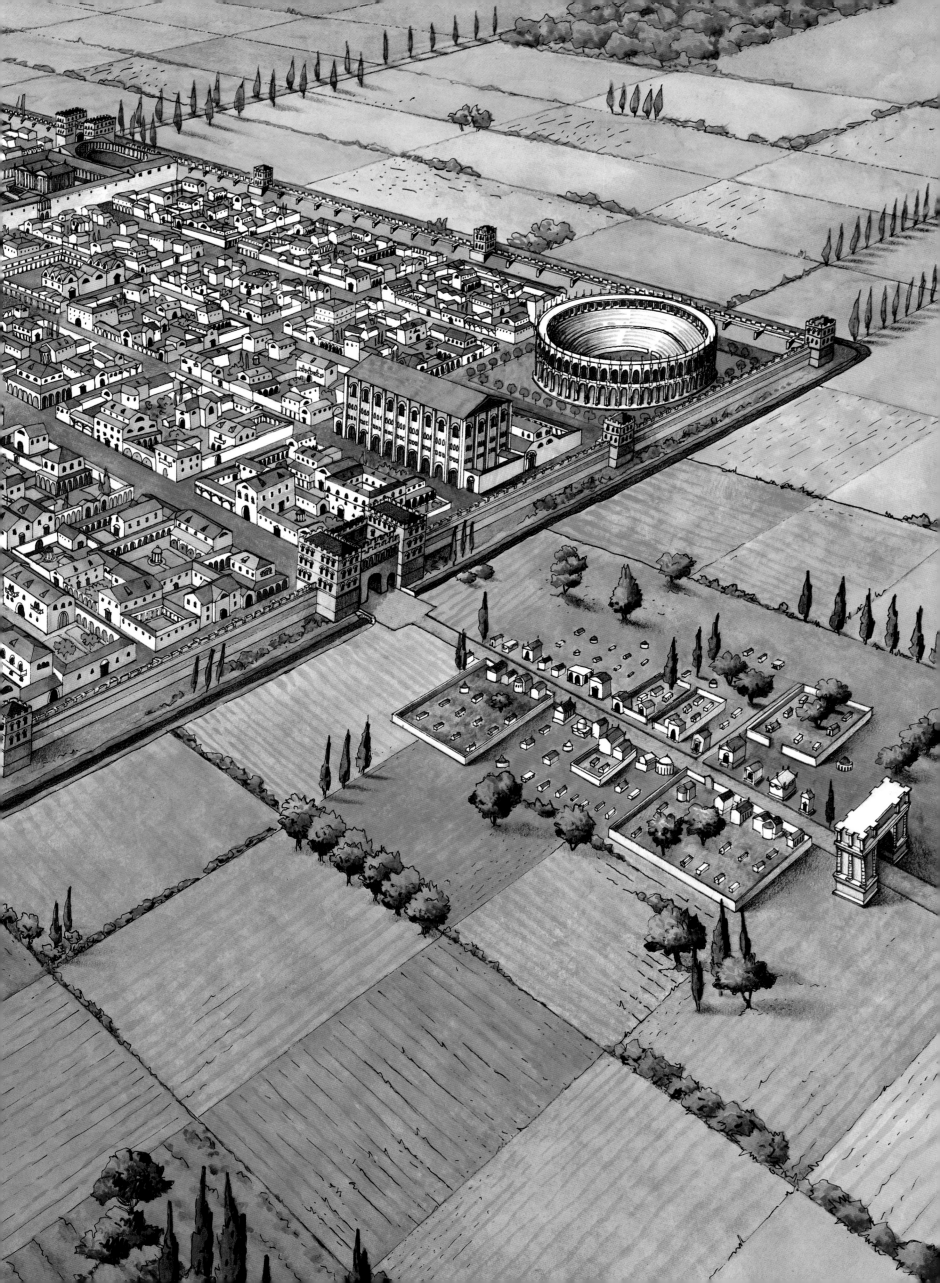

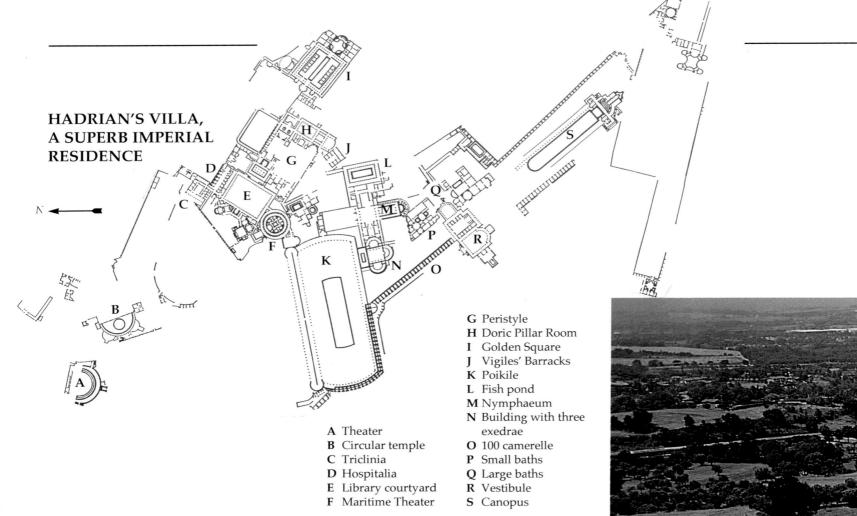

HADRIAN'S VILLA, A SUPERB IMPERIAL RESIDENCE

N ←

A Theater
B Circular temple
C Triclinia
D Hospitalia
E Library courtyard
F Maritime Theater

G Peristyle
H Doric Pillar Room
I Golden Square
J Vigiles' Barracks
K Poikile
L Fish pond
M Nymphaeum
N Building with three exedrae
O 100 camerelle
P Small baths
Q Large baths
R Vestibule
S Canopus

Tivoli (the ancient Tibur) is situated to the southeast of Rome on the Tiburtine-Valerian Way near the Anio Falls. The city came under Roman influence at the beginning of the 5th century B.C., but its relations with Rome were by no means peaceful until the time of the Allies' War, when it became a municipium and obtained Roman citizenship. In the Augustan era it became one of the most fashionable resorts for wealthy Romans. Cassius, Maecenas, Horace, Quintilius Varo, Catullus, Sallust and Augustus all stayed in Tivoli, and Hadrian built his splendid villa at the foot of the town. In addition to the beauty of the area, particular attractions for the Romans were the ancient Sanctuary of Hercules and the Sibylline Oracle, as well as the sulphur baths in the plain below.
It is difficult to reconstruct the plan of the ancient city on the basis of the surviving monuments. Little remains of the city walls and gates; the acropolis had its own wall.
The area where the basilica and forum stood has been identified. On the south side of the forum stand the well preserved remains of a rectangular building with vaulted roof, probably the Food Supplies Office, as two interesting mensae ponderariae (the official samples used for measurements in local

trading transactions) were found there. At the eastern end of the Acropolis, facing the overhanging rock where the Anio forms the famous waterfall, stand two temples: the rectangular, tetrastyle (having four frontal columns) Ionic Temple of the Sibyl and the Temple of Vesta, which is circular with a Corinthian colonnade. Both date from the first half of the 1st century B.C., and constitute a very attractive feature in the surrounding countryside.
Outside the city walls, in the Grotta Oscura district, are the ruins of the grandiose complex known as the Sanctuary of Hercules the Victor. The building, with its beautiful scenic layout, partly built on strong terraces, dates from the 1st century B.C., although it was rebuilt to some extent in the Flavian era. This place of worship is closely linked from an architectural standpoint with other contemporary sanctuaries in Latium, like those of Jupiter Anxur in Terracina and Fortuna Primigenia in Palestrina, and with the Tabularium in Rome. All these buildings are examples of the frenetic construction work carried out in the region around the mid-1st century B.C. Tivoli is now mainly famous for the grandiose Hadrian's Villa, situated on a large plateau on the Tiburtine Hills, to the southwest of the town. The huge

156-157 *Hadrian's Villa was built near Tivoli between 118 and 133* A.D. *by Emperor Hadrian, who wished to recall the places and monuments he had visited during his long travels. In the foreground can be seen the ruins of the four-sided portico and what is called the fishpond.*

157 top *The Maritime Theater, surrounded by a portico and a ring-shaped canal, was actually the small villa to which Hadrian liked to retire to meditate alone, isolated from the rest of the world. The great swimming pool of the* poikile *can be seen in the background.*

complex of buildings, which occupies a site of some 300 acres, is one of the most interesting archaeological sites in Italy. Built on the site previously occupied by a villa of the Republican period, it fits perfectly into the surrounding landscape, apparently spontaneously but actually in accordance with a precise design. In accordance with a fashion already introduced in the Republican period, Hadrian, an admirer of the Hellenistic tradition, drew on famous models for inspiration when building his residence, freely imitating the places and monuments in various parts of the Empire that had made the greatest impression on him.

Hadrian's Villa is famous for the numerous architectural forms

158 Hadrian, a highly cultivated man, loved all forms of art and was fond of architecture. This propensity is evident in the scenic layout of Canopus, the most attractive part of the villa, which occupies an artificial valley to the south of

the complex. The monument was designed to reproduce the Temple of Serapis at Canopus, in Egypt, and the canal that connected that town to Alexandria. The half-dome of the Serapeum stands out in the foreground.

159 top Along the banks of the lake occupying the central part of Canopus ran an elegant colonnade where numerous copies of famous Greek statutes stood, including the four caryatids of the Athenian Erechtheum.

represented, and in particular for the great variety of vaulted ceilings, accompanied by an interesting use of light and visual effects. It is also important because excavations have brought to light numerous sculptures, including the caryatids of Canopus, imitations of those of Erechtheum, and other copies of originals by Phidias and Polycletus. The complex was built between 118 and 133 A.D. At first, the work was limited to restructuring and extending the existing buildings, to which baths, a gymnasium and a hall for official banquets were added. All the rest was added gradually, as the villa acquired its final monumental aspect. The entire area was served by a system of underground passages (some of which were suitable for carts), designed to provide a kind of independent service network so that the prestige of the upper levels remained intact. The main access to the villa was on the north side, served by a road leading off the Tiburtine Way which ran alongside the Valley of Tempe, so called because it resembled a famous place of the same name in Thessaly. Here stood the hospitalia, a building used as dormitory for the praetorians guarding the entrance. Nearby are two rooms known as Libraries; they are actually two summer triclinia, which are part of the older section of the building. The area occupied by the Maritime

159 bottom Various statues of Antinous, Hadrian's favorite, who drowned in the Nile (perhaps intentionally) during a trip to Egypt while he was in the emperor's retinue, have been found in the Canopus area. Hadrian nurtured an unhealthy passion for the young Bithynian, and deified him after his death. Some consider that the emperor's passion was due to the sad, sensual beauty of the boy, which may have made more of an impact on Hadrian's restless, aesthetic, melancholy spirit than any real physical attraction. However it may be, in the classical period homosexual love was not considered particularly scandalous; on the contrary, it was lauded by many poets.

Theater, one of the most attractive places in the complex, is reached from the back of one of these rooms. This section is formed by a circular retaining wall with an inward-facing portico that separated the structure from the rest of the villa, and a canal surrounding a circular islet, which once had two small bridges. On this artificial island was a miniature villa designed for rest and seclusion, built around a courtyard with a fountain, and completed by a small bath-house. Famous precedents are probably the residence of Augustus on the Palatine Hill, and earlier still, the palace of Dionysius the Elder in Syracuse. Beyond the Maritime Theater is the central part of the villa, comprising the courtyard of the libraries, the palazzo, the nymphaeum, the Doric Pillar Room with the Barracks of the Vigiles at the side, and finally, the Golden Piazza, surrounded by a large peristyle and a portico with two aisles. The Doric Pillar Room, actually a basilica, leads to the Throne Room, which probably constituted a kind of palatial hall, used for solemn sessions of the Imperial court. On the north side of the Golden Piazza there is a vestibule with an octagonal plan, the roof of which constitutes one of the most outstanding examples of a segmental dome; on the south side there is a large, complex semicircular nymphaeum, possibly a summer triclinium. One of the short sides of the poikile, a large piazza surrounded by porticoes that constituted a kind of xystus (the place destined for walks and learned conversation that formed an integral part of the gymnasia of Greek inspiration) is built onto the west wall of the Philosophers' Room, near the Maritime Theater. To the east is another set of buildings, the most famous of which are the so-called Stadium, and the summer cenatio (the dining room used for official banquets). The set of rooms which follows includes the Small and Large Baths, the Vestibule and the Canopus. The latter is one of the most famous architectural complexes of the ancient world; it occupies a large, narrow valley and consists of a long channel with the short convex side decorated by a colonnade with mixtilinear architrave. Along the two longer sides of the lake run other colonnades, originally embellished by copies of famous Greek statues. The valley is closed by the Serapeum, a large semicircular exedra surmounted by a half-dome with alternate flat and concave segments.

A huge, sigma-shaped (Σ) triclinium couch actually identifies the building as the impressive, elegant summer cenatio. Its plan is inspired by those of Egyptian temples, and fits in well with the adjacent lake; in fact, in ancient times Alexandria was connected by a channel to the city of Canopus, where a famous Temple of Serapis stood. The channel and the town were famous for parties and banquets, an echo of which can be seen in the famous Nile mosaic at Palestrina. Antinous, a very handsome young man who was a favorite of Hadrian's, drowned at Canopus, and the emperor fell into a black despair. It is thus no accident that the loveliest statues of the youth were found here.

160-161 This delicate mosaic from Hadrian's Villa is a copy of the original by Sosos of Pergamum, a Greek artist much admired by Pliny. Mosaic art, imported from the Hellenistic world, encountered great success among the Romans, and was further refined during the Imperial age. From the 2nd century A.D. the technique became so perfect that mosaic artists could compete in skill with painters, seeking ever more subtle nuances of expression. This type of decoration featured various styles and trends, but the main types were the geometrical and figurative naturalist styles. The tesserae, generally cubic, might be made of stone or glass paste, depending on how they were to be used. They were fixed to the backing with a layer of adhesive mortar on which the basic design was drawn. The various kinds of wall and floor mosaics included opus vermiculatum, which allowed highly detailed work to be performed because of the very small size of the pieces and the wide range of colors, and opus sectile, made with larger, irregular, colored marble chippings.

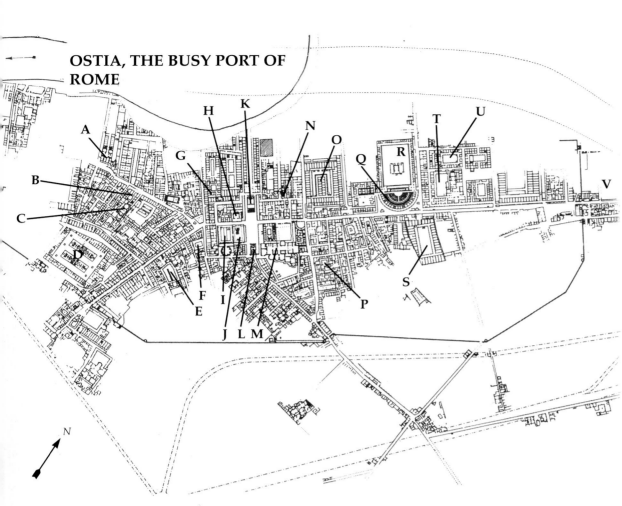

OSTIA, THE BUSY PORT OF ROME

A Trajan's Markets
B Serapis House
C Seven Seers' Baths
D Houses with garden
E Trajan's Schola
F Macellum
G Horrea Epagathiana
H Curia
I Round Temple
J Basilica
K Capitolium
L Temple of Rome and Augustus

M Forum Baths
N House of Diana
O Large Horrea
P Domus of Fortuna Annonaria
Q Theater
R Guild Forum
S Horrea of Hortensius
T Baths of Neptune
U Vigiles' Barracks
V Porta Romana necropolis

162-163 Ostia, once situated between the mouth of the Tiber and the sea, from which it now lies several miles away, was the main port of Rome until the 2nd century A.D., when it was gradually supplanted by the nearby Portus Romae. In the Imperial age it was a rich, cosmopolitan city populated by a busy middle class of traders and businessmen; once abandoned it fell into ruin, and was covered by the sands of the Tiber. It is now one of the most important archaeological sites in Italy.

163 top The great hexagonal port excavated by Trajan to extend the one built by Claudius, which had become antiquated, still survives, not far from Fiumicino International Airport. The new port area developed rapidly, attracting some of the workers from Ostia who soon moved there, founding a new town which was called Portus. Trajan's port was 393 yards square, and covered an area of 80 acres.

The name of Ostia, the ancient trading center of Rome, derives from the word ostium, *meaning entrance, as it was near the mouth of the Tiber. According to tradition, it was founded by King Ancus Martius but the oldest remains, dating from the beginning of the 4th century B.C., relate to the original nucleus of the Roman colony. The town, built as a typical military camp* (castrum), *enclosed by rectangular city walls and intersected by two perpendicular main roads, probably already had some temples, but no forum.*

In the mid-Republican age Ostia was still basically a military outpost by the sea, although its port already played an essential role, guaranteeing corn supplies for Rome. During the Punic Wars it was one of the bases for naval operations against Carthage, and at one time had a permanent detachment of 30 ships. As in the case of many other towns in Latium, Ostia was transformed from a military camp to a trading town during the Republic, in the age of Sulla. The new city walls enclosed an area of some 170 acres (30 times the size of the original castrum), *which was slightly increased in the Imperial age. This period brought a great construction boom, partly due to*

the introduction of new building techniques that were gradually adapted to the requirements of increasingly complex, dynamic architecture. Numerous temples were built in the town, including the grandiose temple of the oracular divinity Hercules. The homes of wealthy families – the typical Hellenistic-Roman domus *featuring an atrium and, in the wealthier houses, a peristyle – began to be built along the main roads.*

In Ostia, unlike Rome, the remains of private buildings have survived intact, so that their development and the variety of their forms can be seen. There were two basic types of dwelling: the domus *(single-family house) and the* insula *(a large multistory tenement block) which, during the 1st century B.C., had* tabernae *(shops) on the ground floor selling all kinds of goods. In the Augustan period Ostia was influenced by the great renovation taking place in Rome; in this case too, it was designed to enhance the dignity of the town. The important Temple of Rome and Augustus was built in the forum area; with its elegant marble decoration, which symbolized a new architectural vision, it was the forerunner of the great monuments of the Imperial age. The theater, with an*

TRAJAN'S PORT

1 Claudius's port (A.D. 42–64)
2 Lighthouse
3 Trajan's port (A.D. 100–112)
4 Navigable canal
5 Course of the Tiber
6 Sacred Island
7 Burial ground

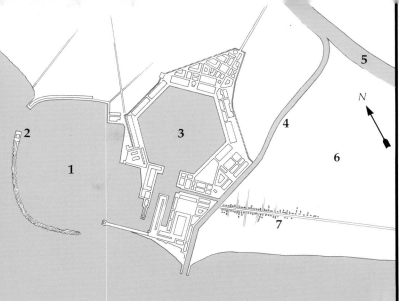

164 bottom left
The Guild Forum was
formed by a huge
quadrangular area
surrounded on three
sides by a portico in
which the offices of
trading and shipping
companies were based;
their businesses were
advertised by mosaic
signs.

164 bottom right The
theater dates from the
age of Augustus, but
was totally rebuilt
under Septimius
Severus. The
auditorium, like the
outer portico, was
entirely reconstructed
during the
excavations.
Behind what remains
of the scaena stands
the Guild Forum.

164-165 The Ostia
excavations have
uncovered numerous
exquisite mosaic floors
that decorated both
public buildings and
private homes.

initial capacity of 3,000 spectators,
which dates from the same period, was
influenced by similar Roman buildings
erected by Pompey and Marcellus.
Together with the porticoed Guild
Square behind it, the theater formed a
magnificent complex. Increasing
numbers of horrea (warehouses used to
store corn and other goods) were built in
various districts of the town,
demonstrating its growing trading
activity. Under Tiberius and Caligula,
Ostia was provided with an aqueduct,
which allowed the construction of
various baths; Claudius ordered the
construction of the first port, north of
the mouth of the Tiber. Until then, the
town's sea trade had been seriously
hampered by the difficulty of access to
the river port, because of the treacherous
sandbanks formed at the mouth of the
Tiber. Large-scale urban renovation,
dictated by the constant increase in
population, was commenced during the
reign of Domitian and completed by
Trajan. Trajan had a large basin with a
perfectly hexagonal shape dug in
addition to the basin built by Claudius,
which was beginning to silt up, thus
permanently solving the problem of the

acquired a largely commercial role.
Those products that could not
immediately be absorbed by the Roman
market, such as corn, oil and wine, were
stored at Ostia. The cargoes of the great
merchant ships were transferred to
smaller boats (codicariae), which were
towed up the Tiber to Rome by teams of
oxen. Society was divided into guilds,
which defended and promoted the
interests of the various trades. Each one
had a headquarters (schola) at which it
held its meetings and ceremonies.
Hadrian, like his predecessor,
reorganized the planning of the town,
giving the forum its final appearance; he
built the great Capitolium (which stood
between two wings of colonnades, like
the Temple of Rome and Augustus in
front of it) and constructed a residential
district with services that included
Neptune's Baths and the Barracks of the
Vigiles. The Garden House complex,
built in a luxury residential district,
also dates from this period. The domus
that symbolized the old town aristocracy
were demolished in many districts to
make room for tenement blocks destined
for the up-and-coming new class
consisting not only of rich, powerful
traders but also of clerical and manual
workers.
This new type of residential building
was developed as a result of the
increasing use of brick and concrete,
which led to the creation of innovative
types of architecture. Numerous
buildings survive, including the more
intensively occupied, working-class
dwellings, which had porticoed
courtyards around which the various
rooms, often decorated with mosaics,
were distributed. The number of
tabernae reached over 800 during the
2nd century; in practice, they were not

165 bottom left Many
of the domus built in
Ostia in the late
Imperial age were
richly decorated.

165 bottom right
In the middle of the
forum stand the
ruins of Hadrian's
Capitolium (the
greatest temple in the
city) dedicated to
Jupiter, Juno and
Minerva.

port of Rome. The modern structure
finally enabled the huge merchant ships
of the Alexandrian fleet, which carried
150,000 tons of corn a year, and the
other ships that traded with the East, to
dock at the mouth of the Tiber instead of
Pozzuoli, which until then had been the
main port of the Tyrrhenian. The small
independent town that developed around
the new dock was called Portus. Trajan
also constructed the curia and the
basilica in the forum, as well as
numerous baths. At this time the town

166-167 The historical development of the various types of urban building can be seen in Ostia. Well documented and quite common, the insula can be considered to be the forerunner of the modern apartment building. This type of tenement building usually had four or five floors, with the main façade overlooking the road and the secondary façade overlooking an inner courtyard or garden; there were numerous windows and balconies. Staircases led to the various apartments (cenacula), the entrances to which opened onto the inner landings. The toilets were sometimes shared; they were usually situated on the ground floor or in small rooms suitable for each apartment, and served by the same sewage pipe. The insulae of Ostia, mainly designed for the middle classes, offered some degree of luxury; they were spacious and airy, decorated with wall paintings and mosaics, and may have had running water, even on the upper floors. In some cases the remains of bathtubs have been found near the room used as the kitchen. This drawing reconstructs the appearance of the House of Diana and the surrounding buildings. The ground floor was occupied by a row of shops; their lofts, illuminated by small windows built into the façade, were occupied by the owners. The pictorial decoration in the upper rooms is based on the remains found in other insulae at Ostia, always featuring simple squares of color, sometimes interspersed with a few rare figures or geometrical patterns. The cross sections of the structures opposite are not the actual ones, but are intended to show a representative sample of the wall and floor decorations used in Ostia.

only retail shops, but also small craft workshops, whose attics were generally inhabited by the owners. Antoninus Pius completed the reconstruction of Ostia begun by Hadrian; the town, which was slightly larger than Pompeii, had 50,000 inhabitants. The major projects included the construction of the Forum Baths, the largest in the town, the Imperial Palace and some large rented tenement buildings, including the House of Diana and the Charioteer's Block.

Ostia, a seaside town, was particularly open to foreign influence, including in the religious sphere. Many Eastern religions became popular under the Antonines, as demonstrated by the presence of numerous shrines of Mithras. Commodus, the last of the Antonines, renovated the theater and, having launched a new corn fleet, reconstructed the great horrea and built new ones. The town, which had reached the peak of its expansion, was going through a very flourishing period. After Commodus, building work came to a halt; the Severus emperors only concentrated on restoration and reconstruction, as they mainly aimed to upgrade trade infrastructures. A new coast road, the Via Severiana, which connected the port of Terracina to Ostia and Portus, was opened. The semi-circular emporium on the Tiber, the extension of the horrea and the rebuilding of the Guild Square and its portico probably date from this period. This unique monument and its mosaics provide some invaluable information about trade in Ostia. The motifs portrayed and the inscriptions relate to shipowners and traders from towns all over the Empire, as well as the local guilds. Among the monumental

buildings erected were the Arch of Caracalla and the round temple, the last great public structure in the town center, possibly terminated under the Gordiani family. The crisis came around the mid-3rd century, at a time of serious political and economic disorder in the Empire. In a few decades many buildings, including horrea and insulae, were abandoned. Much of the town's business activity was transferred to Portus, and the need for close control of supplies led to the concentration of all power in the hands of the praefectus of the Rome Food Supplies Office. Under Diocletian and Constantine the situation improved; by now, however, Ostia was no longer a flourishing trading town, but an administrative and representative center. Some buildings were constructed, but only in the areas along the main streets, whereas the inner districts were gradually abandoned. While the insulae began to empty, the construction of some noblemen's domus – secluded luxury mansions like the old homes of the Republican aristocracy – recommenced. During the 5th century, the crisis became irreversible. Building activity came to a standstill, and wells were dug in the public streets because even the aqueduct had fallen into disuse. Ignored even by the Visigoths led by Alaric, the town of Ostia was now devoid of interest. In the second half of the 6th century, during the Greek-Gothic war, it was used after the fall of Portus to send supplies to Rome along the Tiber. It was finally wiped out by Saracen raids in the 9th century. Unlike Pompeii, Ostia suffered a slow, gradual decline, and this made its historical development, which can be identified in the excavations for at least nine centuries, highly complex.

HERCULANEUM, A CITY STILL SHROUDED IN MYSTERY

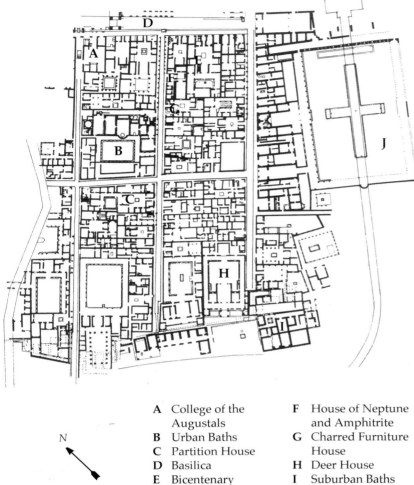

Key to plan

A	College of the Augustals	**F**	House of Neptune and Amphitrite
B	Urban Baths	**G**	Charred Furniture House
C	Partition House	**H**	Deer House
D	Basilica	**I**	Suburban Baths
E	Bicentenary House	**J**	Palaestra

N

Herculaneum (now Ercolano), a famous Campanian town situated some five miles east of Naples, was destroyed by the eruption of Vesuvius in A.D. 79. Its name is based on the legend according to which it was founded by Hercules. First Greek, then Samnite, it was subjugated by Rome in 307 B.C.; it was stormed by Sulla's faction in 89 B.C. during the Allies' War, then given the status of a municipium, to which Roman colonists were sent. Many patrician villas were built in the Republican period.

It was long believed that Herculaneum, which was far less badly hit by the hail of debris that destroyed Pompeii, Oplontis and Stabia, was later covered by the mass of mud that built up on the slopes of the volcano as a result of the violent cloudbursts that followed the cataclysm. It was therefore thought that most of the inhabitants managed to escape, perhaps by sea; in fact, very few skeletons were found in the town during the excavations. However, more recent studies and the discovery of hundreds of human remains in the port area demonstrate that the town was inundated by a cloud of toxic gas, and then buried

168 top left In the Gem House, named after a cameo dating from the age of Claudius that was found in it, the atrium with its *impluvium* is well preserved; it led, via an *adytum* with two columns, to the *tablinum* and the garden behind.

168 bottom left The Urban Baths, which stand in the center of the town, date from the Julio-Claudian age and have a traditional design. The shelves where bathers' clothes were placed can be seen along the walls.

168 right This picture shows the atrium of the Telephus Relief House, an aristocratic residence built on several stories, with a very irregular plan. The bright red plaster and the different materials used to make the columns are interesting.

under a flow of low-temperature lava. Only those who fled to Naples at the first sign of the eruption survived; the others, perhaps reluctant to leave their homes, hesitated too long, and when they eventually decided to flee, it was too late. In a panic, they tried to escape the fury of the elements by using the boats still moored along the docks, but the increasing violence of the waves defeated every attempt. They desperately took refuge in the service buildings surrounding the port, where they were surprised by the poisonous gases emitted

169 The Suburban Baths, dating from the Flavian age, are very luxurious, and present some innovative architectural features such as light and air shafts. An example can be seen in this vestibule, where light penetrates from an opening above the arches. The basin in the center collected water from a spout concealed in the bust of Apollo.

by Vesuvius, and died of suffocation. Their very well-preserved skeletons (over 200 of them) constitute invaluable material for the study of the lifestyles, diseases and diet of the ancient Romans. In the days following the eruption the pyroclastic flow invaded the streets, reaching a depth of 53 feet at some points. As it slowly dried, it solidified to the consistency of tufa and preserved the things it covered, including organic materials such as wood, leather, papyrus, vegetable fibers and food. The great interest aroused by Herculaneum as regards the study of homes and furnishings and the exceptional discovery of written documents and literary manuscripts (the famous papyrus scrolls) is due to this outstanding state of preservation. The first attempted excavations, dating back to the early 18th century, led to the discovery of the theater, which was stripped of its wealth of marble and bronze statues. Between 1738 and 1765, on the orders of Carlo II of Bourbon, numerous shafts were dug; this caused much damage, but enabled the magnificent Villa of Scrolls to be found.

From 1828 to 1865 an attempt was made to use the same technique as in Pompeii to uncover the entire town, but the work was abandoned because the volcanic rock was too hard. Later excavations were interrupted because the modern town, which was built on the site of Herculaneum, was too close. The excavations were only systematically recommenced in 1927; to date, seven *insulae* have been uncovered.

Therefore, much of the town, including some major public areas, still remains to be discovered.

Although the area already excavated is quite small, it reveals a perpendicular

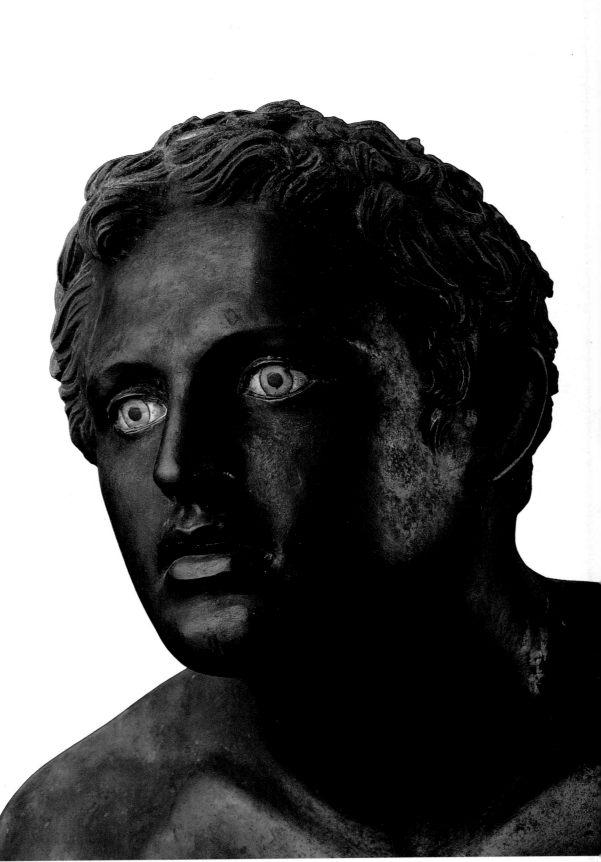

170 An outstanding collection of works of art, consisting of some 90 bronze and marble sculptures comprising copies of classical and Hellenistic masterpieces, portraits of leading Greek personalities and decorative subjects, was found in the Villa of Scrolls, discovered in 1750. This magnificent statue of one of the Danaides, found in the peristyle of the wealthy residence together with four similar female figures, is part of the first group. It was originally believed that the five girls were performing a religious dance, but it later became clear that they were carrying amphoras, now lost. The group was thus associated with the myth of the Danaides, the pretty daughters of Danaus who killed their husbands on their wedding night and were condemned in Hades to pour water incessantly into a bottomless well. Because of its exceptional luxury it is believed that this villa belonged to Lucius Calpurnius Piso, Caesar's rich father-in-law.

171 This splendid male face belongs to a statue portraying a wrestler tackling his adversary, also portrayed in bronze. The sculptural group was found in the Villa of Scrolls, and is now on display at the Naples Archaeological Museum, where many works of art from the excavations at Pompeii and Herculaneum are exhibited. Recent investigations led to the rediscovery of this famous villa in Herculaneum, explored by means of underground passages that were sealed in 1765 and then "lost."

layout, the surface of which is a fifth of that of Pompeii. The town was originally surrounded by walls, and divided into terraces sloping down to the sea. Public buildings are well represented by the theater (which has been explored in detail by underground passages but still buried), the Forum Baths, the Suburban Baths and the gymnasium. The theater, with its typically Roman layout, must have been very elegant; the stage was preciously decorated with exquisite marbles and old yellow, cipolin and African marble columns, while the entire building was embellished with countless bronze statues and sculptures. The gymnasium, surrounded by porticoes and occupied in the center by a cross-shaped swimming pool decorated with a bronze fountain, must have been equally monumental.

However, the true face of Herculaneum is revealed on examination of its dwelling houses. The domus was transformed most rapidly, already heralding the vertical development that became widespread in later decades. Typical of this transitional period is the grid house, the classic apartment building, which was cheap and rational in its use of space. The Wooden Partition House and the Charred Furniture House are also particularly interesting.

As the town was smaller than Pompeii, art can be said to be represented there to a greater extent, in view of the many bronze sculptures found in public buildings, homes, and especially in the Villa of Scrolls, a mansion located 66–82 feet deep in an area to the northwest of the present archaeological site.

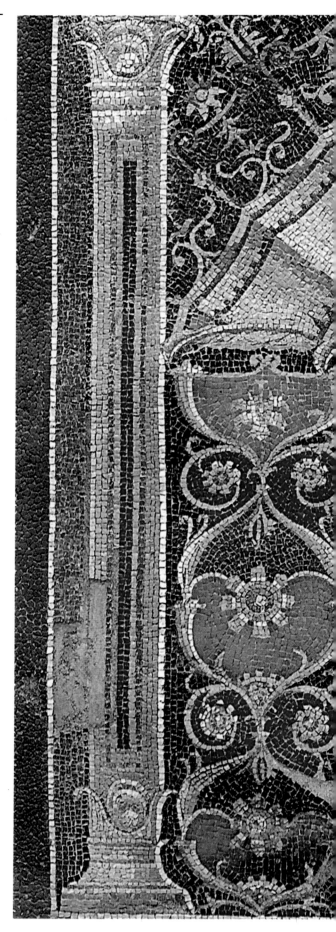

The building is still buried under two petrified layers, the first of which was formed in A.D. 79, while the second was produced by the eruption of lava in 1631. The great importance of the villa, explored by underground passages, lies in the numerous sculptures found (58 bronze and 31 marble) and the library of papyrus scrolls. One thousand-seven-hundred and eighty-five scrolls have been found so far, but many have been lost, because in the mid-18th century they were mistaken for lumps of coal. They contain philosophical writings, mostly by the epicure Philodemus of Gadara, and some Latin texts, including De Bello Actiaco. Unlike Pompeii, Herculaneum was not a mainly industrial and trading town; its principal activities must have been crafts and the minor arts. This is demonstrated by the numerous surviving tabernae, including the workshops of potters and marble carvers, weavers and dyers, pasta makers and small wine producers. Its peaceful nature and pleasant atmosphere, recorded by Greek geographer Strabo, probably made it a resort, frequented by the aristocracy of Rome and nearby Naples. Their luxurious peristyle homes were quite large, forcing the poorer citizens to extend their homes upwards; the result is a very interesting variety of types. However, only further excavations, which are very difficult, will reveal the many secrets still concealed in the buried town.

172 bottom and 173 bottom The huge inner rooms of the College of the Augustals (the priests who presided over the worship of the deified emperor associated with Rome) are decorated with magnificent wall paintings. The fresco depicting Hercules (the hero after whom the city was named) with Minerva and Juno is particularly fine.

172-173 The Neptune and Amphitrite House is named after a splendid mosaic panel depicting two marine deities that decorates one of the walls of the outdoor triclinium. The house must have belonged to a wealthy merchant with elegant, rather elitist tastes, who was definitely an art lover. This is demonstrated by the numerous bronzes and marble reliefs found in the various inner rooms, the luxurious decoration of the triclinium, and the fact that the subject of the mosaic was quite rare in the Roman world whereas it was common in Greek art, indicating the owner's aspiration to elegance.

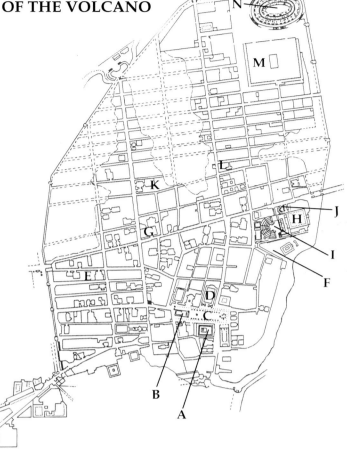

A   Temple of Apollo
B   Temple of Jupiter
C   Forum
D   Eumachia's
    Building
E   Vettius House
F   Triangular Forum
G   Central Baths
H   Gladiators'
    Barracks
I   Theater
J   Odeon
K   Centenary House
L   Pacuius Proculus's
    House
M   Large palaestra
N   Amphitheater

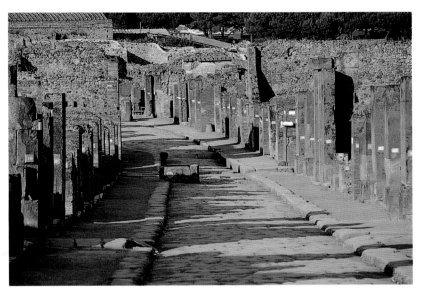

Ancient Pompeii was founded on the southernmost slopes of Vesuvius around the end of the 8th century B.C. by a group of Oscan peoples. It was later ruled by the Etruscans, and for a short period by the Greeks. Towards the end of the 5th century it fell into the hands of the Samnites, who ruled it until 310 B.C., when it became a town allied to Rome. Following the Allies' War it was raised to the status of a municipium, and the inhabitants, belonging to the Menemia tribe, were granted Roman citizenship. In 80 B.C., after the Civil War, it was made a colony, with the name of Cornelia Veneria Pompeianorum, by P. Cornelius Sulla, the dictator's nephew.

As a result of patronage by members of Sulla's party, the town was renovated; major public buildings such as the baths, the odeon, the capitolium of the forum and the amphitheater were erected, and the streets were paved. In time, the old and new inhabitants mingled, and the Oscan language was retained in addition to Latin, which became the official language of the colony. The town was administered by around a hundred decurions, aided by

174 The Temple of Apollo, which dates from the 2nd century B.C., stands near the Forum, in the middle of a peristyle formed by 48 Corinthian columns. A bronze statue of Apollo holding a bow, now replaced by a copy, stood on one of the longer sides in front of the portico. The sanctuary was being restored after the earthquake of A.D. 62.

175 top Public fountains were very common along the streets of Pompeii; forty have been found so far, situated at intervals of not more than 88 yards. This means that anyone who did not have a private water supply always had a source of water just a few yards from home.

175 center The ruins of the basilica, dating from the late 2nd century B.C., stand in the western corner of the forum. They represent one of the oldest surviving specimens of this kind of building, used as a courthouse and for business meetings. This building style developed until it became characteristic of early Christian sacred architecture.

175 bottom The Great Theater was built between the 2nd and 3rd centuries B.C.; although it was extended in the time of Augustus, it is only slightly influenced by Greek building styles. The auditorium is built onto the slope of a hill, not supported by masonry structures as was typical in later Roman architecture.

176 top Within certain limits, painting was the most original expression of Roman art. This photo shows a room in the Vettius House, one of the most magnificent homes in Pompeii. When this domus was extensively restored after the earthquake of A.D. 62, generous use was made of wall paintings, which blend the Third and Fourth styles to create extraordinary perspective effects with bright colors; scenes with mythological subjects alternate with architectural views.

the duumvirs and aediles, who formed a kind of Senate. There were also various religious authorities, from the Augustales to the guardians of the cult of the Lares compitales. Like Rome, Pompeii was organized in districts, divided into vici and pagi, which had shrines to the Lares erected at the crossroads. The names of these districts are often recorded in the electoral posters painted on the façades of the houses. Beginning in 27 B.C. a period of intense Romanization took place in Pompeii. This led to a reshuffle of the ruling political class, in which the supporters of Sulla were excluded and new clans more closely allied with the Imperial house predominated. In this political context, new artistic and architectural styles in line with the official culture of Rome were introduced.

On 5 February of A.D. 62, a disastrous earthquake struck Pompeii and other nearby towns, including Herculaneum. Pictorial documentation of the earthquake survives in the reliefs on the lararium in the home of Lucius Cecilius Jocundus, which portray many of the town's buildings under the effect of the shock wave. The damage was so severe that it was still being repaired over 10 years later. Trade, which until then had constituted the main activity in Pompeii, gave way to frenetic construction work and the associated speculation. But the worst was yet to come.

One morning in A.D. 79, a pine-shaped cloud blotted out the cone of Vesuvius. This was the warning sign of the terrible eruption that was shortly to wipe out the town, bombarded for four solid days by a hail of lapilli that reached a depth of several yards. The lapilli were accompanied by toxic gas and a rain of

176 bottom Pinarius Cerialis was a skilled stone and cameo cutter who owned a small but tastefully furnished house. The frescoes on two walls of a cubiculum on the ground floor are inspired by a theater set. One portrays the characters of Iphigeneia in Tauris, the tragedy by Euripides that inspired much Pompeiian painting, while the other (shown here) depicts the Judgement of Paris. The scene demonstrates a perfect technique and great mastery of spatial organization. It is a great pity that painters did not sign their works at that time; the only painter's name to have survived in all of Pompeii is that of one Lucius, of whom nothing more is known.

176-177 Still lifes, a fairly common subject, not only in Pompeii, demonstrate the sensitivity and expressive skill of the Roman painters. Oddly enough, wall painters were held in lesser consideration than easel painters, and Pliny opined that only the latter were worthy of glory. Unfortunately, the materials used were highly perishable, with the result that very few examples of paintings on tablets have survived from the Roman age, and hardly any from Italic sources. With a few worthy exceptions, therefore, the pictores parietarii (wall painters) were skilled decorators with an inventive imagination rather than true artists.

ash, together with frequent earth tremors. Many fugitives suffocated, fell to the ground in various poses and were buried by the volcanic material. The imprints left by their bodies in the tufa, later discovered by archaeologists and filled with plaster, constitute the most dramatic evidence of the destruction of Pompeii. A detailed account of these tragic moments was written by Pliny the Younger, an eyewitness to the catastrophe, in which his uncle, the famous naturalist Pliny the Elder, admiral of the fleet stationed at Misenum, died in an attempt to bring aid to the victims on the beach of Stabia. Pliny the Younger recounted the terrible events of those days to Tacitus in the following words: "You could hear the groans of the women, the cries of the children and the clamor of the men; some loudly sought their parents, others their children, others again their spouses, and recognized them by their voices; there were some who, for fear of death, invoked it; many raised their arms to the gods, but still more said there were no more gods, and that this was the last night of the world...." Pompeii can justifiably be considered the most famous place in the world in the history of archaeology. The buried town was discovered in 1748, and the first systematically conducted excavations began in 1860. Restoration work soon followed, and was perfected over the years with the use of increasingly sophisticated technologies that have even enabled the species of trees and bushes grown in the gardens of Pompeii to be identified.

Today, although around a fifth of the

178 Mosaic art reached outstanding levels in the Roman world, as demonstrated by this Nile scene, discovered in a Pompeiian villa. For their subjects, the craftsmen were often inspired by famous paintings that were reproduced in the form of large cartoons. The pieces forming the design were laid by museiarii, *and the background by* tessellarii.

178-179 Mosaic workers generally obtained the material they needed locally, but for shades of color unobtainable from local stones they had to use imported stones. The use of tesserae *made of glass paste, from which any shade could be obtained, was introduced for this reason. One of the first known examples of the use of this material is in the* Faun House, *in the black background of the mosaic that shows a very realistic picture of a cat pouncing on a quail. This practice became very common, especially for seascapes in blue shades and the brightest green leaves.*

urban area still remains to be excavated, Pompeii has been resurrected from the darkness, and is visited by millions of tourists and researchers. The archaeological site testifies to the culture and lifestyle of a town whose existence was abruptly cut off and sealed up forever, just at the time of its greatest glory; a town that never knew the fate of neglect and decadence suffered by others. Only excavations clearly revealed the various stages of its evolution.

Pompeii reached the height of its development in the Samnite period, when the buildings essential to public life (the forum square, the triangular forum complex, the basilica, the Samnite Gymnasium and the Stabian Baths) were constructed, together with atrium homes and the mighty fortifications. The great public works of Sulla's period fitted neatly into the previous layout of the town, completing and enriching it. The gymnasium next to the amphitheater, the macellum (market), Eumachia's Building, the Temple of Fortuna Augusta and the so-called Temple of Vespasian were built in the Julio-Claudian era, but the layout of the town remained basically unchanged. In Roman times the town's water was provided by a branch of the Serinus aqueduct, the water from which was conveyed to the castellum near the Vesuvius Gate and then to the baths, the public fountains and the wealthier homes. Pillars for pressure, generally installed near the fountains, supplied water to the various districts. Pompeii had two forums. The first,

surrounded by a Doric colonnade surmounted by an Ionic gallery, presented a systematic distribution of its buildings when it was destroyed. On the short sides stood the Capitolium and curia, while all around were temples, the basilica, the indoor market, the macellum, two triumphal arches and the original Eumachia's Building, named after the patron of the weaver's and dyers' corporation, the busiest industry in the town.

The use of the second forum, built in a narrow triangular space, revolved around the theater, the oldest part of which dates from the 2nd century B.C., and the odeon, a sort of small indoor theater. The amphitheater, which could hold up to 20,000 spectators, was located in the southeastern corner of the

180-181 The largest mosaic surviving from Classical times was discovered in the Faun House in 1831; it is made with tiny tesserae, and portrays the Battle of Issos fought in 333 B.C. between Alexander the Great and Darius III. This extraordinary work is believed to have been inspired by a Greek painting of the 4th century B.C.; the mosaic, made with local materials between the 1st and 2nd centuries B.C., makes very effective use of light and shade, though employing a very limited range of basic colors. The scene is handled very dynamically, and great care is evident in the characterization of the various personalities, especially the Macedonian commander, who bursts bare-headed into the midst of the riders crowding around the Persian monarch. Although this is an exceptional example of technical mastery, the lack of independent creativity is felt even here; however, strange as it may seem, in the Roman world the concept of copying did not have the disparaging value attributed to it today.

CENTENARY HOUSE

The Centenary House is so called because it was excavated in 1879, the 18th centenary of the eruption that destroyed Pompeii. It was a large residence, magnificently decorated with sculptures and oscilla (marble and bronze discs with bas-relief decorations hanging from the architraves), the oldest part of which dates from the 2nd century B.C.; it was later altered on various occasions, and combined with an adjacent house. The walls of the large main atrium were decorated with small pictures in the Fourth Style; in the peristyle garden there was a marble fountain surrounded by rose bushes. It is this domus, shown in cross section from the atrium to the peristyle, which illustrates the inner pages.

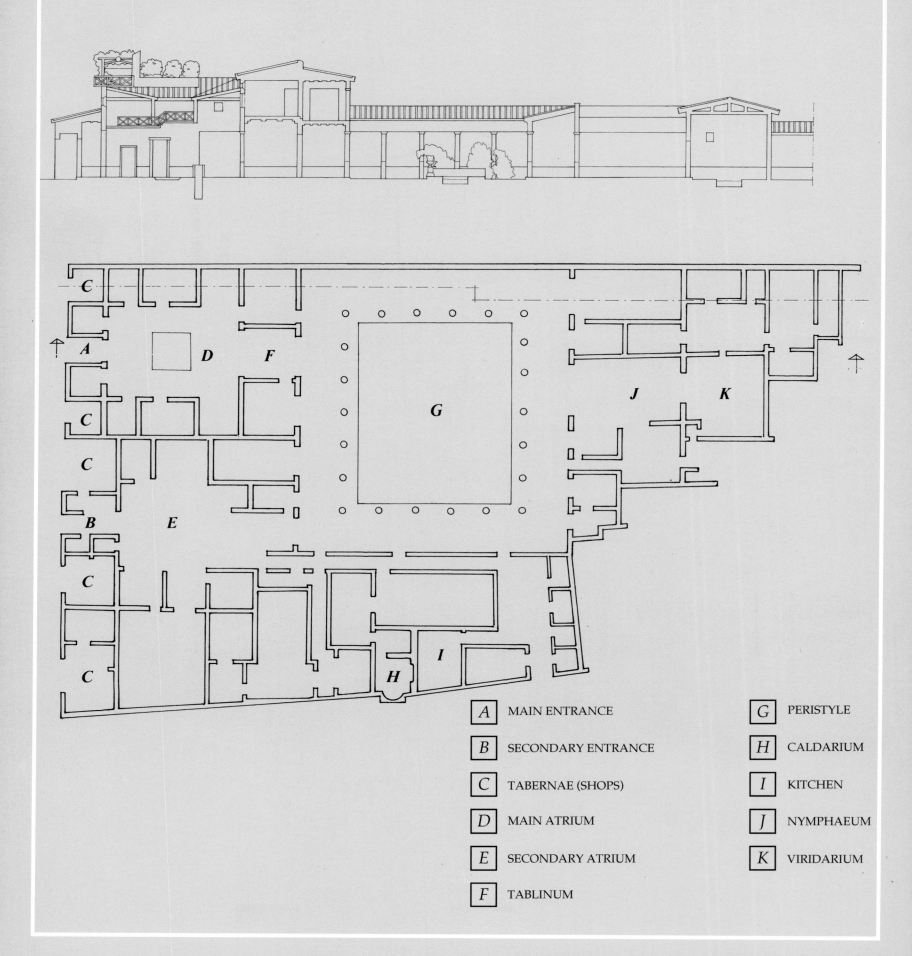

A	MAIN ENTRANCE
B	SECONDARY ENTRANCE
C	TABERNAE (SHOPS)
D	MAIN ATRIUM
E	SECONDARY ATRIUM
F	TABLINUM
G	PERISTYLE
H	CALDARIUM
I	KITCHEN
J	NYMPHAEUM
K	VIRIDARIUM

THE VILLA OF MYSTERIES

187 *The Villa of Mysteries, built in the mid-3rd century* B.C. *and subsequently extended and embellished on various occasions, is named after the famous frieze (a* megalografia, *i.e., a series of life-sized paintings) that shows the salient stages of an* initiation rite into the Dionysian mysteries. *The extraordinary pictorial complex, with its 29 life-sized figures, the work of a Campanian artist in the 1st century* B.C., *runs along the walls of a room entered through a single door. The interpretation of* the various scenes is doubtful, because little is now known of the mystery rites; the picture reproduced here is thought to show the reading of the ritual by a boy, or the education of the young Dionysus.

CENTENARY HOUSE: THE MAGNIFICENT RESIDENCE OF A WEALTHY POMPEIIAN

town. Built in the early years of the Roman colony, it had a series of twin staircases built onto the outside of the structure. Numerous gymnasia and baths completed the range of public buildings.

However, the fame of Pompeii is mainly associated with its private buildings. Such comprehensive evidence of the Roman home in all its aspects, from the structures to the decorations and household furnishings, is to be found nowhere else in the world, except for Herculaneum and Ostia. The development of the domus, the most common type of home in Pompeii, began in the 4th century B.C. The surviving specimens include those dating from the Samnite era, with Tuscan atrium and massive façade, the Republican houses of Hellenistic type with a peristyle, stuccoed walls and a façade with architectural elements, and the mansions of the Imperial age, with their complex plan, finely painted walls, galleries and ornamental gardens.

Many wall paintings survive, showing the development of tastes in decoration. What is called the First Style, a style of Hellenistic influence that flourished between 200 and 80 B.C., was an imitation in colored stucco reliefs of marble cladding made of squared blocks. The Second or Perspective Style, consisting of architectural or landscape views, became common in the 1st century B.C. The Third Style,

fashionable until around A.D. 40, was of a flat, far more schematic, ornamental nature. The Fourth Style, popular after the earthquake of A.D. 62, was exuberant and imaginative, with a wealth of optical illusions.

The local aristocracy lived in elegant mansions, sometimes huge (up to 3,600 square yards), and often decorated with mosaic or colored marble floors. In many cases they included shops that gave onto the street, mainly rented out to freedmen or managed by servants for the retail sale of the master's goods. The many famous houses in Pompeii include the Vettius House, the Faun House and the Tragic Poet's House. There are also numerous examples of the two forms of villa (rustic and patrician) scattered over the suburban area. Particularly magnificent for their rich wall decorations are the Villa of Mysteries and the Villa of Oplontis, while the Boscoreale Villa at Pisanella is very interesting as a study in farm organization.

In addition to dwellings, there were many businesses in Pompeii, especially along Via dell'Abbondanza, one of the main roads: workshops, dyers, inns (cauponae), thermopolia where drinks were served, lodging houses and even gambling houses (tabernae lusoriae). Furnishings, including silverware, crockery of various types of manufacture, furniture, glassware and various implements, have been found in both domus and shops, in an exceptional state of preservation.

Of similar interest are the numerous inscriptions, painted signs and graffiti still visible on the walls of the town, which offer a vivid picture of life in Pompeii.

188 bottom This magnificent example of Fourth-Style painting decorates the triclinium of the Vettius House; imaginative architectural elements are combined with a small picture of Apollo, Artemis and a sacrificial bull. Although Pompeiian paintings are exceptionally well preserved, they now lack the gloss that made them shine like mirrors. This proverbial shine is mentioned by numerous authors, but it is not known how it was obtained. It is thought that they may have been covered with waxy substances or polished with marble dust, but the experts do not yet agree.

188-189 The lower part of the triclinium in the Vettius House features a pretty frieze with a black background populated by cherubs engaged in a variety of occupations. Although the Pompeiian villas appear opulent to us, the very few items of furniture they contained must have made them seem rather bare, which explains why the walls of every single room were extensively decorated. The wealth of the decorations obviously depended on the financial resources of the owner and the skill of the craftsmen. This home, in fact, belonged to two rich merchants with elegant tastes.

190-191 In this scene from the megalografia in the Villa of Mysteries, Silenus offers a drink to a young satyr, while another satyr raises a theatrical mask above his head.
Pompeiian wall paintings (and those dating from the Roman age in general) were made by the fresco technique (i.e., by applying the paint to the wall while the plaster was still damp), and have proven to withstand the ravages of time even better than Renaissance frescoes. Although detailed studies have been conducted, the true nature of the paint application technique and the reason for the durability of Roman paintings is still not fully understood.

However, it is certain that the calcium carbonate film that formed on the paint (following a reaction between the slaked lime in the plaster and the air) plays an important part.
The materials used to obtain the various pigments are well known: they ranged from Spanish cinnabar for bright red to copper oxides for green and resinous charcoal for black. Two paint works have been discovered in Pompeii.
Some colors required rather laborious preparation, which increased their price; it was therefore laid down by law that the client had to supply the most expensive ones, while the painters provided the others.

THE ROMAN EMPIRE AND ITS POWER CENTERS IN THE ANCIENT WORLD

*192-193
This lively scene of
battle between
legionnaires and
barbarians, which
decorates what is
known as the Ludovisi
Sarcophagus, is an
example of the tireless
Roman spirit of
expansionism; with*

*the aid of a military
practice that
developed into a
veritable art form,
supported by firm
faith in the cultural
supremacy of Rome,
it led to the formation
of one of the largest
and longest-lived
empires in history.*

*The frequency of battle
subjects in Roman art
is symptomatic of this
warlike bent.
In this case, the
commander on
horseback has been
identified with
Hostilian, son of
Decius, who ruled
from A.D. 249 to 251.*

THE FORMATION AND ORGANIZATION OF THE ROMAN PROVINCES

The term "province" generally indicated a territory situated outside Italy that had been annexed to Rome peacefully or following a conquest, and was under the jurisdiction of a magistrate of proconsular or propraetorian rank, i.e., a citizen who belonged to the senatorial class and had held the highest offices in the senatorial career. In the Republican age there was a sharp distinction between the legal status of the inhabitants of Italy, who enjoyed certain privileges, and that of all the other inhabitants of the Empire, who were obliged to pay a property tax. This difference was gradually attenuated, and Caracalla eventually granted Roman citizenship to all inhabitants of the empire in A.D. 212. However, complete equality was only granted under Diocletian, who placed the territory of Italy on a par with the provinces.
The provincial dominion of Rome began with the acquisition of Sicily, Sardinia and Corsica between the First and Second Punic Wars. Hispania citerior and Hispania ulterior were soon added. Four new praetors who held civil, military and administrative powers were created to govern these territories. When they took office they issued an edict specifying the rules that would govern the administration of the cities and populations belonging to the province. In 146 B.C. Macedonia, comprising Illyria and Epirus, fell within the sphere of influence of Rome, and in the same year the Province of Africa was created, corresponding to the territories of Carthage, which had been destroyed. In 133 B.C. Rome inherited from Attalus III the Kingdom of Pergamum, which became the Province of Asia, and finally, around 120 B.C., the Province of Narbonnese Gaul was constituted.

This obviously required modifications to the existing administrative structure, which was unable to deal with the needs of territories situated further and further away from Rome, or with the changing political conditions. The practice of extending command after its conclusion (prorogatio imperii) was, therefore, instituted; under this system, after holding office for a year, consuls and praetors became proconsuls and propraetors, and thus continued to be part of the government administration system.
Between 133 B.C. and 31 B.C., the year of the battle of Actium, a series of military operations led to the creation of the provinces of Pontus, Syria and Cilicia. In the meantime, the rulers of Cyrene and Bithynia had also bequeathed their kingdoms to Rome. At the same time, the internal political situation was gradually deteriorating, and there was a real risk of dictatorship; this could easily have happened if a single person had held major powers for too long a time. Pompey, therefore, established that a five-year interval must elapse between appointments as an ordinary magistrate and a promagistrate.
In 58 B.C., Julius Caesar made extensive new conquests; in the course of numerous military campaigns he defeated Numidia (which constituted Africa nova) and Gallia comata, corresponding to the present central and northern France, together with part of Belgium and Germany. In 49 B.C. he extended Italian territory by granting Roman citizenship to all inhabitants of Cisalpine Gaul (corresponding to the present northern Italy).
Under Augustus, the number of provinces considerably increased. After the victory at Actium, Egypt fell

194 top Saint-Rémy-en-Provence, the ancient Glanum in Narbonnese Gaul, still features numerous Roman relics; one of the most interesting is the monument of the Julians, a three-story cenotaph dating from the 1st century B.C.

194 bottom The theater of Merida, which dates from 15 B.C., was donated to the rich Spanish city by Augustus's son-in-law, Agrippa. After careful restoration the scaena has been partly reconstructed and decorated with the original statues.

195 Built at the end of the 1st century A.D., the Temple of Diana in Merida is a magnificent example of a peripteral Corinthian temple, i.e., a temple surrounded by at least one row of columns standing at a distance from the wall of the cella, which in this case has not survived.

into the hands of Rome, soon to be followed by the Alpine regions (the Maritime Alps, the Cottian Alps, Raetia and Noricum), Dalmatia, Pannonia and Lusitania (corresponding to the present Portugal), and Galatia in northeast Anatolia. The provincial administration was then radically modified; those territories requiring a military garrison were placed under the direct control of Augustus, while all the others were left to the Senate. The provinces having thus been divided into two groups (imperial and senatorial), the system of government was changed.

In the case of the senatorial provinces, the Senate had to choose the governors internally from former consuls (this was compulsory for the two prestigious provinces of Asia and Africa) or praetors. All governors, chosen by lot, received the title of proconsul, and held office for a year (unless extended), aided by a number of officials dealing with specific sectors. The emperor could influence the appointments by virtue of a special prerogative called imperium proconsulare maius, which placed him above all the governors.

The imperial provinces were ruled by magistrates called legati Augusti propraetore, chosen by the emperor from among the senators; former consuls were appointed for the provinces with the largest military contingents, and former praetors for the others. They too were aided by other officials, and the duration of their office was at the emperor's discretion. Other minor provinces were also placed under the direct control of Augustus; these were governed by members of the equestrian order, which administered them under the title of procuratores.

Egypt, which differed from the other provinces because of its special administrative, economic and cultural traditions and a whole series of thousand-year-old customs, was treated differently, on a par with the emperor's private property. It was administered by an official of the equestrian order (a praefectus) to whom command of the legionary troops was given; past experience had warned Augustus of the danger that Egypt could become a territorial power base for the senators, in opposition to the Imperial power. Finally, Augustus left some regions to client kings, and allowed some cities or sanctuaries to maintain a degree of independence. In various provinces some towns had their own statutes or privileges, which fell into disuse with time. Tax exemptions existed, for example, in the civium romanorum colonies, to which military colonists had originally been sent, while other towns retained the titles of liberae or foederatae, although their inhabitants were not Roman citizens but peregrini. The principles laid down by Augustus remained in force until the 2nd century, when the changes that were to lead to Diocletian's general reorganization began to take place.

In the East, all the features of independence that had so far been allowed in the individual provinces gradually disappeared; in the West, gradual Romanization took place, aided

196-197 Theatrical performances, circus races and gladiatorial games were some of the most typical social events in the Roman world, and were very popular throughout the Empire. As a result, public entertainment buildings (like the superb theater of Aphrodisias in present-day Turkey) are to be found in every province.

196 bottom left Miletus, an ancient city in Asia Minor, entered the Roman sphere of influence in the 2nd century B.C. and flourished during the Empire. Nearby stands the great sanctuary of Apollo, the Didymaion, built in the Hellenistic era; the frieze with the Gorgon's head is part of an extension built in Hadrian's time.

196 bottom right Aphrodisias was the most flourishing metropolis in the Province of Caria. The most original of the city's monuments is the tetrapylon (a detail of which is shown here), a building in the shape of a four-faced arch supported by sets of columns rather than pillars. It dates from the mid-2nd century A.D.

197 top Pergamum, capital of the kingdom ruled by the Attalus dynasty, in Asia Minor, became Roman in 133 B.C., and reached the peak of its development in the Imperial age, especially under Trajan and Hadrian. The Kizil Avlu, perhaps a basilica or a sanctuary consecrated to an Oriental deity, dates from that period.

198-199 Petra, the ancient capital of the kingdom of the Nabataeans in present-day Jordan, became the capital of the Province of Arabia in A.D. 106.
The city stood in a deep valley hollowed out by a river; in view of the limited space available, the main Nabataean monuments (mostly tombs and temples) were excavated in the surrounding rock faces. Roman artistic influence can mainly be seen in the architectural façades constructed between the mid-1st century and the late 3rd century. The most spectacular monument in Petra demonstrating Roman influence is the building known as the Monastery, a monolithic temple with a 128-foot-tall façade.

by the foundation of new colonies and the massive presence of legionary camps in the border areas.

Such territorial extension as took place during this period was mainly caused by the strengthening or defense of borders. The two Germanys, the **agri** decumates and Noricum, in practice, guaranteed the security of the Rhine-Danube border. Under Claudius, Britannia was conquered, and the provinces of Thrace, Lycia and Pamphylia were instituted. The Province of Moesia was also constituted in the Julio-Claudian era. Finally, Judaea, already a client kingdom, became an equestrian province after its conquest by Titus.

However, it was Trajan who advocated a true expansionist strategy; after conquering Dacia, with its wealth of gold mines, he also declared Arabia, Assyria, Mesopotamia and Armenia maior provinces.

Hadrian, who advocated a more prudent policy, preferred to abandon some of the territories conquered by his predecessor and concentrate more on defending the borders; Hadrian's Wall in Britannia is one such defense.

Under Septimius Severus, Assyria and Mesopotamia again became provinces and the province of Numidia was instituted; Syria and Britannia were divided in half, and some regions were removed from Galatia to make defense of the borders easier and prevent a single governor from obtaining command of too many legions.

Under Caracalla's **Constitutio Antoniniana**, Roman citizenship was granted to all subjects of Rome in A.D. 212. Conditions in the Empire were particularly difficult at this time. In the East, the Sasanians were becoming increasingly strong, while in the West, the barbarian world was in turmoil. The result of this barely controllable situation was increasing political instability, combined with a serious economic crisis aggravated by continual wars. The unity of the empire was severely tested; the rebel Postumus, one of Gallienus's generals, founded an **imperium** Galliarum consisting of Gaul, Britannia and Spain, and in A.D. 260 an independent kingdom was proclaimed in Palmyra by the local sovereign, Odenatus, who was granted the title of **dux** orientis.

The reform initiated in this period, generally attributed to Diocletian, led to the creation of a highly fragmented structure, designed to deal with the many serious problems relating to border defense and the work of the provincial administration officers. For this purpose, the territory of the individual provinces was reduced, with the result that their number increased to around 90; thus split up they were easier to manage, but lost their historical and cultural individuality. They were governed by a member of the equestrian order, the **praeses** or **corrector**, except in the case of Africa, Asia and Achaia, still governed by a proconsul, who reported to the emperor in person. Egypt continued to be governed by a **praefectus**. All that was left to the governor of each province was civil jurisdiction, as the military jurisdiction was handled by a **dux**, sometimes responsible for more than one territory. The new provinces were grouped into 13 dioceses governed by **vicarii**, which in turn depended on the four prefectures of the praetor. The **vicarii** were directly responsible to the emperor, and the various governors, now deprived of military power, became easy to control. As well as aiding border defenses, the separation of military and civil power was mainly designed to prevent imperial acclamation of governors appointed to major territorial bases with large

198 bottom This magnificent mosaic, portraying Artemis surprised while bathing, is housed in the museum of the Syrian town of Suweida, the ancient Dionysias. Numerous Hellenistic and Roman ruins are to be found in what was once a flourishing caravan town, demonstrating the spread of western artistic influences in Syria.

199 bottom In Roman times, Petra developed in the valley bottom after the riverbed was filled in to make room for the forum, surrounded by various temples, a gymnasium, baths and shops. The main road was straddled by a triumphal arch with three archways, razed to the ground by an earthquake.

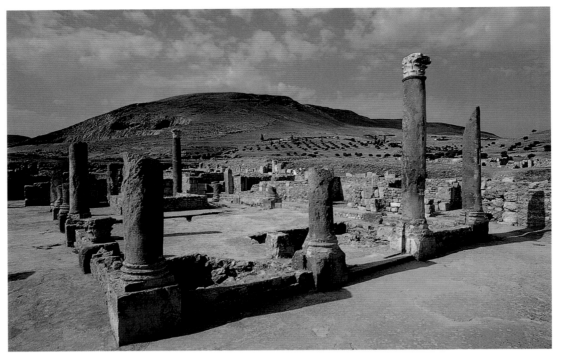

201 Sufetula, a Roman town near present-day Sbeitla in Tunisia, was probably founded in the 1st century A.D., and flourished mainly under the Antonine and Severus dynasties. The most interesting of the important ruins, which are very well preserved, is the capitolium, with its highly original design, consisting of a set of three separate temples, each dedicated to a deity of the Capitoline triad.

garrisons, which were generally elicited with gifts of cash obtained from illegal taxes. Italy was placed on a par with the other territories in the Empire (thereby losing a series of tax privileges) and divided into two dioceses, Italia annonaria (roughly comprising northern Italy), governed by the vicarius Italiae, and Italia suburbicaria (corresponding to the center and south of the country), governed by the vicarius Romae. The work of Diocletian was carried on by Constantine and his successors, who further perfected the already complex bureaucratic system. The serious problem of territorial integrity and the financial resources needed to keep the army efficient were their main objectives; the costs were borne by the inhabitants of the various provinces, who were subjected to increasingly heavy taxation. The great barbarian invasions brought this complex provincial system to an end in the West, but it survived in the Eastern Empire, though radically modified. One of the most interesting sources, which gives a detailed picture of the organization of the Empire at this period, is the Notitia Dignitatum. The richly illustrated manuscript presents numerous dating problems, but is generally believed to refer to the mid- or late 4th century, especially as regards military organization. The document describes the civil and military offices of the Eastern and Western Empires in minute detail, in order of importance, and lists the territorial divisions, coordination structures and the various

202-203 Dougga, the ancient Thugga, is one of the best-preserved Roman towns in the Tunisian Maghreb. Annexed to the Province of Africa by Julius Caesar in A.D. 46, it became a municipium in A.D. 105 and a colony in A.D. 261.
The terraced layout and irregular plan of the town demonstrate its Punic origin, while the forum, the great theater, the baths, the Temple of Caelestis, and the capitolium (shown here) constitute eloquent signs of intensive Romanization.
The town, which had around 5,000 inhabitants, prospered as a result of the cultivation of the fertile surrounding plain, with its wealth of springs.

military contingents responsible for organizing the border defenses.

In conclusion, the colonies, as a direct emanation of the mother country of which they were to some extent a territorial extension, constituted the basic means whereby Roman civilization (language, customs, legal system, art and culture) spread beyond the narrow confines of Italy. At the same time, the colonies absorbed and modified all the external stimuli which made the Roman empire so unusual.

The colonies were the symbols of power and the testing grounds of a complex society that became increasingly sophisticated but also demanding and difficult to handle. They incorporated a huge variety of experiences, externally manifested by continually developing monumental structures that were often more innovative than the official ones. These experiences, transferred and assimilated to varying extents, often influenced the development of tastes in the very capital of the Empire. Not only Roman architecture but also its poetry, decorative arts, applied sciences and religion ceaselessly absorbed new influences, then modified them and finally irradiated them to the furthest corners of the Empire in a continuous feedback cycle. Despite the due distinctions, financial and intellectual exchanges between the various provinces

were continuous. The olive oil produced in Africa was sold at high prices in Rome, tin from the mines of Britannia was exported everywhere, carts made in Gaul traveled the roads of the entire Empire, and Greek and Jewish historians recorded the feats of Roman generals. This ability to absorb such different elements and use them to regenerate itself, while still retaining the essence of its own specific cultural features, was one of the distinctive features of Roman civilization, together with the tireless drive to extend its borders.

Shrewd merchants and great travelers, the Romans journeyed as far as Zanzibar and Samarcand, traded with Begram, in Afghanistan, and along the Ganges, and reached the banks of the Huang-ho in China and the southernmost tip of India. In addition to spices and the finest fabrics, precious metals and objets d'art they imported to Rome and the other cities of the Empire a wide variety of ideas and stimuli, which in turn influenced distant peoples and cultures. For example, a statue of Lakshmi, the Hindu goddess of fertility, was found in Pompeii, and archaeological digs in China, India and southern Arabia have discovered glassware, bronzes and coins with the effigies of the Roman emperors. The Roman heritage is still evident in many present-day countries whose territories formed an integral part of the Roman Empire. More or less evident traces of Roman colonization remain in the place names of regions and towns, sometimes even in those of countries, in the languages and dialects spoken in Europe today (such as Romanian), in the presence of a large number of towns founded at the time of the Republic or the Empire, and even in the routes of many of the major roads that are still used, from Scotland to Syria, from Spain to Hungary. The immense architectural, historical and cultural legacy of ancient Rome is thus tangible in numerous aspects of contemporary civilization, and further details of it are still being discovered as a result of tireless international research.

202 bottom Cuicul (now known as Djemila, in Algeria), which became a colony under Nerva, reached the height of its splendor between the 2nd and 3rd centuries. A mainly agricultural town, it was quite wealthy and decorated with some public monuments, including the surviving temple dating from the Severus dynasty.

203 top Not far from Thugga stands a tower-tomb dating from the 2nd century B.C. Though of Punic origin, this monument is of great interest because the same architectural design is frequently repeated in the mausoleums erected in numerous regions of the Empire, confirming the heterogeneous nature of Roman art.

204-205 The Romans, who were skilled builders, solved the problem of the water supply for the various towns in the Empire by diverting springs, some of which were very far away from the towns. Pipes ran inside masonry aqueducts that sometimes, as in the case of Segovia, had to cross valleys and natural depressions on a series of arches. The water was conveyed into a tank (the castellum aquae), from which it was distributed under pressure to the town's water network. The Segovia aqueduct is one of the most grandiose in the Roman world; built of granite blocks without mortar, it is 800 yards long and 95 feet high.

204 bottom The Los Milagros aqueduct at Merida is another spectacular example of Roman hydraulic engineering in the Iberian peninsula. Built in the 1st century A.D., it brought water to the town from a spring three miles away, crossing the Rio Albarregas valley on a series of arches 913 yards long.

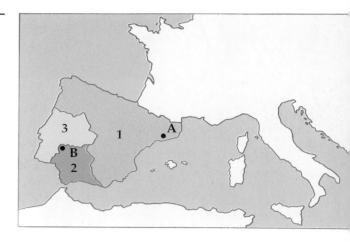

THE IBERIAN PROVINCES, LANDS WITH A HEALTHY ECONOMY

1 Tarraconensis
2 Baetica
3 Lusitania
A Tarragona
B Merida

205 bottom This marble portrait of Augustus, dating from the early 1st century A.D., was found in Merida and is housed in the local National Museum of Roman Art. As demonstrated by his covered head, the emperor is shown here in his capacity as Pontifex Maximus (High Priest), the leading religious authority of the Roman state. Octavian was appointed to this office in 12 B.C. when he had already obtained supreme command of the army and legal, political and administrative power.

Roman dominion over the Iberian provinces began during the Second Punic War. During the decades that followed, the Romans had to deal with numerous rebellions by the indigenous populations, culminating in the great uprising of the Celtiberians in 133 B.C., which concluded with the taking and destruction of Numantia by Scipio Aemilianus.

The war against Sulla conducted by Sertorius, leading troops consisting of natives, Italics and Romans, was crucial to the Romanization of the peninsula. The victories of Caesar in Spain, namely at Lerida in 49 B.C. And Munda in 45 B.C., represented important landmarks in the crisis that led to the final disappearance of the Republic.

Clashes with the tribes of the western Atlantic coasts and those of the far northwestern regions of Cantabria, Asturia and Galicia continued for some time, until Augustus decided to put an end to them once and for all by sending Vipsanius Agrippa, one of his most loyal assistants. As life in the Spanish provinces was fairly peaceful during the Empire, a single garrison was left there, constituted by a legion stationed in Hispania Tarraconensis in a place named Legio after it (now León). The widespread adoption of Roman civilization by the population is demonstrated by the numerous monuments and major public works built in the peninsula, as well as the almost total prevalence of the Latin language and the Roman religion. Some famous personalities came from Spain, including Seneca, Martial, Lucan, Quintilian and the emperors Trajan, Hadrian and Theodosius.

The Iberian provinces made a major contribution to the economy of the Empire, mainly in terms of mineral and agricultural resources, but also (though to a much lesser extent) as regards the products of their industries. These included the salting and preservation of fish, which flourished on the southern and Atlantic coasts.

One of the main exports was oil. In the Roman world there was enormous demand for oil, which was used not only in food, but also for personal hygiene and lighting. Spanish oil was imported to Rome between the 1st and 3rd centuries. It was mainly produced in Baetica, and was shipped on freighters in amphoras of an average capacity of 15 to 18 gallons and a roughly spherical shape, often bearing seals and inscriptions indicating the weight of the

206 left Italica, founded by Scipio in 206 B.C., is the oldest Roman town in Spain. However, it was overshadowed by the nearby and more flourishing Seville (Hispalis), and became a municipium at a very late date. Two of the greatest Roman emperors, Trajan and Hadrian, were born here. Under Hadrian the town underwent radical building work in accordance with Hellenistic patterns. The magnificent homes with mosaic floors uncovered during archaeological digs date from that period.

206-207 The Italica amphitheater, one of the largest in the Roman world, could hold 25,000 spectators. It dates from the period when Hadrian embellished the town with extensive building works. The rooms and the service tunnels under the arena are very well preserved.

207 bottom left The bridge over the Tagus near Alcantara was built under Trajan between 105 and 106 A.D. at the expense of 11 Lusitanian municipia. The bridge, which has six arches (the longest of which has a 40-yard span) is 157 yards long, and was designed by the architect C. Julius Lacer to withstand the sporadic but violent flooding of the river.

207 bottom right Evora, in present-day Portugal, was one of the most important Roman colonies in Lusitania. Founded by Caesar with the name of Liberalitas Iulia, its greatest splendor came in the 2nd century A.D. The Temple of Diana, of which 14 elegant Corinthian columns on a tall podium survive, belongs to this period.

container and the oil, the exporter's name and the date.
When these the ships reached Rome the oil was decanted and the amphoras were destroyed, as they were difficult to re-use. The Testaccio artificial hill (in Latin **mons testaceus**, *or hill of shards) was formed by a pile of amphora fragments, mostly of the Spanish type, from the nearby river port. The Testaccio (which was not the only hill of shards in Rome) is 100 feet high and occupies an area of 24,000 square yards, which gives some idea of the scale of these imports. Spanish oil, which was exported as far as Germany and Britannia, was replaced by African oil in the mid-3rd century. The Iberian peninsula was also the main producer of metals in all the Roman world; gold, silver, iron, tin, copper and lead were widely exported in the form of ingots, not only to Rome, but also to the other provinces. At the time of Polybius, 40,000 miners worked in the Cartagena*

silver mines in an area of 100 square miles. The exceptional purity of Spanish iron allowed the production of high-quality weapons, soon imitated by the Romans.
The law governing the copper and silver mines of Aljustrel in Lusitania (the **lex metalli Vipascensis**, which dates from the reign of Hadrian) describes the exploitation of the Spanish mining resources.
Recently, following excavations and

prospecting, some interesting technical information about the operation of the mines was discovered. In particular, the remains of some specimens of the "Archimedes screw" were found. This was a mechanical device used to drain underground water, allowing a huge amount of water to be sucked out with minimal force. Large waterwheels, the remains of which have also been found in the Spanish mines, were used to increase the height of the water raised.

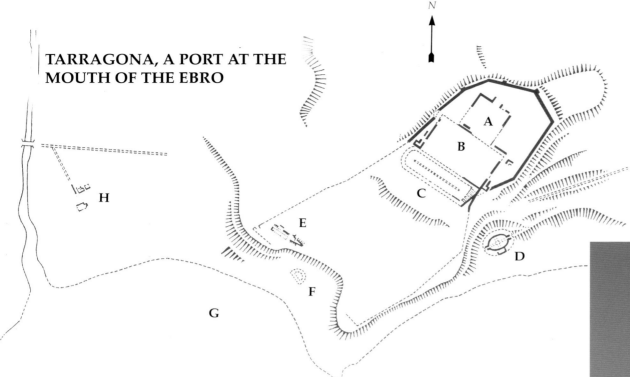

TARRAGONA, A PORT AT THE MOUTH OF THE EBRO

A Sacred enclosure
B Provincial Forum
C Circus
D Amphitheater
E Urban Forum
F Theater
G Port
H Necropolis

The ancient Tarraco, originally a city of the Hergetes, was the capital of Hispania Tarraconensis, also known as Hispania Citerior. It was already a colony under Caesar, and in 16 B.C. Augustus confirmed its status as capital of the region. Built near the mouth of the River Ebro, it developed considerably, and the Romans constructed a port, which no longer survives. The port district contains the remains of the theater, the amphitheater and a macellum, while the remains of the circus, the building known as Augustus's Palace, the forum, and what was probably the provincial governor's residence, dating back to the second half of the 2nd century A.D., are located in the upper town.

A temple dedicated to Augustus was built by Tiberius, and restored under Hadrian and Septimius Severus. The existence of other temples, such as that of Capitoline Jupiter and Minerva, is known almost solely from historical sources. What is believed to have been the governor's residential complex is very unusual; it is formed by the union of the circus and the actual palace, connected at the eastern corner and located on the boundary of two districts of the town. Five aqueducts supplied Tarragona's drinking water; the main one, called the aqueduct "de las Ferreras," crosses a deep valley on two rows of superimposed arches. There are various necropolises and the remains of numerous villas with interesting mosaic floors in the vicinity of the town. The arch of Barà, built by Trajan's lieutenant, Lucius Licinius Sura, is situated some 12 miles from the town. Tarragona, an important center of the Imperial cult and a very active market trading in the wine and linen produced in the region, was seriously damaged by Franco-Alemanni raids in 260 A.D., and later devastated by the Arabs.

208-209 The Las Ferreras aqueduct, some 2.5 miles from the town, is the most spectacular of those that have survived in the eastern regions of the Iberian peninsula. It is 716 feet long, and was built by the drystone wall technique. At the top of the arches, the channel through which the water ran (the specus) is still very well preserved.

209 top left Tarragona was one of the few cities in Hispania in which an amphitheater was built, confirming the social and political importance of this colony.
The amphitheater, dating from the first half of the 2nd century A.D., was partly excavated in the rock of the hillside that slopes down to the beach.

209 top right The circus, built in the late 1st century A.D., completed the official program of building work in ancient Tarraco. It was 1,072 feet long, and designed in accordance with the style typical of this kind of building, which was destined for chariot racing. A large part of the vaulted tunnels and some of the outer façade survive.

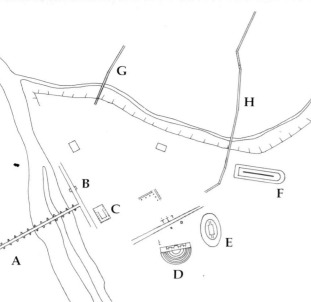

A 60-arch bridge
B Trajan's Arch
C Temple of Diana
D Theater
E Amphitheater
F Circus
G San Làzaro Aqueduct
H Los Milagros
  aqueduct

MERIDA, THE TOWN OF AUGUSTUS'S VETERANS

Emerita Augusta (the ancient name of the town of Merida) was founded in 25 B.C. by decree of Augustus by the veterans and emeritus soldiers of the 5th Alaudae and 10th Gemina legions as a military outpost. It became a flourishing trading center, and later, capital of Lusitania. Its impressive ruined monuments make Merida one of the major archaeological centers on the Iberian peninsula. The theater, amphitheater and circus, built in the same area outside the city walls, are very well preserved. The entire scaena of the theater, which has been totally rebuilt in recent years, has survived. The bridge over the Guadiana River, whose 60 arches span a distance of 871 yards, is one of the longest to survive from the Roman period. The town was supplied with water by three aqueducts; large sections of the ones called Los Milagros and San Lazaro have survived. The first, 82 feet high, winds along an 913-yard route on 37 huge piers made of alternating rows of granite and brick. It was supplied by a reservoir called Persephone's Lake, which is interesting for its large dam.

In the town can be seen the so-called Trajan's Arch, the remains of Diana's Temple and the small temple of Mars, two mausoleums, a home converted into a Christian basilica, and some sections of the turreted city walls. The excavation of a sanctuary of Mithras has brought to light an impressive complex of marble sculptures; other equally important sculptures have been found in the necropolises and during the theater excavations.

Merida maintained its importance during the Christian and Visigoth periods, as demonstrated by historical, artistic and epigraphic references.

210 top Merida, founded as a military outpost for the control of Lusitania, soon became one of the wealthiest towns in the Iberian peninsula. This prosperity is demonstrated by the many archaeological finds made in the urban area and the numerous monuments still visible today. This photo shows one of the exquisite mosaics that decorated a private house near the amphitheater.

210 center Three large aqueducts served the town; the one shown in this photo is called the San Làzaro aqueduct. In Merida, as in all the other cities of the Empire, the operation of the aqueducts and all matters relating to the water supply were handled by a magistrate called the curator aquarum.

210 bottom The bridge over the Guadiana is one of the most spectacular applications of the arch dating from the Roman age.

211 The town's magnificent theater could hold up to 6,000 spectators. After lengthy rebuilding work on the scaena (the most attractive in Europe) the building was restored to its original function, and now houses top-level theatrical and musical seasons every year.

GAUL AND GERMANY, THE CORNERSTONES OF THE EMPIRE

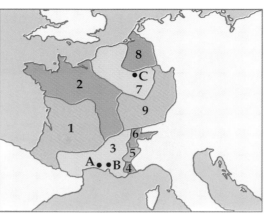

1 Aquitania
2 Lugdunensis
3 Narbonensis
4 Alpes Maritimae
5 Alpes Cottiae
6 Alpes Graiae et Poenine
7 Belgica
8 Germania Inferior
9 Germania Superior
A Nîmes
B Orange
C Trier (Trèves)

Transalpine Gaul occupied the huge territory between the Atlantic Ocean, the Pyrenees, the Mediterranean, the Alps, the Rhine and the North Sea. The region had a mainly Celtic population, together with Germans on the Rhine border and Iberian populations in the area of the Pyrenees. Along the Mediterranean coast there were numerous settlements of Greek origin, the main one being Massilia (Marseilles), a flourishing trading center.

The social system, which was the feudal type and based on a mainly agricultural economy, was ruled by an aristocratic oligarchy over which the priestly caste of the Druids exerted considerable influence. The main deities, partly identified with the Roman pantheon, were Teutatis, Taranis, Epona, Rosmerta and Cerunno. Ethnic, religious and cultural unity did not prevent frequent

rivalry and conflicts, exploited by the Roman conquerors, whose task was facilitated by the absence of towns, as the Gauls preferred villages and fortified hills.

Contacts between Gaul and Rome began in the mid-2nd century B.C., when Rome came to the aid of its ally, Massilia. The first colony (Narbo Martius, now Narbonne) was only founded in 121 B.C., after the victorious military campaign against the Arverni tribe, which had attempted to set up a Gallic state. Shortly afterwards the Province of Narbonnese Gaul (later called merely Provincia, hence the modern name of Provence) was set up, and trade and political/military alliances were encouraged.

There were frequent rebellions by various tribes, however, including uprisings by the Cimbrians and the Teutons, put down by Caius Marius in 102 and 101 B.C. In the Battles of Aquae Sextiae and the Raudian Fields. Caesar's victory over Vercingetorix at Alesia in 52 B.C. finally gave Rome possession of the whole of Gaul, which from then on was strongly Romanized. When it was permanently reorganized, Augustus divided the region into Gallia Narbonensis, Aquitania, Gallia Belgica and Gallia Lugdunensis, and this system lasted until the time of Diocletian. The population was divided into 64 civitates, corresponding to the original tribes. Every year their representatives attended the Conventum Galliarum, *which met near the altar of Rome and Augustus at the confluence of the Rhône and the Saône, to discuss common affairs and exert a limited right of control over the acts of the Roman governors.*
The towns, which were considerably

212-213 The Arles amphitheater, which dates from the late 1st century A.D., is the best preserved in France together with the one in Nîmes; it is 449 feet long on the major axis, and can still hold 12,000 spectators.

212 bottom left An aqueduct over 30 miles long, with a difference in height of only 56 feet, conveyed water diverted from a source near present-day Uzès to Nîmes. To cross the River Gardon, the Roman builders erected the Pont-du-Gard, which is 907 feet long and just under 161 feet high.

212 bottom right Augustodunum, present-day Autun, was one of the main cities in Lyonnese Gaul, and became famous in the 3rd century for its school of rhetoric. The town still has many Roman ruins, including the beautiful monumental door of St. André built into the great city walls, which date from the age of Augustus.

213 The Temple of Augustus and Livia, built c. 10 B.C., is the most famous Roman monument in Vienne, the ancient Colonia Iulia Vienna Allobrogum. Very similar to the one in Nîmes, it is also a Corinthian hexastyle temple on a tall podium.

extended and embellished with monuments, acquired a typically Roman appearance, and theaters, amphitheaters, circuses, bath complexes, basilicas, arches, bridges and aqueducts, numerous remains of which still survive today, were built everywhere. Gallo-Roman art constituted a combination of the Hellenistic-Roman experience and Celtic art and, unlike the art of other provinces, had its own independent characteristics. These

214 top and 215 bottom This splendid goblet and great silver crater are part of the treasure of Hildesheim, found near the German town in 1865. Consisting of over 60 items, it was perhaps the traveling kit of a high Roman official of the age of Augustus, seized in an attack by a Germanic warrior who hid it and was then unable to retrieve it. Beginning in the 1st century B.C. the possession of silverware was considered a status symbol; this represents another sign of the gradual Hellenization of Roman society and culture.

included funeral sculptures, the most celebrated examples of which consist of decorated pillars portraying the activities of the deceased, special votive monuments dedicated to Jupiter, which were especially frequent in north and east Gaul, and finally, the practice of decorating the entire surface of triumphal arches with sculptures. Gaul had a flourishing economy, represented by the products of agriculture, industry and trade between the north and the Mediterranean. Some

examples are the wines of Narbonnese Gaul, which were Rome's main export during the Flavian age, and a type of ceramic called **terra sigillata**, which was very popular and exported throughout the Empire. According to sources, gold was abundant and easily obtainable; in fact, Gaul was one of the few countries of the Mediterranean able to mint its own gold coins.

The two provinces of Roman Germany only comprised a small part of the huge territory that the Romans called by that name. Caesar's campaigns in Gaul had taken the legions as far as the Rhine, in order to safeguard the Gallic provinces. From 12 to 9 B.C., Drusus fought courageously there, endeavoring to pave the way for unification of the various Germanic populations that, once pacified, were to meet at a religious and political center similar to the one established in Lyons for the Gauls. For this purpose, he consecrated a large altar for the federal cult, associated with the worship of Rome and Augustus, in the

territory of the Ubii, on the left bank of the Rhine.

The premature death of Drusus first slowed, and then jeopardized the conquest of these lands. Although their fortunes fluctuated, the Roman armies suffered some serious defeats at the hands of the warlike Germanic tribes for several years, until the time of Tiberius. Particularly tragic was the defeat of Varus in A.D. 9 by the barbarian chief, Arminius, when three legions were annihilated. Recent excavations have identified the site of the terrible battle, in the Kalkriese area. Helmets, fragments of breastplates, arrowheads, javelins and a whole range of Roman coins whose latest date is A.D. 9 have been discovered.

It is interesting to note that the remains found coincide with what Germanicus witnessed, according to Tacitus: "In the middle of the field, bones shone whitely, piled up or dispersed...scattered all around were fragments of arrows and limbs of horses; and human skulls were impaled on tree trunks. In the nearby sacred woods rough altars could be glimpsed, on which the Germans had sacrificed the tribunes and the leading centurions."

Of the two Roman provinces, Upper Germany stretched from Lake Geneva to the confluence of the Vinxtbach and the Rhine, by way of Confluentes (Koblenz) and Bonna (Bonn). The only region on the far side of the Rhine that was included was Taunus. Lower Germany reached as far as the North Sea, including part of what is now the Netherlands.

Opposite Colonia Claudia Ara Agrippinensium (Cologne) stood the fortified camp of Divitia (Dentz), which acted as a bridgehead. In those sections where the border was not constituted by the Rhine, a fortified limes protected the province against the barbarians. For a length of 237 miles it consisted of a vallum (rampart) reinforced by palisades, preceded by a ditch and protected by fortified camps of various sizes. Many of them have been identified and excavated, with the result that the entire line of the limes has been reconstructed. The Saalburg limes, all parts of which have been reconstructed, is particularly famous.

The two Germanys were basically military provinces, as can be deduced from the surviving monuments. As regards the economy, a characteristic product exported on a large scale to Rome was glass articles. Some exquisite specimens, made in the workshops of Cologne, still survive.

214 bottom Augst, a few miles from Basle, was founded with the name of Augusta Raurica c. 40 B.C. Situated at the intersection of the roads that crossed the Alps to connect Gaul with the Danube provinces, this military colony had a strategic position. The main archaeological remains were discovered around the forum and theater area; this photo shows the podium of a temple dating from the 2nd century B.C.

215 top The funerary stele, or pillar, of the legionnaire Gnaeus Musius is part of the archaeological collection of the Magonza Landesmuseum. The town, known as Magontiacum, grew up around the military camp founded under Augustus near the confluence of the Main and the Rhine. The great castle, manned by two legions, was an important base for the control of Upper Germany for a long time. Many similar steles have been found in the local military necropolises.

NÎMES, THE PRIDE OF NARBONNESE GAUL

Called Nemausus in Latin after a mythical son of Hercules, Nîmes was a Latin colony inhabited by soldiers from Antony's army. Under Augustus it was given the name of Colonia Augusta Nemausus, and was part of Gallia Narbonensis (Narbonnese Gaul). It soon became one of the most flourishing and Romanized towns in the region. Some very important public monuments were built in its territory, and imposing remains of many of them still survive. In the town, at the crossroads between the cardo and the decumanus, near the site of the forum, is the Maison Carrée, one of the best preserved hexastyle temples, initially

dedicated to Agrippa, and later to Caius and Lucius Caesar.

In the area to the south of the town is the large amphitheater with two rows of arches, which dates from the second half of the 1st century A.D. and is very similar to the one in Arles; the structure is still used for shows of various kinds. No trace remains of the circus, which must have been located in the same area. In the northwest part of the town there is a huge monumental complex: around the sacred spring of Nemausus stand the remains of the theater, whose terraces exploit the natural slope of the hill, a nymphaeum and numerous temples.

216 bottom Nîmes was one of the most flourishing towns in southern Gaul; its prosperity is demonstrated by the outstanding collection of Roman art housed in the local Archaeological Museum.

216-217 The Maison Carrée is a perfect example of a Corinthian marble temple on a podium; it is the most complete of the similar buildings that have survived from the age of Augustus. Its excellent state of preservation is due to the fact that it was reused for various purposes as during the Middle Ages; it was converted into stables, then a church, and then the first city museum. It is now an exhibition center.

The so-called Temple of Diana is of particular interest; it was built in the Augustan period and extended and enhanced under Hadrian by setting it in a scenic complex that wound along the slope of the hill.

Nîmes was supplied with drinking water by an aqueduct 31 miles long, of which the spectacular Pont-du-Gard, with its three rows of arches, still survives.

217 bottom left
Nîmes amphitheater, dating from the 1st century A.D., presents some quite advanced construction methods that allowed 23,000 spectators to enter and exit quickly, due to a system of five concentric tunnels built at different levels and intersected by passages and staircases constructed in a radial pattern.

217 bottom right
The Temple of Diana was part of the sacred complex of the Nemausus spring, built under Augustus; part of the great barrel vault of the cella survives. Due to the excellent state of preservation of its numerous monuments dating from the Imperial age, Nîmes has become famous as "France's Rome."

ORANGE, A COLONY FOUNDED BY JULIUS CAESAR

Under Julius Caesar, the town of Orange (Arausio) was the site of a colony of veterans belonging to the Second Legion, commanded by Tiberius's father. The foundation of the colony was celebrated with the construction of a triumphal arch, one of the most impressive of those still surviving. It consists of a central archway and two smaller archways at the sides, has a frontage of 64 feet and is 62 feet high. It is decorated with a lively battle scene and also portrays war trophies, groups of chained prisoners and a naval trophy commemorating Caesar's victory over Massilia (Marseilles). The dedication, probably to Tiberius, was added later, after the Sacrovirus revolt was put down.

The other major Roman monument in Orange, the theater, is outstanding for the exceptional state of preservation of the scaena, the back wall of which is 340 feet long and 121 feet high. At the top, the brackets used to support the poles of the velarium (protective awning) are clearly visible. The interior, which originally had three tiers of columns, features a wealth of decoration, including statues and friezes with centaurs, maenads, eagles and garlands. The outer façade is outstanding for its totally regular surface, while the auditorium still has acoustics of exceptional purity.

Not far from the theater are the remains of a large temple and a building with an exedra and parallel walls. This is perhaps the only example of a gymnasium discovered in Gaul.

The division of the territory of Arausio is documented by some very rare fragments of marble cadastral maps relating to the administration of the colony, which are housed in the local museum.

218 top The theater of Orange dates from the end of Augustus's reign and the beginning of Tiberius's. The exceptional interest of the building is due to the perfect state of preservation of the scaena wall and the exceptional acoustics of the auditorium, which still enable theatrical performances to be staged. A statue of Augustus 11.5 feet high stands in the central niche.

218 center The triumphal arch was built in the northern area of the town to commemorate its foundation by Caesar.

218 bottom The reliefs decorating the triumphal arch portray a battle between Roman soldiers and barbarian warriors, evoking the conquest of Gaul.

219 The Orange theater is the only one in which the triumphal statue of the emperor has survived; it was in fragments when found but was pieced together and placed in its niche, which features a bowl-shaped vault.

TRIER, A FLOURISHING TOWN OF THE LATE EMPIRE

A Warehouses
B Baths
C Forum
D Porta Nigra
E Constantine's Palace
F Aula Palatina
G Baths of Constantine
H Circus
I Amphitheater

220 and 221 top right
The Aula Palatina,
though much restored,
dates from A.D. 310; it
was the audience
chamber of
Constantine's Palace.

221 left
This fragment of a
funeral monument,
portraying a wine
cargo ship, originates
from the town of
Neumagen.

221 center right
Porta Nigra, dating
from the early 4th
century, was built
in the northern side
of the city walls.

221 right bottom The
ruins of the Imperial
baths, built by
Constantine and
converted into a
barracks in the 4th
century, were reused
in the Middle Ages to
house the church of
Santa Croce.

Augusta Treverorum (Trier or Trèves) in Gallia Belgica (Belgic Gaul) was founded by Augustus between 19 and 16 B.C. It was a very wealthy, prosperous town that reached the peak of its glory in the late Imperial period, when it became the residence of many emperors. In A.D. 287 Diocletian chose it as the capital of the western part of the Empire, and especially under Constantine, the town was embellished with many major monuments. Its decline began in the early 5th century, when the legions stationed on the Rhine were recalled to Italy. The northern access to the town features the magnificent Porta Nigra, dating from the 4th century, the best-preserved surviving city gate. The 100-foot-high gate had a large inner courtyard, enclosed between two towers connected by a twin gallery. Another major monument is the Aula Palatina, a grandiose legal basilica erected by

Constantine in A.D. 310. It is a huge rectangular room with no aisles and an enormous apse. The ancient brick building, which survives as far as the roof, has two rows of tall arched windows. The nearby Imperial Baths complex, also commissioned by Constantine, was never completed.

The structure was preceded by a large palaestra, and a nymphaeum constituted the façade of the outer portico. Apart from the large residential villas in the neighborhood of the town, other monuments include the Roman bridge over the Moselle, the small but well-preserved amphitheater dating from the 1st century A.D., the richly decorated Baths of St. Barbara, built in the last 30 years of the 3rd century, and the remains of a palazzo under the cathedral, probably belonging to the residence of Constantine's mother, St. Helena, where some interesting panels with busts of women were found.

221

BRITANNIA, A PROVINCE UNDER STRICT MILITARY RULE

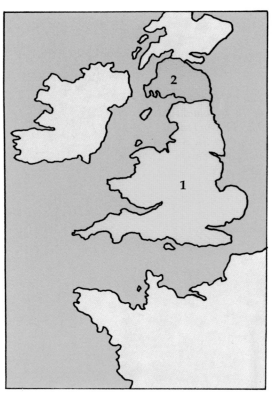

The Romans came into contact with the populations of Britannia in 55 B.C., when Julius Caesar led the first military expedition there, followed by a second one the next year. The conquest of the region was mainly formal, however, and it was only really subjugated in A.D. 43, under Emperor Claudius.

The northern boundary, along which Hadrian built his celebrated wall, ran between the mouths of the Tyne and Solway rivers. Later, Antoninus Pius moved the limes further north, and ordered the construction of a second fortified line, which only remained operational until the time of Commodus. At the time of the Roman conquest, Britannia had a mainly agricultural economy and good mineral resources. The geographer Strabo listed the main goods of the island as follows: "Wheat, cattle, gold, silver, hides, slaves and excellent hunting dogs." Gold deposits were located in Wales, Scotland and Cornwall, and silver (obtained by refining argentiferous lead), copper and tin were mined in many areas. Some mines in Cornwall produced copper associated with tin, a coincidence that probably led to the local production of bronze. Other major copper mining centers were situated in North Wales. Tin was also quite important, at least until the 3rd century A.D., when it was supplanted by Spanish tin. However,

1 From A.D. 43 to 406
2 From A.D. 142 to 180

Britannia was mainly famous because it was one of the main lead production areas in the Imperial age. The deposits were so rich that, as Pliny wrote, it became necessary to pass a law to restrict excessive production.

The interest of the Romans in the products of Britannia was facilitated by the many landing places along the coast, especially frequent in the south opposite Belgic Gaul, such as Dubrae (Dover), Anderida (Pevensey) and Regulbium (Reculver). Colonization began in the Thames basin, where the most densely populated towns on the island were located. Of these, Londinium (London) was already an active river port, from which the Roman road system developed.

A great thoroughfare that started here led east to Camulodunum (Colchester), an important colony founded by the Romans and the headquarters of the Imperial cult, then continued to Lindum (Lincoln) and Eboracum (York). Another busy commercial road was the one that led from Londinium across Calleva Atrebatum (Silchester) to the land of the Silures (Wales), where it reached the towns of Venta and Isca Silurum, and then branched off to Glevum (Gloucester).

The problems that faced the Romans in Britannia mainly related to security of transport across the channel and the particular geographical conformation of the island, with its very uneven territory. Dealings with the local customs were aided by long experience acquired in Gaul, whose population presented strong cultural similarities to

222 bottom
This series of niches was part of the changing room of the baths at Cilurnum (Chesters), one of the 17 great fortified camps along Hadrian's Wall.

222-223 The remains of ancient pillars flank the neoclassical columns in the baths at Aquae Sulis (Bath). This town was already famous in the Imperial age for its hot healing springs; in 1796 the great Pump Room, a magnificent thermal spa including an archaeological museum with many interesting exhibits, was built on the huge complex of the Roman baths, which dated from the 1st century A.D. and was continually extended until the 5th century.

223 top The remains of the Verulamium Theater can still be seen near St. Albans in Hertfordshire. The town, founded c. A.D. 49, became one of the most important in Britannia during the 3rd century.

that of Britannia, especially in the fields of religion and mythology.

Tacitus described the inhabitants of Britannia as follows: "The physical appearance of the inhabitants differs…the inhabitants of Caledonia have red hair, and the size of their limbs bears witness to their Germanic origin; the Silures are mainly dark-skinned and curly-haired, and the fact that they occupy the part of the country which lies opposite Spain seems to demonstrate that the ancient Iberians crossed the sea and occupied those places. Those who live in the regions nearest to the country of the Gauls resemble the latter.…" Britannia was one of the least peaceable and least Romanized provinces in the Empire. The various conflicts include the skirmishes in 54 B.C., which culminated in the battle of the Tamesis (Thames) between Caesar, with five legions and 2,000 horsemen, and the Britons, commanded by King Cassivellaunus. On that occasion,

224 top Helmets like this one (dating from the late 1st century A.D., found during excavations at the fort of Ribchester in Lancashire) were not worn in battle, but only for parades and tournaments. *Hyppica gymnasia* were a kind of mock battles in which two teams of horsemen, protected by finely decorated breastplates, fought to demonstrate their skills. These events, which always attracted large crowds, were presided over by the military and civil authorities of the neighboring villages and forts.

224 bottom The superb golden torques found at Snettisham in Norfolk perhaps belonged to a leading figure in the local tribe called the Iceni. This kind of heavy collar was a very common ornament among the Celtic populations; for example, the famous Dying Galatea wore a similar necklace. Celtic art, especially in Gaul, was strongly influenced by the Roman world, and indeed almost suffocated by it. However, in Britannia this influence was weaker, and local styles continued to be used.

Caesar's Seventh Legion confronted the powerful enemy combat chariot (assedum), drawn by a pair of horses, with a crew consisting of a driver and a fighter armed mainly with a bow. Another particularly dramatic event took place in A.D. 59, when the attempted conquest of the Isle of Mona (Anglesey), the center of the Druidic cult, triggered a general insurrection led by Boudicca, the widow of Prasutagus, King of the Iceni. After the defeat suffered by the Roman army at the time of Commodus by populations that had come down from the north, in A.D. 197 Septimius Severus divided the province into Upper Britannia and Lower Britannia, and this arrangement remained in force until Diocletian further split the territory into four zones.

The barbarian invasions, which began in the 4th century, culminated in A.D. 406, when Britannia was finally abandoned by the Roman legions after the invasion of Gaul.

225 top The treasure trove of Thetford in Norfolk, one of the greatest finds of Roman gold and silver to be made in Great Britain, was discovered by chance in 1979. Among the numerous precious objects is this gold buckle consisting of two parts hinged together; the rectangular frame is decorated with the figure of a dancing satyr, and the arch with two horse heads. In view of the quality of the workmanship, this jewel is believed to have been made in continental Europe around the mid-4th century.

225 bottom This large silver plate dating from the 4th century A.D. is part of the treasure found at Mildenhall in Suffolk; it is one of the most exquisite specimens of toreutic art to have survived from ancient times. At the center is the face of the god Oceanus, surrounded by a number of sea creatures; the outer strip is occupied by 14 satyrs and maenads engaged in bacchic rites. The entire 34-piece set perhaps belonged to a wealthy Roman-British landowner or a local official.

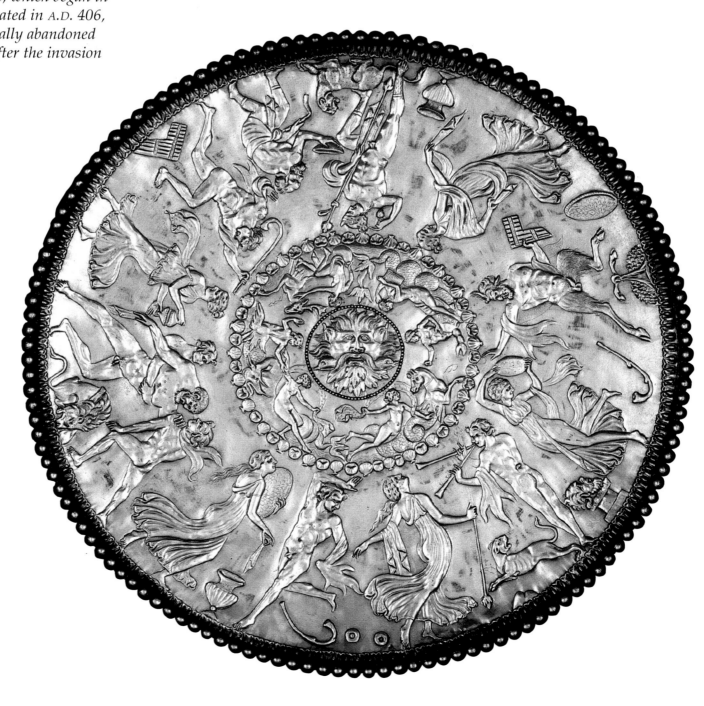

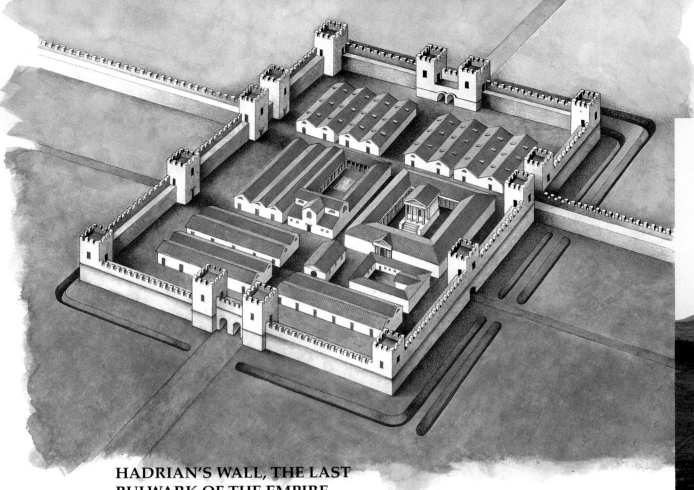

HADRIAN'S WALL, THE LAST BULWARK OF THE EMPIRE

226 top This drawing shows what the fortified camps built along Hadrian's Wall may have looked like. Strong walls surrounded the barracks in which the garrison was quartered; at the center stood the commander's quarters, a small bathhouse and the Temple of Rome and Augustus.
Small towns with homes for the soldiers' families, emporia, inns, temples and bath complexes grew up around the main forts.

226-227 This picture shows a stretch of Hadrian's Wall near Housesteads. This bulwark against the Caledonian populations, manned by 15,000 auxiliary soldiers, consisted of a wall 80 Roman miles long (about 72.5 miles), with a wide ditch and a military road running alongside it. Forts and watchtowers were built at regular intervals along the entire length of the rampart, which was around 20 feet high.

Hadrian's Wall, the complex of military engineering works that constituted the limes (boundary) of Britannia under Hadrian, was built after the emperor's visit to the province in A.D. 122 The immense fortified line, completed five years later, reflected Hadrian's theories about border defense, which no longer had offensive purposes, but was designed to strengthen the territories already conquered. The 72.5-mile-long wall ran from the Solway Firth to the mouth of the River Tyne, marking the boundary between Roman Britain and Scotland. The construction of the wall, which was preceded by a ditch measuring on average 26 feet wide and 8.2 feet deep, bears witness to the skills of the Roman engineers and soldiers, who adapted its design to the lay of the land and set up quarries and brickworks in the area. At first, instead of stone they actually used clods of turf, which are still visible at some points. The limes was defended by auxiliary cohortes and alae from various parts of the Empire, which were quartered in numerous fortified camps incorporated in the line of the wall. The legions were stationed in decentralized locations behind the wall. The mile castles, so called because they were built every mile, were designed to defend openings in the wall, and could house around 50 men. The vallum (rampart), which consisted of a ditch (approximately 20 feet wide and 10 feet deep) and two embankments built at the sides, ran parallel to the nearside of the

wall. The vallum was only interrupted in the mountainous area now called the Crags. It deviated from the wall to surround the forts, and opened at the border crossing places. The last and most crucial element was constituted by the roads. In fact, the limes could be described as a clever pattern of military roads designed to aid movements parallel to and across the border. Communications in the east-west direction were guaranteed by various highways, especially Stanegate; this road connected Corstopitum (Corbridge) to Luguvallum (Carlisle), forming a curve on the nearside of the defensive line, and secondary roads led off it to each fort along the limes. From the south, two more highways, together with a myriad of minor roads, connected Eburacum (York) to Corstopitum and Deva (Chester) to Luguvallum. Seventeen military camps were situated along the wall. Those which are best known nowadays are the camps at Cilurnum (Chesters), which is quite well preserved, and Vindolanda (Chesterholm), where important relics of garrison life have been found. From Maia (Bowness), Hadrian's limes continued along the Cumberland coast to the Solway Firth. Here, it consisted of a system of forts and towers, with no other defensive structures such as the ditch, wall and rampart, as the presence of the sea made them superfluous. The outposts situated north of the wall included the forts of Banna (Bewcastle) and Castra Exploratorum (Netherby).

A Castra Exploratorum (Netherby)
B Banna (Bewcastle)
C Bribra (Malbray)
D Alauna (Maryport)
E Derventione (Papcastle)
F Olerica (Old Carlisle)
G Luguvallum (Carlisle)
H Vereda (Old Penrith)
I Bravoniacum (Kirly Tore)
J Verterae (Brough)
K Corstopitum (Corbridge)
L Longovicium (Lonchester)

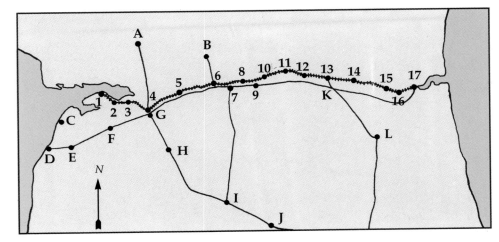

1 Maia (Bowness)
2 Congavata (Drumburgh)
3 Aballava (Burgh-by-Sands)
4 Petriana (Stanvix)
5 Uxellodunum (Castlesteads)
6 Camboglanna (Birdoswald)
7 Magna (Carvoran)
8 Aesica (Great Chesters)
9 Vindolanda (Chesterholm)
10 Borgovicium (Housesteads)
11 Procolitia (Carrawburgh)
12 Cilurnum (Chesters)
13 Hunnum (Halton)
14 Vindobala (Rochester)
15 Condercum (Benwell)
16 Pons Aelius (Newcastle)
17 Segedunum (Wallsend)

THE DANUBE PROVINCES, REGIONS OF STRATEGIC IMPORTANCE

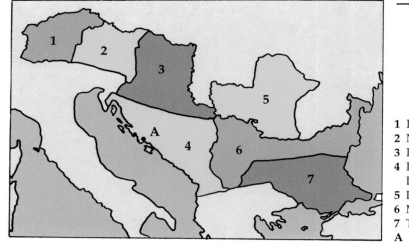

1 Raetia
2 Noricum
3 Pannonia
4 Illyricum or Dalmatia
5 Dacia
6 Moesia
7 Thracia
A Split

228 The base of Trajan's column is entirely covered with magnificent decorations portraying Roman and barbarian weapons overlapping in apparent disorder. Some breastplates typical of the Dacian armored horsemen are recognizable by their "fish-scale" appearance.
The conquest of Dacia, which was rendered difficult by the resistance offered by the warlike local populations, was the last episode of Roman imperialism in the Danube territories. Despite increasingly violent barbarian attacks, the last strongholds on the Danube were held until the 5th century.

229 This large fibula made of gold and semiprecious stones, an exquisite product of what is known as Dacio-Roman art, is part of the treasure found at Pietroasa in present-day Romania. The fibula, which portrays a stylized eagle, dates from the 4th century A.D. and is clearly influenced by barbarian designs. The Danube regions, and Dacia in particular, were intensively Romanized, as demonstrated by the development of numerous towns; the local craftsmen were naturally influenced by styles imported by the Roman colonists, and then elaborated on them to produce wholly original styles, even after the withdrawal of the occupying troops.

The Danube provinces comprised a huge territory, bounded to the west by the Germanys, to the north (except for Dacia) by the Danube, to the east by the Black Sea, and to the south by Cisalpine Gaul and Achaia. The province consisted of seven regions: Raetia (Rhaetia), Noricum, Pannonia, Illyricum, Dacia, Moesia and Thracia (Thrace). Raetia, like Noricum, came into contact with the Romans as a result of trade that originated in Aquileia. The region was inhabited by Celtic populations, mainly concentrated in the Rhône and Rhine basins, that were organized in independent cantons. Largely because of the impenetrable territory of the region, the process of Romanization was not very effective, and there were very few major towns. Those that did exist included Augusta Vindelicum (Augsburg), Cambodunum (Kempten), Brigantium (Bregenz) and Castra Regina (Regensburg). The real importance of these territories lay in the road network that crossed them, which was of great commercial and military value. Their few agricultural and mineral resources were scarcely sufficient to meet local requirements.

Noricum was inhabited by Celtic-Illyrian populations. Before its subjugation it was a kingdom, whose capital was Noreia (Neumark), and its kings had friendly dealings with Rome for many years. The province was fairly Romanized, partly because of the high level of Italic immigration. The main wealth of the region was constituted by metals, especially gold, lead and iron; the iron mines became the most famous in the entire Roman world in the Imperial age. Ovid and Pliny also recount that exceptionally high-quality steel was made there. It is believed that a method (probably unknown to the Greeks and Romans) of making steel from iron by using a percentage of manganese in the casting, was developed in Noricum around 500 B.C. The art that developed in this province in the Roman age represented a combination of Italic and Celtic-Illyrian influences. In the field of architecture, in addition to the sanctuaries of the Romanized Celtic deities, public buildings also closely imitated the Roman patterns. Pannonia only became an independent province after the great insurrection of the Danube populations, which took place between A.D. 6 and 9, was put down. Various legionary camps were set up to defend the region against the barbarians from over the Danube, and they eventually became important centers of Romanization. The main towns of the region, in fact, developed from the military camps and neighboring indigenous communities called canabae, formed by craftsmen, merchants and camp followers. Although the economy of

Pannonia mainly revolved around agriculture and mining, a flourishing business was also conducted by the traders who settled along the major highways crossing the province from west to east. Savaria (Szombathely), for example, was a major road junction from which roads led to Vindobona (Vienna), Brigetio (Szöny), Poetovio (Ptuj) and Siscia (Sisak), after which it was possible to continue as far as Salona (Solin) in Illyricum. Again in the field of transport, an important role was played by the major rivers, including the Danube, the Drava and the Sava. Roman influence, which was strongest in the western part of the region, had to contend with an indigenous substratum, mainly Celtic and partly Illyrian, that had previously produced the La Tène civilization, whose influence was still strong in the arts. There were also some Greek influences in the eastern areas.

Illyricum, situated on the opposite shore of the Adriatic to Italy, had attracted the attention of Rome in the 3rd century B.C. because of piracy by the indigenous tribes living there. The wars designed to consolidate Roman rule over the Dalmatian and Liburnian tribes continued throughout the 2nd century B.C., and much of the 3rd. The province was greatly extended under Augustus. From the time of the Republic, immigration by Italic traders who joined forces in guilds led to the Romanization of the coastal towns and the islands. The coastal area was thus very different from the inland areas, where the indigenous populations assimilated Roman civilization far more slowly. The main resources of this region consisted of iron, gold and silver mines, stock-rearing, and corn, grape and olive growing.

The major towns were Doclea (Duklja), Scodria (Skutari) and Salona (Solin),

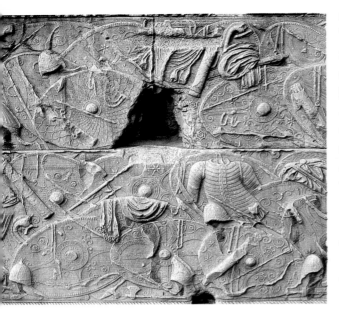

(Alba-Iulia), Napoca (Cluj) and Ulpia Traiana Sarmizegetusa, the headquarters of the Imperial legate. Dacia was finally abandoned by Aurelian in A.D. 270 under pressure from barbarian attacks. The Romans had to intervene in Moesia to limit the mass of populations not subjugated by Rome that infiltrated the conquered territories with continual raids and incursions. Military activity in the region was extensive, especially under the Flavians, and border security always represented the main concern of the Imperial legates. This province was one of the most heterogeneous because of the great variety of the land and the

which was the birthplace of Diocletian and an important ecclesiastical metropolis in the Christian era. Not far away Diocletian built his magnificent palace, around which the city of Spalatum (Split) developed.
Rome undertook military campaigns against Dacia (not always successfully) in the time of Domitian, following continual raids by the local populations against the garrisons in Moesia. However, it was Trajan, in the course of two successive campaigns between A.D. 101 and 107, who eventually overcame the resistance of Decebalus, King of the Dacians, and finally conquered the region. The various stages of the Dacian Wars are vividly portrayed in the reliefs on Trajan's Column, which often show the Dacians wearing their characteristic headgear, the pileus. After the Roman occupation, numerous colonists flocked to the lands across the Danube, and it was mainly they who, together with the legions stationed there, helped make the region one of the most intensely Romanized in the Empire. The main resources of Dacia were ores, especially iron, silver and gold; after the conquest, Trajan brought some 182 tons of gold and 165,500 tons of silver to Rome as war booty. The excellent quality of the iron objects still surviving and the tools used to make them demonstrate the high level of technical expertise achieved by this population in the field of metallurgy. The province was served by an extensive road network along which numerous towns developed, including Apulum

populations who lived there, ranging from the Celtic-Illyrian tribes in the west to the Thracian tribes in the east, and the Greeks in the towns on the Black Sea coast. This meant that there was a great variety of cultural aspects, in addition to the work of Romanization performed by the legions stationed along the Danube, whose main camps were at Singidunum (Belgrade), Noviodunum (Isaccea), Viminacium (Kostolac), Ratiaria (Arcar) and Oescus (Ghighen). The numbers of municipalities and colonies were very small, and the province as a whole retained a rather rustic nature within the official Roman context. The outstanding

funeral and triumphal monuments of the region include the Tropaeum Traiani, erected in South Dobruja (Romania), at what is now the village of Adamklissi, to commemorate Trajan's Dacian conquests. The rich figured decoration of the impressive building constitutes one of the most magnificent complexes of provincial Roman art still surviving.
Thracia, formerly the kingdom of the indigenous tribe called the Odrisi, and later long disputed between Macedonia and Syria, was the last region on the nearside of the Danube to become a Roman province, when Claudius seized it in A.D. 46. Numerous towns, such as Flaviopolis, Hadrianopolis (Edirne) and Trajanopolis, were founded to aid the pacification process. At the same time, particular attention was given to developing the road network which connected the Aegean to the Black Sea. Romanization was most intense in the coastal areas, which were influenced by the process of civilization conducted by the Greeks, whereas in the inland areas the Romans long had to contend with bellicose local populations. In any event, the tribal organization of the Thracians was maintained even after the conquest, and most of the inhabitants retained their own customs and religion. A characteristic feature of this region were the emporia, the sites of periodic markets located along the main highways between Europe and Asia. The towns of Serdica (Sofia), Beroe (Stara Zagora) and Philippopolis (Plovdiv) were also important road junctions. The region was of little political

230 top
The continuous bas-relief, over 650 feet long, which winds around Trajan's Column, faithfully depicts the various stages of the two Dacian campaigns conducted by Trajan. The reliefs feature a wealth of detail that is invaluable to comprehension of Roman military organization. They show legionnaires engaged in constructing fortified camps, sappers building a huge bridge over the Danube, soldiers forming the testudo or storming enemy towns with the use of war engines, standard-bearers with the banners of the cohorts, buglers and horn players, and even field hospitals. It also faithfully depicts the various uniforms, weapons and models of breastplate worn at the time of the battles described.

231 The grandiose Tropaeum Traiani was built in A.D. 109 in Lower Moesia (in the area of what is now Adamklissi in Romania) to commemorate the emperor's victories over the Dacians. The monument consisted of a massive cylindrical pile made of concrete faced with blocks of limestone and decorated with a frieze surmounted by a crenellated parapet. The conical roof was covered with fish-scale-shaped stone tiles. A tall hexagonal pedestal at the top of the roof supported the great war trophy, at the base of which there were perhaps some male and female figures symbolizing the regions and populations subjugated by Trajan. The total height of the structure was around 105 feet. The metopes forming the decorated strip, mainly showing military subjects, are designed in accordance with popular local taste; they are, therefore, believed to belong to a reconstruction of Trajan's Trophy, dating from the time of Constantine. They are actually one of the most interesting surviving specimens of provincial Romano-barbarian art.

and economic importance until the 3rd century, when it became the site of battles with invading barbarian populations. It was long disputed between the Empire of the East and the Empire of the West until it was finally conquered by the former, constituting a crucial defensive outpost. This turbulent political situation corresponded to the rise of Byzantium, already a flourishing city founded by Megara, which was magnificently rebuilt by Constantine beginning in A.D. 323. The city, called Constantinople from A.D. 330 onwards, became the new capital of the Roman Empire, and eventually of the Byzantine Empire. The defense of the Danube borders was one of the most difficult military and political problems facing the Empire; for this purpose numerous sections of the limes were protected by camps, watchtowers, fortresses and barriers. These provinces, which constituted Rome's bulwark against barbarian invasions from the east, therefore had a largely military character, and their internal stability was always of vital importance.

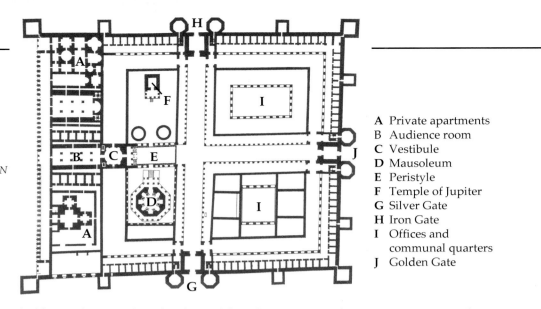

SPLIT, THE CITY THAT WAS ONCE DIOCLETIAN'S PALACE

→ N

A Private apartments
B Audience room
C Vestibule
D Mausoleum
E Peristyle
F Temple of Jupiter
G Silver Gate
H Iron Gate
I Offices and
   communal quarters
J Golden Gate

The ancient Spalatum developed in the 7th century, in and around the palace built by Diocletian as his residence from the time of his abdication in A.D. 305 to his death in 313. As a result of this circumstance, many of the structures in the complex have been preserved to the present day as a rare and magnificent specimen of a late Empire residence. The general layout resembled that of military camp, while the large portico overlooking the sea was inspired by the contemporary fortified country villas. The building, which presented a trapezoidal plan, had large opus quadratum walls, at the corners of which stood strong square towers; only the southwest tower has been totally lost. Of the four gates that opened

halfway along each side, the Gold and Silver gates are the best preserved, while the one overlooking the sea was little more than a glorified opening.
The southern area, now the most intact, contains an interesting complex consisting of two areas, separated by what is called the Peristyle: the Imperial mausoleum to the east, which was converted into a cathedral in the Middle Ages, and a tetrastyle temple to the west. The Peristyle, a huge unroofed rectangular area bordered by arched porticoes on the two longer sides, is closed by a four-column pronaos featuring an interesting arched tympanum of Syrian inspiration. It was probably a hall used for open-air performances. Seen from the exterior, the

mausoleum is an octagonal structure, surrounded by a peribolos of columns with trabeations, while inside it is circular, with a series of alcoves separated by columns. The roof is pyramidal, and the building is raised to house the burial chamber. The tetrastyle temple in the western area, later used as a baptistry, rests on a very tall podium; the cella, one of the best preserved from ancient times, has a vaulted roof, and the interior, like the frame of the main doorway, is richly decorated.

232 top left
Diocletian's Palace at Split is of exceptional interest in view of the fact that hardly any Imperial residences survive from the late Imperial period.

232 bottom left
The Peristyle, which has become the most characteristic square of the city, is closed on the south by a pronaos with four columns, surmounted by a triangular pediment with an arch on the two central columns.

232 right
This aerial photograph shows the interior of the Silver Gate, with what remains of the large cavaedium.

233 Numerous blocks of hewn stone that were part of the trabeation of the colonnaded road can be seen in the area around the Peristyle.

234-235
This reconstructional drawing demonstrates the huge size of Diocletian's fortified palace, which covered an area of almost 12 square miles.
It was surrounded by massive walls 10 feet thick, and the interior space was divided by two right-angled avenues. The two quarters in the foreground must have been used as offices

and barracks; next came the mausoleum, on the left, and the temple, perhaps dedicated to Jupiter, on the right. In the middle was the peristyle, followed by a vestibule and a rectangular hall leading to the Imperial apartments.
The section of the walls overlooking the sea was perhaps embellished with a hanging garden.

GREECE, ON THE PATH OF ANCIENT SPLENDORS

1 Achaia
2 Epirus
3 Macedonia
A Atene

236 left The statue of Antinous found at Delphi, the work of a skilled local sculptor, is one of the many surviving portrayals of Hadrian's favorite. It denotes a marked return to the themes of classical Greek statuary in the treatment of the body, but the ambiguous beauty and markedly sensual face are typically Hellenistic.

Roman intervention in the Hellenic peninsula began as early as the 3rd century B.C., at the time of the battles between the Macedonian kings and the Greek cities led by Athens. Rome, called on to defend the latter, at first did nothing to exploit the supremacy it gained after the victory of Cinoscefale against Philip V and, at least in appearance, restored Greece to freedom. However, when the Roman legions finally defeated the Macedonian army at Pydna in 168 B.C., the expansionist aims of Rome became clear, and the Greeks' aversion to their new conquerors was soon manifested. In 146 B.C., after one of many rebellions, this one resulting in the destruction of Corinth, Greece was relegated to the status of a province. It was divided into Macedonia and Achaia, and also included Epirus. In 88 B.C., driven by the desire for freedom, Athens joined the anti-Roman campaign conducted by Mithridates VI, King of Pontus, which ended tragically two years later with the siege and subsequent sack of the city by Sulla. From then on, Greece was one of the most peaceful provinces in the Empire, consoled by the remembrance of its glorious past and its fundamental role in the culture of the Mediterranean basin. The economy of Macedonia flourished as a result of the reopening of the gold and silver mines and better exploitation of its copper and iron resources. The Macedonian towns were allowed to keep their traditional form of government and were granted numerous immunities. Some of these towns, like Dyrrachium, Pella and Philippi, were massively colonized by Roman veterans. The most important monument in the region is the Arch of Galerius in Thessalonica, outstanding for its unusual

architectural form and its rich sculptural decoration.

Achaia, which in practice included the entire Peloponnese and the islands as far as Crete, together with the Cyclades, Attica, Boeotia and Euboea, gained new prosperity, as it was situated at the hub of an important system of sea routes leading to Piraeus, the ports of the Cyclades and the landing places on the Isthmus of Corinth. Under Caesar and Augustus numerous towns flourished once more, but the region mainly became important under Nero (who in A.D. 67 gave the Greeks their freedom, and also exempted them from paying tributes), and later under Hadrian, especially in the case of Athens. Epirus, which only became an independent province in the 2nd century A.D., played little part in the life of the Empire, except for some coastal towns such as Actium (the most important port in the region, founded by Augustus to commemorate his victory over Antony), and a few inland towns such as Dodona, famous for the Sanctuary of Zeus. Epirus, which had no major highways, only had some degree of importance because of the strategic value of its naval bases. During the Roman dominion, many towns throughout Greece retained their traditional magistratures, and there were many free city-states such as Athens, Sicyon, Delphi and Tespie. Sanctuaries and sports venues continued to be active as centers of national gatherings. The most famous of these were the stadium and sanctuaries of the Isthmus, followed by Actium and Nicopolis, where Augustus instituted triumphal games. Under Hadrian, Athens was the headquarters of the Panhellenic amphictyony.

In practice, though subjugated, Greece conquered Rome with the greatness of its culture, and successfully introduced the basic themes of its art to the Romans.

236-237 The construction of the Olympieion in Athens, which began in the 4th century B.C. and was frequently interrupted, was completed by Hadrian c. A.D. 130. It was made entirely of valuable Pentelicus marble, and was the largest Corinthian-style temple in ancient times.

*237 bottom
The Wind Tower
in Athens was built
around the mid-1st
century B.C. to house
the waterclock
designed by
Andronicus of Cirrha;
its name is due to
the fact that it was
surmounted by a
bronze Triton that
acted as a weather
vane.*

ATHENS, THE BEACON OF CLASSICAL CIVILIZATION

After its sack at the instigation of Sulla in 86 B.C., and a period of rather unstable political equilibrium with Rome, Athens enjoyed the Imperial favor under Augustus. The other two pro-Greek emperors, Nero and Hadrian, were particularly generous to the city, which had by now come to symbolize classical civilization. When the city was destroyed by the Heruli in A.D. 267, only the Acropolis survived, thanks to its strong walls. After this disaster, from which it never fully recovered, Athens only regained part of its original glory under Theodosius. The university, still flourishing, was finally suppressed by Justinian in A.D. 529. Apart from a few monuments, evidence of the Roman presence in Athens coexists with remains of the classical period, and can be traced in the form of more or less conspicuous restoration and renovation work on nearly all the city's public buildings. The main monuments built under Augustus were the Odeon of Agrippa in the central part of the agora (marketplace), the Temple of Augustus and Rome on the Acropolis, opposite the Parthenon, a stoa (colonnaded covered walk) in the Ceramicus district, and what is known as the "Roman agora," Little is known of building activity under the Julio-Claudian and Flavian emperors. The library of T. Flavius Pantainos and the funeral monument of G. Antiochus Philopappus, an Attic citizen and Roman consul, date from the age of Trajan. The generosity of Hadrian, celebrated as the second founder of the city, led to the construction of a stoa and a magnificent library to the north of the Roman agora, the completion of the Olympieion (the largest Corinthian temple in the ancient world), a gymnasium, and the restoration of the Theater of Dionysius. The library, of which little remains, must have been especially magnificent; according to the sources, it had a four-sided portico with 100 precious marble columns, and the rooms had gilded ceilings and alabaster walls.

A gymnasium and some public buildings, including two baths, are still part of what is called Hadrian's Town, entered through the triumphal arch named after him. The activity of Herodes Atticus, who restored the stadium and covered it with marble, and built the new Odeon on the slopes of the Acropolis at his own expense, dates from the period of the Antonines.

238 top The façade of Hadrian's Library consists of 14 Phrygian marble Corinthian columns surmounted by a broken trabeation with very well-balanced lines. Hadrian, who was an admirer of Hellenism, wished to embellish Athens with outstanding monuments, and lavished huge sums on their construction.

238 bottom Situated at the border between the old part of Athens and the new Roman districts, Hadrian's Arch, now stripped of the columns that flanked its archway and of the statues standing on the attic story, broke away from the building tradition typical of this kind of structure, demonstrating an evident fondness for Athenian architecture.

238-239 *Herodes Atticus built a magnificent Odeon at the foot of the Acropolis around* A.D. *161, which is still outstanding for the extensive use of arches and vaults in its construction. This structural element symbolizes the changeover from rectilinear Greek architecture to curvilinear Roman architecture.*

A Roman Temple
B Agrippa's Odeon
C Hadrian's Library
D Roman Agora
E Wind Tower
F Dionysius Theater
G Hadrian's Arch
H Olympieion

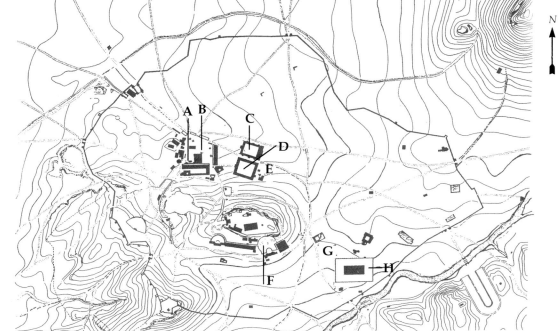

N

ASIA MINOR, THE LEGACY OF KING ATTALUS

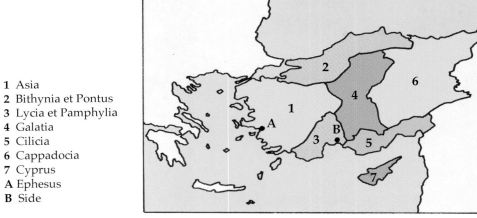

1 Asia
2 Bithynia et Pontus
3 Lycia et Pamphylia
4 Galatia
5 Cilicia
6 Cappadocia
7 Cyprus
A Ephesus
B Side

The Roman presence in Asia Minor began in 133 B.C. with the legacy bequeathed by Attalus, King of Pergamum, and continued with the annexation of the neighboring kingdoms. The most important towns in the Asian provinces were the ancient Greek colonies of Ionia, scattered along the coasts at the estuaries of the great rivers, which experienced a construction boom. Right from the outset, the wealth of the region attracted a large number of Italics, mainly traders and tax collectors, whose greed caused the serious discontent that led to a terrible revolt in 88 B.C., during which 80,000 people died. Unrest continued during the civil wars, and it was only with the advent of Augustus that the fortunes of Asia began to improve. A period of peace and prosperity that lasted until the mid-3rd century now began, as demonstrated by the numerous grandiose buildings,

still surviving, that were constructed in all the towns of the province. Ruins dating from the Roman period are scattered all over Asia Minor, not only in the major towns such as Ephesus, Pergamum, Miletus and Halicarnassus, but also in those minor towns that were already flourishing, and continued to prosper. Sardis, Mylasa, Labraunda, Magnesia on the Maeander, Laodicea and Apamea are some of the best-known examples. The sanctuaries and religious federations carried on as usual; they were tolerated by the Romans, who merely introduced the worship of Rome and Augustus. In the artistic and cultural field, the Aphrodisia school of sculpture, whose artists were active in Rome and in Africa, became very important. Literature and science, which boasted two major centers of knowledge in the medical schools of Ephesus and Pergamum, were equally fertile. The main sources of wealth in these provinces were agriculture and trade; priceless goods from the Orient were conveyed to the Mediterranean ports along the ancient royal highway of the Achaemenids and the numerous roads built by the Romans. The purple-veined marble from the quarries of Synnada in Phrygia and the red Portasanta marble of Chios were highly prized. Marble was transported on special ships called naves lapidariae, and unloaded at the port of Ostia. It was then conveyed up the Tiber to the deposit at the foot of the Aventine, which is still called Marmorata (Marble Hill) today. It was usually transported in the form of rough-hewn blocks, ready to be finished when it reached its destination. Asia Minor was also famous for sheep-rearing and the production of wool and parchment, which, with papyrus, constituted the most common writing surface in ancient times. The parchment from Pergamum was renowned, while almost all the other towns were known for trade in textiles and woolen garments, the quality of

which was guaranteed by the weavers' and dyers' guilds. Fabrics dyed with purple, a dye obtained from a mollusk, were highly prized. In Hierapolis (now Pamukkale), wool was washed in the natural hot springs to fix its color. The region was also rich in ore deposits, especially silver and gold. The abundance of gold originated the legend of King Croesus (near whose kingdom the auriferous River Pactolus still flows), and was often mentioned in ancient texts, beginning with the Iliad.

240 top left During the Imperial age Aphrodisias was embellished with great public monuments, including the enormous hippodrome.

240 bottom left The present appearance of the Theater of Miletus dates back to its rebuilding in the 2nd century A.D.

240 right This picture shows a detail of Hadrian's Temple in Ephesus.

241 The Tetrapylon of Aphrodisias acted as a monumental entrance to the sacred area occupied by the Temple of Aphrodite, the patron goddess of the city.

242-243 The great theater of Aspendos, built in the 2nd century A.D., is the best preserved in Asia Minor. The town became Roman as early as 133 B.C., and was prosperous and powerful in the Imperial age.

EPHESUS, BELOVED OF ARTEMIS

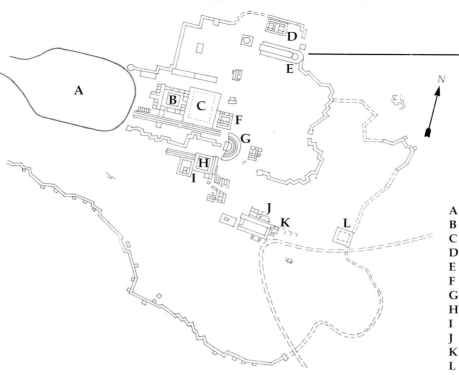

Ephesus, the center of the cult of Artemis and the birthplace of great philosophers, was one of the most densely populated and wealthiest cities in the ancient world. Built at the mouth of the Lesser Maeander, at the end of the great "Royal Highway" leading from the interior, it had a long and eventful history. It became part of the Kingdom of Pergamum, and was included by Attalus III in the legacy left to the Romans, who made it the capital of the Province of Asia. It maintained its primacy even after its sack by the Goths in A.D. 263. It soon recovered, but was destroyed by the Arabs in the mid-7th century. Although nothing remains of the great temple dedicated to Artemis, goddess of the fertility of the earth, which was restored for the last time in the Hellenistic period, the architectural heritage of Ephesus is still very rich, and clearly influenced by the long Roman presence in the area. The main road of

the town was Via Arcadiana (so called because it was rebuilt by the Emperor Arcadius in the 4th century), which ran from the theater to the port, lined with colonnaded porticoes. The theater, though of Hellenistic origin, was extensively transformed during the Empire. The same fate awaited the stadium, which was converted under Nero so that it could be used for gladiatorial games and wild beast hunts. New construction work included numerous porticoes, built to embellish the main roads of the city, fountains and **nymphaea**, *which used the water conveyed to the city by C. Sextilius Pollio at the time of Augustus. Among the major monuments dating from the Roman period are the Odeon (a small roofed theater built by wealthy citizen P. Vedius Antoninus at the time of Antoninus Pius), the Serapeum (a grandiose octastyle temple dating back to the 2nd century A.D.), the Temple of Domitian, the Temple of Hadrian (a small, very elegant, richly decorated building) and the Library of Celsus. The latter, outstanding for its grandeur and luxury, was donated to the city by benefactor Titus Julius Aquila Polemeanus to honor the memory of his father, a senator under Trajan. The front, preceded by a stairway, presents an unusual sequence of alternating doors, windows and niches with allegorical statues in a complex, lively architectural decoration typical of Hadrian's era. Inside was a burial chamber containing the sarcophagus of Celsus Polemeanus; this was unusual in the Roman world, as permission was only occasionally given for particularly meritorious citizens to be buried inside public buildings.*

A Port
B Port Baths
C Verulanus Square
D Vedius gymnasium
E Stadium
F Theater gymnasium
G Theater
H Agora
I Library of Celsus
J Odeon
K Baths
L East gymnasium

244 The Library of Celsus (the upper part of which can be seen in the background) stands next to the agora, *a large square area surrounded by porticoes.*

245 left The Gate of Hercules stood at the beginning of the Via dei Cureti, one of the main roads of the town (one of the reliefs after which the gate was named is shown here).

245 center right The commercial agora, *with numerous shops lining all four sides, was reconstructed in Corinthian style in the 3rd century.*

245 bottom right Built in the 3rd century B.C. on the slopes of Mount Pion, the theater was extended in the Roman age until it could hold 24,000 spectators.

246 left
The temple dedicated to Hadrian, an elegant example of Roman-Hellenistic art, has an interesting pronaos with two columns between pillars, with mixtilinear trabeation. The four bases in front of the columns supported the statues of Diocletian, Maximian, Constantius Clorus and Galerius.

246 right
Four niches in the façade of the Library of Celsus each contained a female statue, allegories of the principal virtues attributed to the famous man. The photo shows the personification of sophia *(wisdom). The entire building was restored between 1970 and 1978.*

247 The magnificent Library of Celsus was built to commemorate Senator Julius Celsus Polemeanus, a magistrate of Ephesus, by his heirs, who also spent a large sum on the purchase of books. Very unusually for a Roman public building, the library also contained the sarcophagus of the great man.

SARDIS, A CITY OF LEGENDARY WEALTH

A Gymnasium or "Marble Courtyard"
B Synagogue
C Bronze House
D Basilica
E Stadium
F Theater
G Temple of Artemis
H Acropolis

An ancient city of Asia Minor, standing at the confluence of the Rivers Hermus and Pactolus, Sardis was long the capital of Lydia, and acquired considerable splendor under King Croesus, who built his magnificent palace there. The city became part of the Kingdom of Pergamum, and was annexed to the Roman Province of Asia in 133 B.C. It was seriously damaged by earthquakes in the time of Tiberius. It rose to new heights of glory under Hadrian, and finally fell into ruin in the Byzantine era. Situated some 60 miles from the coast along the Persian "Royal Highway," which connected the Aegean to the regions of Mesopotamia, it was a city of great economic and cultural importance. In particular, due to the abundance of gold obtained from the River Pactolus, the first true metal coins are believed to have been minted here as early as the 7th century B.C. The ancient urban area has been extensively excavated by archaeologists, who have uncovered the remains of a great Ionic temple dedicated to Artemis, built in the 4th century B.C. and restored in the Hellenistic period, and numerous buildings dating from or altered during the Roman period, when the life of the city revolved around a great colonnaded highway running east-west. These include the stadium, the theater, a basilica, some bath complexes and the gymnasium, which also included a synagogue. Generous use of finely carved marble cladding can be seen in these buildings. The scenic entrance courtyard to the gymnasium, extensively reconstructed by archaeologists and now known as the Marble Courtyard, is a spectacular example of what is known as Roman Baroque, dating from the age of the Severus dynasty. The annexed synagogue, the largest surviving from ancient times, was decorated with splendid mosaic floors and a majestic marble table, with eagles portrayed on its supports. The integration of local art with Roman art is particularly evident in the statuary, the paintings found in numerous tombs in the necropolis, and the mausoleum of Claudia Antonia Sabina, in which a magnificent sarcophagus with architectural motifs framing full-relief figures was found. A large aqueduct, donated to the city by Emperor Claudius, provided the town's water supply, conveyed to the population by means of a complex system of earthenware pipes. Nowadays, Sardis is a popular archaeological site, one of the best-known in Turkey.

248 left In Asia Minor, as elsewhere, the fusion of Roman and local styles gave rise to entirely new types of structure, as demonstrated by the Marble Courtyard in Sardis, a scenic structure with two rows of columns facing towards the gymnasium.

248-249 The presence of a synagogue next to the Sardis baths and gymnasium complex demonstrates that the local, Jewish and Roman communities peacefully coexisted for many years, in line with the Imperial policy of cultural assimilation.

249 bottom The fact that the supports of the great marble table in the synagogue are decorated with two eagles (a clear breach of Jewish law, which prohibited the portrayal of living creatures in places of worship) may be explained by the distance from Palestine, which led to the attenuation of religious precepts. The magnificent marble inlay work in the building indicates the wealth of the local Jewish community.

THE EASTERN PROVINCES, A MELTING POT OF RACES AND CULTURES

1 Armenia
2 Mesopotamia
3 Assyria
4 Syria et Palaestina
5 Arabia
A Baalbek
B Caesarea
C Gerasa
D Palmyra

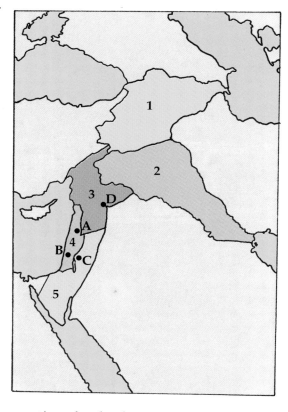

The term "Eastern Provinces" refers to the vast territory that to the east, constituted the furthermost boundary of the Roman Empire, and included Armenia, Assyria, Mesopotamia, Syria et Palaestina and Arabia. The history of these regions was eventful and intricate; Rome had to deal with local situations that were often very different, and with the Parthian Empire, whose ever-threatening power equaled that of Rome.

250 top and center Anjar, in present-day Lebanon, was situated in the Beka'a Valley; it was a caravan town on the road that connected Beirut with Damascus. The Roman town, with its right-angled layout, flourished between the early 1st and late 3rd centuries, and was also fairly prosperous in the Byzantine period, of which numerous relics remain.

The situation was also made more complex by the presence of large desert regions inhabited by nomadic populations that were difficult to keep under control.

By far the most important of these provinces was Syria et Palaestina. Syria, in particular, experienced great prosperity under the Severus dynasty, partly thanks to Julia Domna, the second wife of Septimius Severus, who belonged to the dynasty of priest-kings of Emesa (Homs). It was largely her doing that a huge influx of Syrian culture and religion spread throughout the West, as far as Rome. Among other things, great jurists, such as Papinian and Ulpian of the Berytus (Beirut) law school, held high office in the administration. Conversely, the Roman occupation had little effect on local cultural life. Greek and Syrian

continued to be the most commonly spoken languages, while Latin was only used in the large cities, as the official language in the administrative and legal fields.

Antioch (Antakya) was one of the largest cities in the eastern part of the Empire, together with Seleucia, Laodicea, Apamea, Berytus and Tolemaide. There were few newly founded colonies. The Roman hold on the surrounding provinces was so precarious that a limes, *consisting of a close-knit network of strongholds connected to an extensive road system was created; it started at the Syrian desert and led from Damascus to Palmyra, as far as the Euphrates and beyond.*

These regions, which were of great military value, also played an important role in the economic sphere. Agriculture gave excellent results, due to the clever use of hydraulic works that enabled large arable areas to be reclaimed from the desert, and the purple and glass industries were also highly prosperous. Their main source of wealth, however, was trade. From the furthest countries of the east, from Arabia, India and China, a wide variety of goods was carried back and forth, from the desert to the sea and vice versa. This was the reason for the particular development of the ports on the Phoenician coast and the great caravan towns of Palmyra, Damascus and Gerasa. Long convoys of camels and mules crossed huge territories on payment of a transit fee, sometimes escorted by armed troops to prevent attacks by marauding bandits.

250 bottom Bosra, in present-day Jordan, one of the main towns in the kingdom of Nabathaea, was refounded by Trajan in A.D. 106. It features one of the best-preserved Roman theaters.

251 The Lebanese town of Baalbek, once called Heliopolis, was universally famous for its sanctuary, which included the splendid temple dedicated to Mercury.

The taxes payable on trade obviously affected the price of the goods carried, which therefore mainly consisted of products of limited size and high value. In addition to government taxes, tariffs were also payable to the various cities crossed by the caravans, which for this purpose were equipped with a range of services designed to accommodate the merchants, animals and goods. The "Palmyra tariff," a bilingual stele in Palmyran and Greek dating from A.D. 137, gives some idea of the goods commonly carried by the caravans: slaves, purple-dye, aromatic oils and spices, prostitutes, fabrics, salt and works of art. The Roman organization in these provinces was highly efficient, especially in the field of communications.

The Romans perfected and improved the existing road network, created by the Achaemenids and exploited by Alexander the Great, which connected the great river and land routes along the Tigris and the Euphrates and the caravan routes that led from Media and

Persia to the Syrian ports and the interior roads of Anatolia. The easternmost towns like Nisibis (Nusaybin) and Singara, in Mesopotamia, had military garrisons. The Eastern Provinces were a melting pot of different races and civilizations, where Greek, Semitic and Roman peoples came into contact with and influenced one another. Christianity spread rapidly here, and these regions became its main headquarters.

This mixture of varied influences is demonstrated by the many archaeological remains still surviving in numerous towns, such as Palmyra, Gerasa, Philadelphia (Amman), Heliopolis (Baalbek), Damascus, Antioch, Apamea and Dura Europos, in which Hellenistic, Roman and Oriental elements blend to produce magnificent and often surprising results.

252 top Be't She'an, founded in the 5th millenium B.C., is one of the oldest inhabited sites in Israel. The town was conquered in 63 B.C. by Pompey, who retained its Hellenistic name of Scythopolis; in the Imperial age it expanded considerably, and major building work was carried out, including the construction of a large colonnaded road.

252 center These two coins celebrate the final pacification of Judaea by Titus in A.D. 70; the bronze one bears the effigy of Vespasian, and the gold one portrays the region as a conquered woman. The Romans responded to the Jewish revolt that broke out three years earlier by destroying the Temple of Jerusalem.

252-253 Be't She'an was originally built on the hill that can be seen at the top right, and only expanded into the plain below in Roman times. A large porticoed road lined with numerous shops started from the theater and continued until it intersected another road; a temple and a nymphaeum were built at the crossroads.

253 bottom The Masada crag stands alone on the shores of the Dead Sea in Israel. The fortress on the summit was built by order of Herod the Great, who added two magnificent residences destined for the court and honored guests, such as Augustus's legates. During the first Jewish revolt against the Romans, the fortress was occupied by 960 Zealots who withstood the siege by the 10th Legion, commanded by General Flavius Silva, for three years. The stronghold was finally stormed in A.D. 73 with the aid of a huge ramp made of wood and crushed stone (visible in the right-hand picture) that enabled the soldiers to breach the walls. All the besieged Zealots preferred suicide to capture.

254 left Numerous excavations conducted at Hama (once known as Epiphaneia), an ancient town in central Syria, have brought to light some valuable late Roman mosaics dating from between the 3rd and 4th centuries A.D. The town was mainly a caravan junction.

254 right This man's face with its dramatic expression is part of a mosaic decoration dating from the mid-3rd century A.D., found in Suweida. Like all Syrian mosaics of the late Imperial period it demonstrates great skill and a marked fondness for color, which is used in a very wide range of shades.

255 This magnificent detail belongs to a large mosaic portraying the marriage of Peleus and Thetis, found in a villa at Philippopolis in the Province of Arabia. The town (now called Shabba, in Syria) was founded around A.D. 244 by Emperor Philip the Arab, born in nearby Bosra. Syrian artists, who were strongly influenced by Hellenistic art and the desire to emulate the results obtained by painters, took mosaic art to a level of great refinement, using tiny tesserae and a very wide range of colors. The subjects portrayed were drawn from Greek and Roman mythology, even in the late Imperial period, until the 4th century.

BAALBEK, DEDICATED TO THE HELIOPOLITAN TRIAD

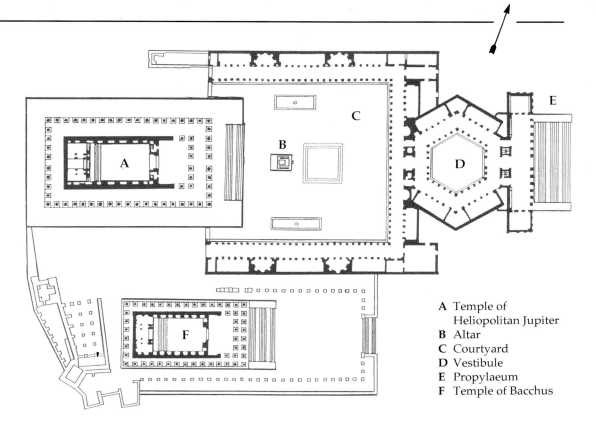

A Temple of
    Heliopolitan Jupiter
B Altar
C Courtyard
D Vestibule
E Propylaeum
F Temple of Bacchus

The most ancient origins and history of Baalbek (situated in what is now Lebanon) are obscure; only its modern name (which means "city of Baal") clearly refers to the god Baal. However, the original religion seems to have been the worship of Hadad, who in the Hellenistic era, was identified with the Sun and, therefore, with Zeus. As a result, the town was named Heliopolis (city of the sun). The city became a Roman colony and the site of a permanent garrison in the Julio-

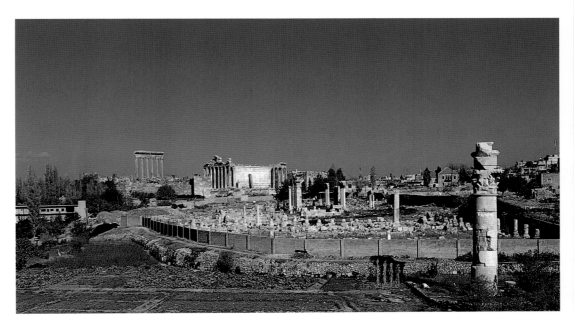

Claudian era, when it was called Iulia Augusta Felix Heliopolitana. Although the city played no active part in trade because of its distance from the major trading routes of the region, its religious importance was promoted by the Romans. The fame of the Sanctuary of Heliopolitan Jupiter is demonstrated by the fact that Trajan himself consulted the oracle before the expedition against the Parthians in A.D. 115. Heliopolis prospered until the first half of the 3rd century; its temples were converted into churches under Constantine and Theodosius, and it later became a bishop's see. However, the Arab invasion hastened its decline, and numerous earthquakes in later centuries reduced it to rubble. The western part of the city

was largely occupied by the impressive sanctuary of the Heliopolitan triad of deities (formed by Jupiter, Venus and Mercury), the ruins of which constitute one of the most important architectural complexes of classical antiquity.
The main temple, dedicated to Jupiter-Hadad, was situated at the end of a huge complex of buildings, and stood on a podium nearly 50 feet high. Not far away stands the much better preserved building known as the Temple of Bacchus, which was actually dedicated to Mercury: this Corinthian peripteral temple is divided internally by elegant Corinthian half-columns. The ruins of the small, round, delicately elegant Temple of Venus are situated on the decumanus maximus of the city.

256 This Corinthian peripteral temple, known as the Temple of Bacchus, was built between A.D. 150 and 200.

257 left
The sanctuary of Baalbek represents the most spectacular achievement of Syrio-Roman art. For the construction of the Temple of Jupiter, Roman engineers found a way of cutting and transporting stone blocks weighing some 800 tons each.

257 right The six monolithic columns of the Temple of Jupiter still standing, which date from A.D. 60, are 62 feet tall.

258-259 This reconstruction of the interior of the Temple of Bacchus, one of the most magnificently decorated in the Roman world, shows its unusual construction features, such as the Corinthian half-columns, the canopy over the votive statue and the coffered or lacunar ceiling.

CAESAREA, THE PORT OF PALESTINE

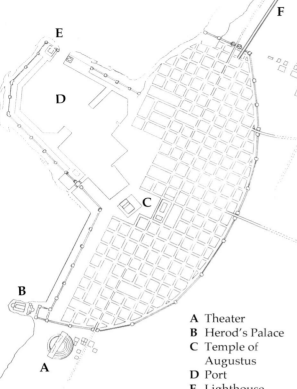

A Theater
B Herod's Palace
C Temple of Augustus
D Port
E Lighthouse
F Aqueduct
G Amphitheater

260 top The discovery in 1951 of this fragment of a red porphyry statue dating from the 3rd century A.D. revived interest in archaeological exploration in Caesarea.

260 center The Caesarea water system, consisting of two aqueducts, was one of the most complex in Palestine. The main pipe, which was five miles long, mostly ran above ground on a series of arches, conveying water from the Mt. Carmel springs to the city.

The origins of Caesarea, a prosperous port on the coast of present-day Israel to the north of Haifa, date back to the Phoenicians. During the Hellenistic period it became known as Strato's Tower. The city was totally rebuilt between 25 and 9 B.C. by Herod the Great who, as part of his policy of friendly relations with Rome, called it Caesarea in honor of Augustus Caesar. The town, also known as Caesarea Stratonis, soon became the main port of the region and one of the busiest in the Mediterranean. After A.D. 44 it became the capital of the Province of Iudaea, later called Palaestina. It was the last Byzantine stronghold to hold out against the Muslim invaders, who eventually stormed it in A.D. 640. The city, which has been extensively excavated during the last few decades, presented the usual right-angled layout, and was enclosed by a perimeter wall 1.6 miles long. The most important monumental buildings include the amphitheater, the hippodrome (where fragments of the porphyry obelisk that decorated the spina and the remains of the metae can still be seen), the baths and the theater.

260 bottom The architecture and art of Caesarea resembled that of many other towns all over the Empire. Each structural element (like this composite capital) represented further confirmation of the supremacy of Rome. It was no mere chance that the town was dominated by the austere bulk of the Temple of Rome and Augustus.

261 The contour of the artificial port built by Herod, now submerged, can be seen through the clear water of the bay. Bottom: The ruins of the roadbed built with spoil by the Crusaders still emerge just above the surface of the water. The promontory in the background, near the theater, was once occupied by Herod's palace.

The auditorium of the theater has been partly rebuilt, and is now used as a venue for concerts. The ruins of Herod's magnificent palace have been discovered on the promontory near the theater. In the forum area stood a great temple dedicated to Rome and Augustus, which was so large that it could be seen from far out at sea.

Caesarea was mainly famed for the great artificial harbor built by Herod, which was divided into two inner docks protected by massive jetties. The tall lighthouse tower stood at the end of one of the jetties. Two long aqueducts provided the town's water supply, diverted from springs at the foot of the Mt. Carmel range. An inscription discovered on a pillar of the main aqueduct states that the structure was restored by the 10th Fretensis Legion during the reign of Hadrian. Among the various finds made during the excavations, a stone fragment bearing the name of Pontius Pilate is of particular historical importance. The ruins of a synagogue with a mosaic floor are also interesting.

GERASA, A PROSPEROUS CARAVAN TOWN

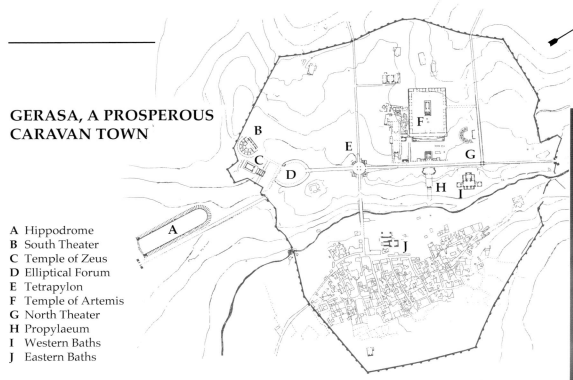

A Hippodrome
B South Theater
C Temple of Zeus
D Elliptical Forum
E Tetrapylon
F Temple of Artemis
G North Theater
H Propylaeum
I Western Baths
J Eastern Baths

This town, whose modern name is Gerash, was situated in a wide valley on the banks of the River Chrysorrhoas in Jordan. Founded by the Semites, it was basically a Hellenistic city before becoming Roman. During the second half of the 1st century A.D. It flourished as a result of caravan trade, and reached the peak of its prosperity in the age of the Antonines. After a period of decline between the 3rd and 4th centuries, Gerasa flourished briefly once again under Justinian. Razed to the ground during the Crusades, it was eventually abandoned, and only repopulated in 1878. The excellent state of preservation of its monuments is in fact due to the long centuries of oblivion. The Roman town has a regular plan, with a highway (the cardo*) running north-south, intersected by two roads running east-west (the* decumani*), which crossed the river on two bridges in the center of the town. Outside the south gate is a triumphal arch with three archways dating from A.D. 130, and next to it a hippodrome with a capacity of 15,000, dating back to the 2nd or 3rd century. At the entrance to the city stands the Temple of Zeus, with eight columns on the façade, built in A.D. 163, and the south theater, whose auditorium held 3,000 spectators. Opposite the Temple of Zeus was the unusual city forum, which has a unique design. Instead of having a rectangular plan it takes the form of an*

elliptical piazza with the longer axis 300 feet in length, surrounded by a portico with Ionic columns that housed a long row of shops. It is believed that the Gerasa Forum played a mainly economic rather than political or religious role, and this hypothesis is supported by its highly decentralized position. The Romans may thus have allowed the great sanctuary of Artemis, situated right in the heart of the town, to retain its status as the focal point of the town's social and spiritual life. The temple

dedicated to the patron goddess of
Gerasa stands in the center of a huge
sacred enclosure with an area of 40,800
square yards, reached from a
magnificent staircase leading from the
cardo maximus. Other monuments
dating from the Roman era were a
second theater in the northern part of
the town, two bath complexes, one on
each side of the river, an impressive four-
faced arch occupying the center of a
circular piazza on the cardo, and a
similar, though less majestic tetrapylon
on the same road.

*262 bottom Gerasa,
an ancient town of
Semitic origin, is a
typical example of the
Romanization
undergone by towns
that became part of the
Empire. Its
perpendicular layout
replaced the far less
regular older layout,
and monumental
constructions were
much in evidence
along the colonnaded
main roads.*

*262-263 The elliptical
forum, also known as
the Oval Piazza, is
certainly the most
unusual monument in
Gerasa, and one of the
most singular
exceptions to the
usual styles of Roman
public architecture.
Built in Ionic style in
the 2nd century A.D.,
it was used solely for
business purposes, not
for political or
religious purposes.*

263

264-265 The architecture of Palmyra demonstrates that Western construction methods were used, although a large degree of stylistic independence was maintained. This can be seen, for example, in the great sanctuary of Bel, whose layout appears uninfluenced by classical tenets, although it is decorated with Ionic and Corinthian capitals.

264 bottom This view of the cella in the Temple of Bel demonstrates the most unusual features of its style, i.e., the fact that the entrance is situated on one of the longer sides, and the presence of windows. In society, as well as in art, local customs continued to predominate, despite the fact that the Palmyrans enjoyed Roman citizenship.

PALMYRA, A SPLENDID METROPOLIS IN THE DESERT

A Diocletian's Fort
B Colonnaded roads
C Forum
D Tetrapylon
E Sanctuary of Ba'alshamin
F Theater
G Monumental Arch
H Temple of Bel
I Monumental tombs

The ancient Palmyra stands in an oasis in the Syrian desert, halfway between the Mediterranean and the Euphrates. It achieved a degree of prosperity as early as the 4th century B.C. due to the abundance of water, which made it the most important caravan town in the region.

It fell into ruin after it was sacked by Antony, but later recovered, especially during the 1st century A.D., when it achieved great prosperity due to its neutrality between the Roman and Parthian empires.

It became a Roman colony in A.D. 183, but was granted independence by Emperor Gallienus in A.D. 261 as a sign of his gratitude to Odenatus, lord of the city, who had defeated the Persians. His widow, Zenobia, who was hostile to Rome, began a strong policy of expansion in Asia Minor and Egypt but was defeated by Aurelian, who destroyed the town in A.D. 272.

The city was conquered by the Arabs in the 6th century, and was finally razed to the ground by the Omayyads. Palmyra is now one of the most famous archaeological sites in the Middle East, due to the excellent state of preservation of many of its monuments.

By virtue of its privileged position between East and West and its very mixed population, Palmyra produced some very unusual forms of art and culture in which Aramaic, Semitic, Hellenistic, and finally Roman elements were blended.

Its architecture reflects this mixture, especially in the impressive sanctuary dedicated to Bel, the Temple of Balshamin (which has the unusual feature of a cella *illuminated by windows), and the great colonnaded road on which stands an interesting triumphal arch with a triangular plan. The Temple of Bel presented elegant decoration and unusual structural features, such as the entrance situated*

on one of the longer sides, the cornice, decorated with triangular crenellations, and the roof, formed by a terrace with a turret at each of the four corners. By contrast, the theater (also quite well preserved) and the Baths of Diocletian are typically Roman.

*265 top
Palmyran art, which flourished between the reigns of Augustus and Gallienus, is a singular combination of local figurative styles and those imported from the Hellenistic-Roman West.*

*265 bottom
The Great Colonnade, about a mile long, was erected in the 2nd century A.D. The most interesting feature of this monument is the presence, about halfway up the columns, of prominent shelves that supported statues of local dignitaries. This is a typically local element, combined with the architectural styles of classical art.*

265

A Aegyptus
B Cyrenaica
C Creta

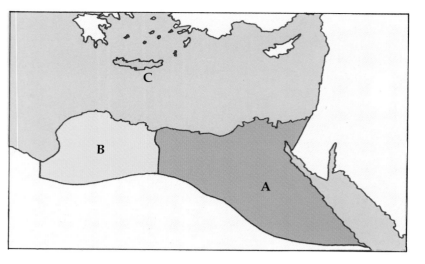

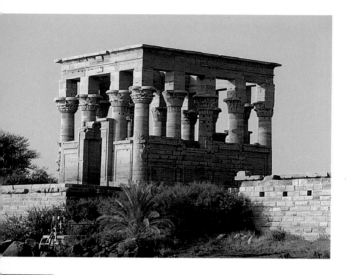

After the death of Cleopatra VII, who committed suicide after her defeat at Actium by Octavian, Egypt was the last of the Hellenistic kingdoms to fall under the Roman sphere of influence. Augustus made it a territory directly ruled by the emperor, who governed it through a **praefectus** Aegypti. Right from the outset the Roman rulers, who inherited the privileges of the Ptolemies, had to deal with the problems caused by conflict between the Greek community (which enjoyed special legal and tax privileges) and the Jewish community. The latter, in particular, organized numerous rebellions, the bloodiest of which took place under Claudius and Trajan. Rome made a rather limited contribution to this region, whereas Egyptian culture exerted considerable influence on the Roman world, especially in the religious and artistic spheres. This influence is demonstrated, for example, by the great success that the worship of Serapis, Isis and Osiris

encountered in Rome. While the new rulers enthusiastically (albeit amateurishly) emulated the architectural and figurative themes of the local tradition (one such example is "Trajan's Kiosk" on the Island of Phylae), perhaps the most original form of art in the Roman period in Egypt was represented by "Fayyum portraits," paintings on wood designed to be placed on the face of mummies.

Very few new towns were founded, and those that were built were mainly represented by military outposts or trading posts in strategic positions. They include Babylon, a fortress dating from the time of Trajan which was built on the site of what is now Cairo, and Antinoupolis, built by Hadrian to commemorate his favorite, Antinous. Egypt played a mainly economic role within the Empire. Large amounts of corn, shipped from Alexandria, were produced in the province, together with valuable raw materials and luxury articles. The goods exported included various types of marble, pink "obelisk" granite from the quarries of Syene (Aswan), grey granite from Mons Claudianus and red porphyry from Upper Egypt. The country also held the monopoly in the papyrus trade, and was famous for its woolen industry, which supplied the Roman army with clothing. Camels were of great strategic value in the military field. During the 2nd century, various camel-mounted units were set up in the region, and these robust animals were also used in Europe, as demonstrated by numerous finds of bones in various parts of Gaul, the Germanys and even Britannia.

Trade with Nubia and Ethiopia

flourished on the southernmost borders of Egypt, which were occupied by legionary garrisons. The various emporia on the Red Sea carried on a flourishing trade with India, from which rare and precious goods arrived; Berenice, for example, was famed as the port used by ships bringing olivines (green gems much prized by the Romans) from Zavargad.

Numerous caravan routes crossed the desert and led along the coasts towards Arabia, Petra and Palestine, or towards Cyrenaica. The latter region was declared a province in 74 B.C., but was later given by Antony to his daughter by Cleopatra. Augustus restored its status as a senatorial province in 27 B.C., annexing it to the island of Crete. Cyrene presented the same difficulties of government as Egypt, because of the violent clashes between the Jewish and Greek communities. The damage caused by a particularly bloody Jewish rebellion in 116 A.D. was partly repaired by order of Hadrian. However, the country's economy, which had begun to recover to some extent since the time of Augustus, was irreparably damaged by the slaughter and devastation committed by both sides. Nevertheless, Cyrene remained famous for its thoroughbred horses, which were still being exported at the end of the 4th century.

Crete was far more peaceful, and the history of the island recounts no particularly outstanding events; as a result, the Roman military presence was limited to a few local garrisons. In both regions Rome pursued a very liberal policy towards the towns, which continued to enjoy numerous immunities.

266 top left Trajan's Kiosk was erected in A.D. 105 on the Isle of Phylae, in Egypt, next to a famous sanctuary of Isis.

266 center Cyrene, a long established and prosperous Greek colony, entered the Roman sphere of influence in 74 B.C., and was made into a joint province with Crete by Augustus.

266 bottom left Gortis became the capital of the Roman province of Crete in 67 B.C. The ruins of the odeon are shown in this photo.

266 bottom right The best-known artistic relics from Roman Egypt are portraits painted in tempera on wood or canvas, which were laid on the face of the deceased.

267 This portrait of a man on canvas, originating from Antinoe, dates from the 3rd century A.D.; its sober lines clearly demonstrate the influence of Roman pictorial styles. Apart from their funerary use, portraits of the same artistic quality must have been common throughout the Empire.

AFRICA, THE GRANARY OF ROME

1 Mauretania
  Tingitana
2 Mauretania
  Caesariensis
3 Numidia
4 Africa
  Proconsularis

A Volubilis
B Timgad
C Sabratha
D Leptis Magna
E Sufetula

Roman penetration into the African continent began after the destruction of Carthage in 146 B.C. The first provinces constituted were Africa Proconsularis and Africa Nova or Numidia, to which Mauretania Caesariensis and Mauretania Tingitana were later added. The African border, which stretched from present-day Morocco to Libya, was by far the longest in the Empire; it was some 2,480 miles long, and bounded a territory whose immense geographical variety was matched by the widely differing cultures and lifestyles of the local populations. The reason why the Romans were so interested in Africa was the strategic position of its ports, control of which guaranteed total domination of the Mediterranean routes, together with the immense agricultural wealth of the region. For this reason the Romans encouraged the development of the ancient maritime towns of Carthaginian and Greek origin, and built many new ones. At the same time they gained control of the hinterland and the trade in valuable goods from the interior of the continent by extending the existing caravan towns and initiating the construction of many more, as in the case of Timgad. An excellent road network connected these towns to the coastal ports, where goods destined for Rome were loaded onto cargo vessels. In the countryside around the towns, scattered over a vast radius, were the farms of the rich local landowners. Numerous dams, traces of which still remain, enabled the seasonal water transported by the wadies to be collected and distributed for irrigation purposes by means of complex channel systems.

The main reason for the prosperity of cities like Sabratha and Leptis Magna was their enormous production of corn and olive oil. The corn trade, which gave Africa its nickname of "Rome's granary," was far more strictly controlled by the government than trade in other products. The importance of a regular supply of this food to Rome was partly political, as even at the time of Augustus some 150,000 plebeians received the public corn dole. The main corn shipping port was Carthage, whose reconstruction was ordered by Augustus. Oil exports also acquired great importance, especially from the 2nd century A.D.; this product was shipped in cylindrical jars, made in the

268 top Carthage, razed to the ground during the Third Punic War, was rebuilt by order of Caesar.

268 bottom The province of Africa was often portrayed as a woman wearing headgear in the shape of an elephant's head, as on this plate, found in Boscoreale, which dates from the 1st century A.D.

268-269
The amphitheater of El Jem, in present-day Tunisia, was the second largest in the Roman world after the Coliseum. The ancient Thysdrus, which stood inland, around 25 miles from the sea, particularly flourished in the 2nd and 3rd centuries as a result of its production and sale of olive oil.

269 bottom
Thuburbus Maius, founded on the site of an earlier Berber settlement, reached the peak of its splendor under the Antonines. Like all the Roman towns in Tunisia, it owed its wealth to olive growing. This photo shows a view of the portico of Petronius, dating from A.D. 225.

270 top This mosaic, dating from the 3rd century A.D., was found in Sousse, in present-day Tunisia. It portrays the mythological episode in which Zeus, disguised as an eagle, carried off Ganymede, "the most beautiful of mortals," to make him the cup-bearer of the gods. Many of the Sousse mosaics are now housed in the Bardo Museum in Tunis.

coastal towns of Tunisia, which were also used to store garum, a popular sauce made of salted, fermented fish entrails, which was a basic ingredient of Roman cuisine. Africa was the largest supplier of this condiment, which was also made in numerous production works along the Mediterranean and Atlantic coasts. Another important item exported from the African provinces was animals (horses for races at the circus, and wild beasts, lions, leopards and elephants for the games held in the amphitheater), which were captured during hunting expeditions and then transported on special ships that took them to destinations far and wide.

The introduction of Roman civilization into Africa had wide-ranging results, as demonstrated by the many monuments that have survived to the present day. In particular, the official language and religion were always the Roman ones, although the country people continued to speak Punic and worship Baal and Tanit, though identified with Saturn and Caelestis. The African provinces reached the height of their glory at the time of the journeys made by Emperor Hadrian, and the construction, cultural and economic development promoted by the Severus dynasty.

From the 2nd century onwards, local people also had a major influence on the political and intellectual life of the Empire. Emperors like Septimius Severus, jurists and writers like Fronto and Apuleius, and the large group of Christian apologists (especially Tertullian and Augustine) represent the outstanding contribution made by Africa to the development of the pagan and Christian cultures of the Roman Empire.

270 bottom The famous mosaic portraying Virgil, which dates from the 3rd century A.D., was found in a villa at Sousse. The seated poet is holding in his lap an open papyrus scroll on which the eighth verse of the Aeneid can be read. On his right is Clio, muse of history, and on his left stands Melpomene, muse of tragedy. It is interesting to note that culture played a very important part in the Roman world because it brought social status.

270-271 This detail of a mosaic floor, found in Sousse and also housed in the Bardo Museum, confirms the high artistic level achieved in the African provinces. The scene celebrates the triumph of Dionysus in his capacity as dominator of the forces of nature and lord of the wild beasts. The mosaic dates from the 3rd century A.D., when the port reached the peak of its development as a result of trade with the interior and shipments of olive oil to Rome in great cargo vessels. Little or nothing has survived of ancient Hadrumetum, apart from the floors of the wealthy local villas.

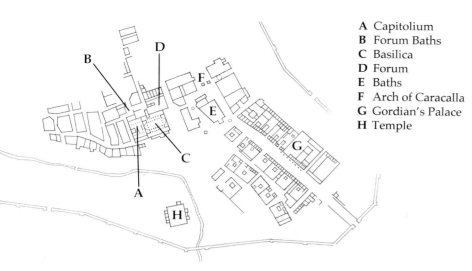

A Capitolium
B Forum Baths
C Basilica
D Forum
E Baths
F Arch of Caracalla
G Gordian's Palace
H Temple

VOLUBILIS, A COLONY ON THE OUTSKIRTS OF THE EMPIRE

Volubilis, an ancient town of Mauretania Tingitana in present-day Morocco, was an indigenous settlement of some importance beginning in the 2nd century B.C., and probably the residence of King Juba II. After falling within the sphere of influence of Rome, it became the headquarters of the Imperial procurator. In 44 Claudius granted the town Roman citizenship, which gave it a new lease on life. The town expanded rapidly during the 3rd century, and even after the region was abandoned under Justinian, it long maintained a semblance of wealth before falling into ruin. The town consists of an original nucleus with an irregular plan, and the Roman districts, designed with the usual right-angled pattern. It is situated on a plateau that slopes steeply down to the south, and is enclosed by a ring of walls dating from the time of Marcus Aurelius. The forum, a huge square with porticoes on four sides, last renovated at the time of Antoninus Pius, is located at the boundary between the original town and the new districts. On the eastern side is the basilica, which has two apses and three entrances; on one of the longer sides there was a series of small rooms, possibly used as offices. The tetrastyle capitolium *(built under Macrinus in A.D. 217) stands on a tall podium to the south of the basilica, facing onto a small square surrounded by porticoes that provided shade for a row of different rooms, which possibly housed colleges. In another square stands the triumphal arch dedicated to Caracalla, the main archway of which was flanked by two small niches, possibly containing fountains. There were two baths, an olive processing works and a number of kilns in the town, and a sanctuary was located outside the walls. A partly underground aqueduct provided the town's water, and*

supplied a fountain at the northern baths. The private buildings demonstrate the high standard of living of the local bourgeoisie, enriched by industrial and commercial activities; some of their homes were fitted with thermal baths. The building known as Gordian's Palace, a large private house that was probably the residence of the provincial governor, stands on the decumanus maximus. *The many mosaics in the town, especially those with geometrical patterns, have apparently influenced the decorative style of the Berber carpets still made today.*

272 top The basilica stands on the east side of the forum. After Mauretania was annexed to the Roman Empire, Volubilis retained its status as capital, and new monuments were erected.

272-273 The Arch of Caracalla is one of the best-preserved buildings in Volubilis. The basin under each of the side niches suggests that two fountain statues stood in them.

273 top Many houses in Volubilis feature a wealth of mosaic decoration, which demonstrates the presence in the city of a large, wealthy middle class of mercantile or industrial origin.

273 bottom All that remains of the capitol is the wide access staircase and the columns of the pronaos, surmounted by Corinthian capitals. Volubilis mainly flourished under Septimius Severus, and until the 3rd century.

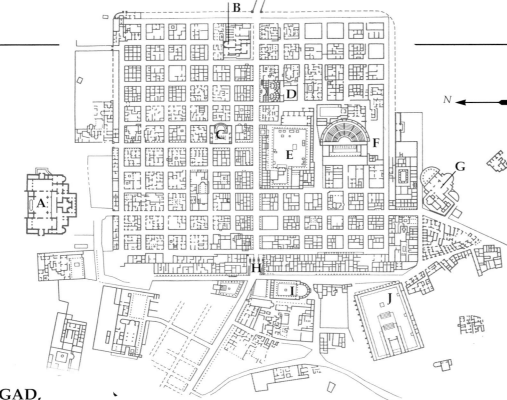

TIMGAD, THE SQUARE CITY

Timgad, in Numidia, was founded in A.D. 100 by Trajan's veterans, with the name of Marciana Traiana Thamugadi. It probably stood on a site previously occupied by an indigenous settlement, no trace of which now remains apart from the name. The layout of the city, with its right-angled axes, reflects that of the typical military camp. It was originally surrounded by city walls, which soon fell into disuse, as demonstrated by various buildings, including the capitolium, that were built outside the original grid and never aligned with it.

The perfectly square city of Timgad was divided in half by the decumanus maximus, which ran east-west. The cardo maximus was interrupted after dividing the northern part of the city in half, as the southern area was largely occupied by the forum and other public buildings, including the theater, whose auditorium exploited a natural depression in the land. The absolutely straight city streets were paved with limestone slabs, and a number of fountains were installed at the crossroads.

The three main city gates stood at the ends of the two main roads, each flanked by porticoes, while traces of a secondary entrance next to a minor cardo remain on the south-facing side. The west gate was constituted by the magnificent, sumptuously decorated triumphal arch of Trajan, with its three archways. The road to Lamaesis (Lambesi), the headquarters of the military commander and governor of the province, started from this gate, while the road to Cirta

(Constantine), the capital of Numidia, started at the north gate. The forum occupied a huge quadrangular area, enclosed towards the outside and surrounded by porticoes, behind which were situated buildings connected with the public life of the city: the basilica, the curia and the rostra.

At the center were numerous triumphal monuments, only the bases of which remain. Inside the original city walls was the market, with two semicircular courtyards along which various shops were situated, no less than 14 bath complexes, and a library. The library, facing onto the cardo maximus, occupied a small rectangular building containing a semicircular room, the wall of which was divided into a number of alcoves designed to contain cupboards for books, consisting of long strips of rolled parchment.

Two temples, dedicated to Ceres and Mercury, stood to the west of the theater, while the Temple of Saturn was situated in the northern suburb.

The temple dedicated to the Capitoline deities was not situated near the forum as usual, but outside the city perimeter. It stood alone on a tall podium, and had a pronaos of six Corinthian columns. A large sanctuary was situated to the south of the town, near a spring, in the area later occupied by the Byzantine fortress.

Also outside the urban quadrangle, towards the west, was another very large market. Residential building is well represented, and the wealthier specimens reflect the typical layout of the African house, with the addition of

elements of partly Hellenistic and partly Roman origin. The remains of fuller's shops, potteries and other industrial works have also been found. Built mainly of stone, with little use of valuable marble, Timgad is especially famous for the mosaics featuring geometrical and plant motifs found in nearly all its public and private buildings. Some buildings dating from the Christian era demonstrate that it was still prosperous during the Late Empire.

274-275 Thamugadi, founded by Trajan as a colony for veterans of the Third Augustea Legion, soon became a rich agricultural market, whose prosperity increased greatly, especially under the Severus dynasty. Its strictly perpendicular layout reveals that it was originally a military camp.

A Great Northern Baths
B Great Eastern Baths
C Public Library
D East Market
E Forum
F Theater
G Great Southern Baths
H Trajan's Arch
I Sertius's Market
J Capitolium

275 bottom Trajan's Arch, with its three archways, constituted the western access to the city. Though situated on the outskirts of the Empire, Timgad was embellished with all the great public monuments common to the other Roman cities, but the use of costly marble was by no means common.

SABRATHA, CITY OF MONUMENTS

276-277 The theater of Sabratha, built between the late 2nd and early 3rd centuries, is one of the best preserved in Africa. The stage front has three tiers of columns of various types, while the platform of the scaena is decorated with elaborate reliefs.

277 top left The columns in the foreground were part of the peristyle of a wealthy villa built in the 2nd century A.D. in the neighborhood of the theater, whose partly restored structures can be seen in the distance.

277 top right Some columns that were part of the vestibule of the Curia have been re-erected in the forum area. The curia, present in all Roman towns, was the senate house in which citizens met to discuss local affairs.

A Justinian's Basilica
B Temple of Serapis
C Capitolium
D Forum
E Basilica
F South Temple
G Temple of Antoninus Pius
H Temple of Liber Pater
I Forum Baths
J Baths
K Temple of Isis
L Theater

Sabratha, an ancient Libyan city on the Mediterranean coast, came under the influence of Rome in 46 B.C., when Caesar deposed the king of Numidia. Already flourishing under Augustus, it reached the peak of its prosperity under the Antonine and Severus dynasties, mainly as a result of its trading activities. Many of the main surviving civil and religious buildings belong to this period. Still flourishing at the beginning of the 4th century, it soon began to decline as a result of increasingly frequent raids by populations from the interior, culminating with its sack by the Vandals after A.D. 455. It experienced a brief period of recovery in the Byzantine age, but after it was occupied and plundered by the Arabs it fell into a state of total neglect. The port and part of the northern area of the town were later swept away by the sea. Archaeological excavations have revealed the monumental appearance of the city, whose layout was influenced by the tortuous, untidy nature of the earlier Phoenician town. The oldest part of Sabratha is occupied by the forum, overlooked by the ruins of the capitolium, the curia, the Temple of Serapis and the Temple of Liber Pater, one of the most popular deities in the African provinces. The capitolium, in particular, has the shape of a typical Italic temple; it stands on a tall podium and is accessed from a side staircase. A large basilica stood on the south side of the huge forum square; not far away was the temple dedicated to Antoninus Pius. The orthogonal-axis design of the eastern part of the city dates from the mid-2nd century A.D.; here stood the Temple of Hercules, the Baths of Oceanus (named after the subject of the mosaic decorating the tepidarium) and the theater, whose scaena is one of the best preserved from the Roman world. To the northeast of this impressive building, on the sea front, is the Sanctuary of Isis, whose temple stood in the middle of a large courtyard surrounded by Corinthian columns. The amphitheater is built in the hollow of a former stone quarry, quite a long way east of the town. Sabratha is also famous for its Christian monuments, which are no less outstanding than its Roman ruins. The most famous is Justinian's Basilica, noted for its splendid mosaics.

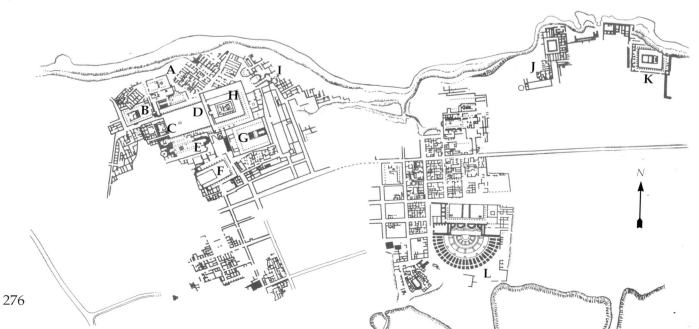

N

278-279 The Leptis Magna market was one of the most flourishing in Africa; caravans from the interior of the continent brought valuable goods, slaves and exotic animals, while huge quantities of olive oil arrived from the country and high-quality garum and salted fish were brought from the coast.

278 bottom The Leptis Magna theater, built in the time of Augustus, was financed by a rich local merchant. The bottom part of the auditorium rested on a natural slope, while the top part was supported by strong constructions filled with crushed stone. The richly decorated stage front was added at the time of Antoninus Pius, in the mid-2nd century A.D.

A Theater
B Markets
C Arch of Septimius Severus
D Hadrian's Baths
E Palaestra
F Nymphaeum
G Temple of Rome and Augustus
H Forum
I Curia
J Temple of Jupiter Dolichenus
K Severian Port
L Lighthouse
M Amphitheater
N Circus

LEPTIS MAGNA, A SUPERB MARBLE METROPOLIS

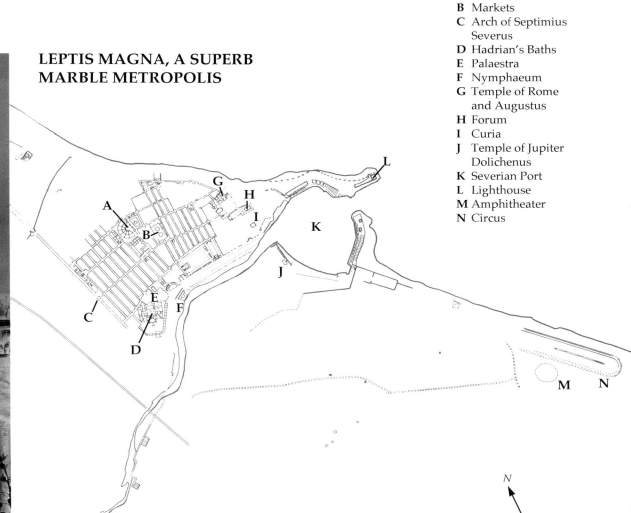

Leptis Magna, a flourishing city in Tripolitania of Phoenician origin, which was the main port of the region between the two Syrtes, became part of the Province of Africa in 46 B.C. after the battle of Thapsus. It became a colony in A.D. 110 under Trajan, and reached the height of its splendor during the reign of Septimius Severus, born there in A.D. 146, who carried out extensive building work in the city. The metropolis, with its superb monumental appearance, became one of the richest in the Mediterranean basin as a result of its exports of valuable goods from the interior (ivory, precious gems, slaves and exotic

animals) and local products. The tuna-salting and garum production industries prospered in Leptis, which was also famous for its olive oil. The city began its decline in the 4th century because of raids by tribes from the interior, and rapid silting of the port caused by a serious error in the design of the dock built by Severus. Subsequent invasions by the Vandals seriously weakened it, and after a brief period of recovery under Justinian, it finally fell into ruin. The basic design of the city's future layout, focusing on two slightly divergent main roads to the west of the Lebda wadi, was already apparent as early as the Augustan age. Due to the generosity of some local benefactors, the city was embellished with numerous monuments in the 1st century, including the Old Forum (around which stood the curia, a basilica, the Temple of Liber Pater, the Temple of Hercules, and the Temple of Rome and Augustus) and a large market. This very interesting market was formed by a rectangular area bounded by porticoes, in the middle of which stood two round pavilions set in octagonal porticoes. Nearby stood the theater (later only than Pompey's

279 bottom A number of Ionic columns that were part of the Temple of Hercules, built in the early 1st century A.D., stand in the area of the Old Forum. The square in front, which was given its first monumental buildings by Augustus, was the heart of the city until it was renovated under the Severus dynasty.

Theater in Rome) and the Chalcidicum, an elegant building erected in A.D. 11 as a trading center. In A.D. 126 Hadrian contributed to the splendor of Leptis by erecting a huge bath complex, including a large palaestra, in the southeastern area. The extensive building program ordered by Septimius Severus was carried out in the area between the cardo maximus and the bed of the Lebda wadi, which was deviated outside the city. A new and grandiose urban highway was built; this impressive colonnaded road, 66 feet wide, began near Hadrian's Baths with a gigantic nymphaeum and led to the docks. On the west side of the road stood the New Forum and Severus's Basilica, with its splendid marbles, statues and relief decorations, often consisting of acanthus volutes, projecting animal figures, and mythological scenes. The same taste for such magnificent baroque

280 left The intensive building activity promoted by Septimius Severus, a native of the town, transformed Leptis Magna into a metropolis with a magnificent appearance. This picture shows one of the Medusas used in the medallions belonging to the architectural decoration of the Severian Forum; it clearly demonstrates that the sculpture tended to emphasize the play of light and shade, to great dramatic effect.

280-281 Architectural styles under the Severus dynasty were luxurious and picturesque, and there was an evident fondness for buildings embellished with apses, niches and colonnaded façades. A good example is the avenue outside the Severian Basilica and adjacent to the Old Forum, which is interesting for the elegant color effects obtained by using different materials.

ornamentation is clearly evident in the large four-faced arch standing at the crossroads between the cardo and the decumanus maximus, whose pilasters and pilaster strips are decorated with friezes similar to those of the basilica, while the sculptural decorations include various political and religious scenes that, in terms of style, already herald Byzantine art.

281 bottom The basilica of the Severian Forum fully reflected the new styles that came into vogue in the late 2nd century A.D. The columns are made of red granite with white marble capitals, the pillars framing the apse are decorated with acanthus volutes, and numerous niches relieve the solidity of the masonry.

282-283 This is what Leptis Magna must have looked like at the height of its splendor: the great colonnaded avenue with the Severian nymphaeum sloped down to the port near which, on the left, stood the Old Forum. Next to the theater were the Chalcidicum and the market. Hadrian's Baths can be seen in the foreground, with the Severian Forum behind them.

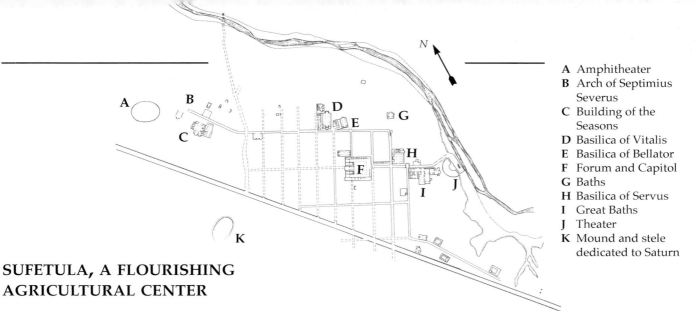

A Amphitheater
B Arch of Septimius
   Severus
C Building of the
   Seasons
D Basilica of Vitalis
E Basilica of Bellator
F Forum and Capitol
G Baths
H Basilica of Servus
I Great Baths
J Theater
K Mound and stele
   dedicated to Saturn

SUFETULA, A FLOURISHING AGRICULTURAL CENTER

The history of Sufetula, a Roman town near Sbeitla in what is now Tunisia, is not recounted by any written source, but archaeological digs support the hypothesis that this major town was founded in the second half of the 1st century A.D. Founded after a military campaign against an indigenous tribe, the town developed at the crossroads of some major highways, which brought it into contact with the main cities of the region. Enriched by olive growing and oil production, Sufetula reached the peak of its splendor between the 2nd and 3rd centuries, when many impressive monuments were built. It soon became a bishop's see, and also prospered

during the Byzantine period, until it was stormed and sacked by the Arabs in A.D. 647. The fairly well preserved ruins have been extensively excavated; much of the urban area has been brought to light, and the subdivision of the center into insulae is clearly apparent. The major monuments of the town include the forum, a square with porticoes on three sides, closed on the fourth side by three tetrastyle temples constituting the capitolium, which were joined by arches to form a single scenic façade. Opposite this complex stands a triumphal arch with three archways, built into the wall surrounding the forum.
It was dedicated to Emperor Antoninus Pius, under whom Sufetula particularly flourished. Other important buildings were an amphitheater with an unusual, almost circular plan, a theater built on the hillside, which slopes down to the nearby wadi, and a large bath complex. An arch named after Septimius Severus, now destroyed, and another dedicated to the first Tetrarchs marked the southern and northern boundaries of the town. The town's water supply was provided by an aqueduct thatcrossed the wadi on a bridge, still in a good state of repair. Five large basilicas, presenting clear signs of reconstruction work, survive from the

284 top The town center of Sufetula was built following the typical division into "centuries," and the insulae presented a rectangular plan. The forum stood in a dominant position. The borders of the town, which was not surrounded by walls, were marked by two triumphal arches.

284 bottom left The triumphal arch dedicated to the Tetrarchs, which has a single archway with a niche framed by columns on each side, features a style that was quite common in Africa. The design of this kind of monument varied from province to province.

284 bottom right The forum area was bounded by a wall that contained a triumphal arch dedicated to Antoninus Pius, dating from A.D. 139, in the form of a monumental gateway. Sufetula mainly prospered between the 2nd and 4th centuries.

285 Unusually, the capitol of Sufetula is not a temple with a single cella, but is formed by three separate buildings.

286-287 The Arch of Antoninus Pius was reached along a colonnaded avenue lined with shops.

284

INDEX

A

Abruzzo, *66*
Achaemenids, 240, 252
Achaia, 199, 228, 236
Acropolis, 238, 239
Actium, 43, 236, 266
Adamklissi, 230, *231*
Adige, *146*
Adrianople, 56
Adriatic Sea, 229
Aegates, 38
Aegean Sea, 230, 248
Aelius Bridge, 132
Aemilian Bridge, *129*
Aemilius Lepidus, 43, 109, 110
Aeneas, 22
Aeneid, 122, *270*
Aequi, 36
Aesculapius, 110
Aetius, 57
Afghanistan, 203
Africa Nova, *see* Numidia
Africa Procunsularis, 268
Africa, 35, 38, 51, 54, 194, 197, 199, *200*, 202, 203, 240, 268, *269*, 270, 276, 278, 279, 284
African coast, 38
Agesandrus, *109*
Agrippa, 122, *126*, 132, *133*, *194*, 216
Agrippina, 46, *46*
Agrippina the Elder, *16*
Agrippina the Younger, *16*
Alaric, 57, 134, 167
Alba-Julia, 230
Alba Longa, 22, 26
Alcantara, *206*
Alesia, *97*
Alexander Severus, 35
Alexander the Great, 56, *181*, 252
Alexandria, 159, 161, 266
Alexandrine aqueduct, 134
Algeria, 203
Aljustrel, 206
Allia, 104
Allies' War, 26, 148, 156, 168, 175
Alps, 38, 213, 215
Alsietine aqueduct, 122
Amiterno, *66*
Amman, 252
Ammianus Marcellinus, 139
Amphion, *110*
Amphitheater of Italica, *206*
Amphitheater of Nîmes, *217*
Amphitheater of Pompeii, 175
Amulius, 22
Anatolia, 197, 252
Ancus Martius, 22, 100, 104, 146, 162
Anderida, *see* Pevensey
Andronicus of Cirrha, 237
Anglesey, 225
Aniene Falls, *146*
Anio Falls, 156
Anjar, *250*
Antakya, 250, 252
Antinoe, *267*
Antinoupolis, 266
Antinous, *159*, 161, 236, 266
Antioch, *see* Antakya
Antiope, *110*
Antonia the Elder, *133*
Antonia the Younger, *133*
Antonine Emperors, 132
Antoninus Pius, 35, 49, *51*, *85*, 167, 222, 245, 273, 278, 284, *284*
Antony, 35, *40*, 42, 43, *43*, *44*, 216, 236, 265, 267
Aosta, 150, 152, 153, *153*
Aosta Archaeological Museum, *152*
Aosta theater, 152, *152*
Apamea, 240, 250, 252
Aphrodisias, *197*, 240, 240
Aphrodite of the Esquiline, statue of, *150*
Apollo, *168*, 175, *188*, 197
Apollo of Veii, 22
Apollodorus of Damascus, *49*,*100*
Apollonius, *113*
Apollonius of Tralles, *110*
Appia Aqueduct, 122
Appian, 130
Appian Way, *130*, 134
Appius Claudius, 104, *130*
Apuleius, 132, *270*
Apulum, *see* Alba-Julia
Aquae Sulis, *223*
Aquileia, 228
Aquitania, 213
Ara Pacis Augustae, *see* Ara Pacis
Ara Pacis, 44, 122, *133*, *144*
Arabia, *198*, 199, 203, 250, *254*, 267
Arabs, 208, 245, 265, 276, 284
Arausio, *see* Orange
Arcadius, 35, 56, *57*, 134, 245
Arcar, 230
Arch of Antoninus Pius, *284*
Arch of Augustus, 152, *153*
Arch of Barà, 208
Arch of Caracalla, *167*, *273*
Arch of Constantine, *117*, 134

Arch of Galerius, 236
Arch of Hadrian, *238*
Arch of Septimius Severus, *104*
Arch of Titus, *104*, 130
Arch of Trajan, 210, *275*
Arena of Verona, *146*
Arians, 55
Arles, 216
Arles amphitheater, *213*
Armenia, 199, 250
Arminius, 214
Arno, 36
Arrian, 130
Artemis, *188*, *199*, 245, 248, 262
Arverni tribe, 213
Arx, *104*, 120
Asia, 26, 194, 197, 199, 230, 240, 245, 248
Asia Minor, 67, *197*, 240, *240*, 248, *248*, 265
Aspendos, *240*
Assyria, 199, 250
Asturia, 205
Aswan, 266
Athanadorus of Rhodes, *109*
Athens, *109*, 236, *236*, 237, 238, *238*
Atlantic coast, 38, 205, 270
Atlantic Ocean, 213
Attalus I, *109*, *110*, *197*, 240
Attalus III, *194*, 245
Attica, 236
Attila, 57
Augsburg, 228
Augst, 215
Augusta Praetoria Salassorum, *see* Aosta
Augusta Raurica, *215*
Augusta Treverorum, *see* Träves
Augusta Vindelicum, *see* Augsburg
Augustales, 176
Augustine, *270*
Augustodunum, *see* Autun
Augustus, 8, 27, 34, 35, 42, 43, *43*, 44, *44*, 46, *46*, 60, 62, 74, *92*, 94, *117*, 120, 122, *122*, *126*, *133*, 144, 148, 152, 156, 161, *164*, 175, 194, *194*, 197, *205*, 206, 208, 210, 213, *213*, 214, *214*, 215, 216, *216*, 217, *218*, 229, 236, 238, 240, 245, 253, 260, 265, 266, 267, *267*, 268, 276, 278, 279
Augustus' Forum, 100
Augustus of the East, *see* Theodosius
Augustus' Palace, 208
Aula Palatina, 221, *221*
Aulus Terentius Varro, 152
Aurelian, 55, 134, 230, 265
Aurelian Wall, 130, 134
Autun, *213*
Aventine Hill, 104, 129, 240
Avitus Bassianus, *see* Heliogabalus

B

Baal, 257, 270
Baalbek, *250*, 252, 257, *257*
Babylon, 266
Bacchanalia, 113
Bacchus, 113
Baetica, 49, 205
Balearics, slingsmen of, 97
Balkans, 56
Banna, *see* Newcastle
Bardo Museum, *270*, *271*
Barracks of the Vigiles, 164
Basilica Aemilia, 109
Basilica Julia, 120, 122
Basilica of Maxentius, 105
Basilica of Neptune, 122
Basilica of Santa Maria degli Angeli, *138*
Basilica Porcia, 109
Basilica Sempronia, 109, 120
Basilica Ulpia, *100*, 132
Basle, 215
Baths of Agrippa, 122
Baths of Caracalla, *110*, 134, *134*, *135*, *139*
Baths of Diocletian, *138*, *139*, 265
Baths of Hadrian, 280, *281*
Baths of Helena, 134
Baths of Neptune, 164
Baths of Nero, 122, 129
Baths of Oceanus, 276
Baths of Santa Barbara, 221
Battle of Cannae, 38
Battle of Actium, 35, 43, 194, 197
Battle of Châlons, 57
Battle of Hadrianopolis, 35
Battle of Issos, *181*
Battles of Aquae Sextiae, 213
Begram, 203
Beirut, 250, *250*
Beka'a Valley, *250*
Bel, *264*, 265
Belgic Gaul, *see* Gallia Belgica
Belgium, 194
Belgrade, 230
Bellona, 62
Benedict XIV, Pope, *113*
Beneventum, 26
Berenice, 267
Beroe, *see* Stara Zagora
Berytus, *see* Beirut
Be't She'an, 252
Bithynia, 26, 159, 194

Black Sea, 228, 230
Boeotia, 236
Bologna, 150
Bonn, 215
Bonna, *see* Bonn
Boscoreale, *269*
Boscoreale Villa, 188
Bosra, *250*, *254*
Boudicca, 225
Bowness, 226
Bregenz, 228
Brigantium, *see* Bregenz
Brigetio, *see* Szöny
Britain, *see* Britannia
Britannia, 16, 35, 42, *45*, 47, 49, *51*, 199, 203, 206, 222, 223, 224, *224*, 225, *225*, 226, 266
Britons, 224
Brundisium, 130
Brutus, 26, 42
Building of Eumachia, 181
Bulla Regia, *200*
Buthier, stream, 152
Byzantine art, 57
Byzantium, 35, 55, *55*, 231

C

Caelestis, 270
Caelian Hill, *98*, 129
Caesar, 26, 35, *40*, 41, 42, *43*, 44, 50, *80*, *97*, 120, 122, 132, 148, 171, 194, 200, 202, 205, *206*, 208, 213, 214, 218, *218*, 222, 224, 236, *269*, 276
Caesarea, 260, *260*
Caesasarea Stratonis, *see* Caesarea
Cairo, 266
Caius Caesar, *133*, 216
Caius Cestius, *130*
Caius Gracchus, 26, 148
Caius Julius Caesar, *see* Caesar
Caius Marius, 26, *40*, *41*, 94, 213
Caledonia, 224
Caligula, 35, 46, 47, 129, 164
Calleva Atrebatum, *see* Silchester
Cambodunum, *see* Kempten
Campania, 22, 26, 116, 146
Campanian Samnites, 36
Campanians, 64
Camulodunum, *see* Colchester
Canopus, *159*, 161
Cantabria, 205
Capitol, 21, 27, *51*, 104, 120
Capitol Hill, 130, 132
Capitoline She-Wolf, 8, 21
Capitoline Temple, *see* Temple of Jupiter Capitolinus
Capitoline Venus, *143*
Capitolium, *164*, *164*, 175, 181, *200*, 202, 273, 274, 276, 284
Caracalla, 35, 54, *54*, 194, 199, 273
Caria, *197*
Carine, 129
Carlisle, 226
Carlo II of Bourbon, 171
Carmen Seculare, 122
Carrhae, battle of, 42
Cartagena, 206
Carthage, 26, 38, 38, *97*, 162, 194, 268, *269*
Carthaginian empire, 38
Carthaginians, 38, *96*
Caryatids of Canopus, 159
Cassius, 26, 42, 156
Cassius Dio, 134
Cassivellaunus, 224
Castel Sant' Angelo, *128*
Castor and Pollux, 110
Castra Exploratorum, *see* Netherby
Castra Praetoria, 129
Castra Regina, *see* Regensburg
Catholicism, 56
Catholics, 55
Catiline, 26, 40, 41
Cato, 42
Cattle Market, 26, 104
Catullus, 120, 156
Caudine Forks, 26
Cecilia Metella, *130*
Celsus Polemeanus, 245
Celtiberians, 205
Centenary House, *182*
Ceres, 110, 274
Cermalus, 130
Cerunno, 213
Chalcidicum, 280
Channel, 222
Charioteer's Block, 167
Charred Furniture House, 172
Chester, 222, 226
Chesterholm, 226
China, 86, 203, 250
Chios, 240
Christian Basilicas, 134
Christian Church, 55, 56, 57
Christian martyrs, *113*
Christian religion, 50
Christianity, 35, 44, 47, 50, *55*, 139, 252
Christians, 35, 50, 55, 55, 56
Chrysorrhoas, 262
Church, *see* Christian Church

Cicero, 26, *40*, 41, 42, 43, 60, 120
Cicero's Villa, *81*
Cilicia, 194
Cilurnum, *see* Chester
Cimbrians, *41*, 213
Cincius Alimentus, 113
Cinoscefale, 236
Circus (of Caligula), 129
Circus Maximus, 70, 104, 129
Circus of Maxentius, *130*
Cirta, 274
Cisalpine Gaul, 146, 194, 228
Civil War, 175
C. Julius Lacer, *206*
Claudia Antonia Sabina, 248
Claudius, *16*, 35, 46, *46*, 129, 132, *162*, 164, *168*, 199, 222, 230, 248, 266, 273
Claudius Aqueduct, 129
Cleopatra VII, 35, 43, 266, 267
Clio, *270*
Cloaca Maxima, 104
Cluj, 230
Colchester, 222
Coliseum, *17*, 27, 47, 70, 71, 74, 77, *98*, 113, 117, 130, 134, 152, *269*
College of the Augustals, *172*
Colleges of Priests, 22
Cologne, 215
Colonia Augusta Nemausus, *see* Nîmes
Colonia Claudia Ara Agrippinensium, *see* Cologne
Colonia Iulia Vienna Allobrogum, *see* Vienne
Column of Antoninus Pius, 34
Column of Marcus Aurelius, 8
Comitia centuriata, 36
Comitia curiata, 24, 36
Comitia tributa, 26, 36
Commodus, 35, 49, 51, 54, 167, 222, 225
Como, 150
Confluentes, *see* Koblenz
Constantine (town), 274
Constantine, 27, 35, *55*, 55, 56, *103*, *105*, 134, 139, 167, 200, 221, 221, 231, *231*, 257
Constantine's Palace, 221
Constantinople Hippodrome, 57
Constantinople, *see* Byzantium
Constantius II, 35
Constantius, 55, 56
Constantius Clorus, *246*
Constitutio Antoniniana, 35, 54, 199
Conventum Galliarum, 213
Corbridge, 226
Corinth, 38, 236
Cornelia Veneria Pompeianorum, *see* Pompeii
Cornelius Fronto, 132
Cornwall, 38, 222
Corsica, 38, 194
Corstopitun, *see* Corbridge
Cottian Alps, 197
Council of the Plebs, 36
C. Petronius Arbiter, 129
Crags, 226
Crassus, 26, *40*, 41, 42, *43*, *130*
Cretan archers, 97
Crete, 236, 267, *267*
Croatia, *147*
Croesus, *see* King Croesus
Crusaders, *260*
Crusades, 262
C. Sextilius Pollo, 245
Ctesiphon, 49
Cuicul, *see* Djemila
Cumberland coast, 226
Curia, 120, 122, 164, 181
Cybele, *81*, 113
Cyclades, 236
Cynicism, school of, 50
Cyrenaica, 267
Cyrene, 194, 267, *267*

D

Dacia, 49, *49*, 199, 228, *228*, 230
Dacian Wars, *100*, 132, 230
Dacians, *49*, 230, *231*
Dalmatia, 197
Dalmatian tribes, 229
Damascus, 250, *250*, 252
Danaides, 171
Danaus, *171*
Danube, 96, 215, 228, *228*, 229, 230, 231
Darius III, *181*
De Bello Actiaco, 172
De reditu suo (poem), 139
Dead Sea, 253
Decebalus, 230
Decius, 55, 192
Delphi, 236, *236*
Dentz, 215
Deva, *see* Chester
Didymaion, *197*
Diocletian, 27, 35, 55, 55, 94, 134, 139, 167, 194, 197, 199, 200, 221, 225, 230, 232, *232*, 246
Dionysias, *see* Suweida
Dionysisus the Elder, 161
Dionysus, 187, *271*
Dioskourides of Samos, *81*
Dirce, *110*

288

BIBLIOGRAPHY

HISTORY AND CIVILIZATION

A.A. V.V., *The Cambridge Ancient History*, Voll. V - IX, London, 1970.

Carcopino, J., *La vita quotidiana a Roma all'apogeo dell'impero*, Bari, 1967.

Connolly, P., *Greece and Rome at War*, London, 1981.

Cornell, T. and Mattews, J., *Atlas of the Roman World*, Oxford, 1982.

Cunliffe, B., *Rome and Her Empire*, Maidenhead, 1978.

Desideri, P., *L'imperialismo romano*, Messina, 1972.

Gabba, E., *Esercito e società nella tarda repubblica romana*, Florence, 1973.

Gibbon, E., *History of the Decline and Fall of the Roman Empire*, London, 1776, new edition 1979.

Levi, M. A., *L'impero romano*, Turin, 1963.

Levi, M. A., *L'Italia antica*, Milan 1968.

Millar, F., *The Roman World and Its Neighbours*, London, 1981.

Moscati, S. (edited by), *Vita quotidiana nell'Italia Antica*, Verona, 1993.

Paoli, U.E., *Vita romana, usi, costumi, istituzioni, tradizioni*, Florence, 1962.

Petit, P., *L'empire romain*, Paris, 1974.

Pisani, Sartorio G. and Liberati, Silverio A.

M. (edited by), *Vita e costumi dei Romani antichi*, Rome, 1986.

Webster G., *The Roman Imperial Army*, London, 1969.

Wheeler, M., *Rome Beyond the Imperial Frontiers*, London, 1954.

ART AND ARCHITECTURE

Adam J-P., *La construction romaine. Materiaux et techniques*, Paris, 1984.

Becatti, G., *L'arte dell'età classica*, Florence, 1965.

Bianchi, Bandinelli R., *Rome, le centre du pouvoir*, Paris, 1969.

Bianchi, Bandinelli R., *Rome, la fin de l'art antique*, Paris, 1970.

Boëthius, A. and Ward-Perkins, J.B., *Etruscan and Roman Architecture*, Harmondsworth, 1970.

Borda, M., *La pittura romana*, Milan, 1958.

Chiolini, P., *I caratteri distributivi degli antichi edifici*, Milan, 1959.

Coarelli, F., *L'oreficeria nell'arte classica*, Milan, 1966.

Mansuelli, G. A., *Roma e il mondo romano*, Turin, 1981.

Mumford, L., *The City in History, Vol. II*, New York, 1961.

Picard, G. C., *L'art romain*, Paris, 1962.

Ragghianti, C. L., *Pittori di Pompei*, Milan, 1963.

Richmond, J., *Roman Archaeology and Art*, London, 1969.

Ward-Perkins, J.B., *Roman Architecture*, London, 1973.

Wheeler, M., *Roman Art and Architecture*, London, 1964.

ARCHAEOLOGICAL SITES

Aurigemma, S., *Villa Adriana*, Rome, 1962.

Bianchi, Bandinelli R. and Becatti, G. (edited by), *Enciclopedia dell'Arte Antica Classica e Orientale*, Rome, 1959-1966.

Bisel, S. C., *The Secrets of Vesuvius*, Toronto, 1990.

Breccia, A.E., *Egitto greco-romano*, Pisa, 1957.

Brizzi, M., *Roma: i monumenti antichi*, Rome, 1973.

Coarelli, F., *Roma*, Milan, 1971.

De Franciscis, A., *The Buried Cities: Pompeii and Herculaneum*, New York, 1978.

Drinkwater J., *Roman Gaul*, London, 1983.

Giuliano A., *La cultura artistica delle province della Grecia in età romana*, Rome, 1965.

Holum, K.G. and others, *King Herod's Dream - Caesarea on the Sea*, New York and London, 1988.

La Rocca, E., de Vos, A. and de Vos, M., *Guida archeologica di Pompei*, Milan, 1976.

Maiuri, A., *Pompei ed Ercolano fra case e abitanti*, Milan, 1959.

Pavolini, C., *Ostia*, Bari, 1983.

Pugliese, Carratelli G. (edited by), *Enciclopedia dell'Arte Antica Classica e Orientale*, Rome, 1994.

Richmond, I.A., *Roman Britain*, London, 1967.

Romanelli, P., *Storia delle province romane dell'Africa*, Rome, 1959.

Romanelli, P., *Topografia e Archeologia dell'Africa Romana*, Turin, 1970.

Romanelli, P., *In Africa e Roma*, Rome, 1981.

Stern, E. (edited by), *New Encyclopedia of Archaeological Excavations in the Holy Land*, Voll. I-IV, Jerusalem, 1993.

Tarrats, Bou F., *Tarraco*, Tarragona, 1990.

Wiseman, F.J., *Roman Spain: An Introduction to the Roman Antiquities of Spain and Portugal*, London, 1956.

PERIODICALS

Archeo, Attualità del passato, De Agostini - Rizzoli Periodici, Via Cassia 1328, Rome.

Archeologia Viva, Giunti Gruppo Editoriale Firenze, Via Bolognese 165, Florence.

ILLUSTRATION CREDITS

PHOTOS

Antonio Attini / Archivio White Star: pages. 146-147, 147 top, 194, 195, 196, 197, 198-199, 199 bottom, 200 top, 201, 202-203, 203 top, 204, 205, 206, 207, 208, 209, 210, 211, 212 bottom, 213, 216, 217, 218, 219, 232, 233, 237, 238, 239, 240, 241, 242-243, 244, 245, 246, 247, 248, 249, 250, 251, 252 top, 256, 257, 262 top, 269 bottom, 272, 273, 284, 285, 286-287.

Marcello Bertinetti / Archivio White Star: pages 55 top, 105 top right, 123 bottom left, 252-253, 253 bottom, 263, 268-269.
Marcello Bertinetti / Archivio White Star "Italian Air Force General Staff permit no. 316 dated 18/8/1995": pages 128-129, 128 bottom, 129 top, 130 top, 138-139, 156-157, 157 top, 158, 159 top, 162-163, 163 top.
Marcello Bertinetti / Archivio White Star "Italian Air Force General Staff permit no. 325 dated 1/9/1995": pages 2-3, 18-19, 98-99, 100 top and center, 101, 123 bottom right, 130 bottom, 131, 134-135.

Massimo Borchi / Archivio White Star: pages 222 bottom, 226-227.

Luciano Ramires / Archivio White Star: pages 212-213.

Giulio Veggi / Archivio White Star: pages 35 right, 67 top left, 96 bottom, 100 bottom, 104, 104-105, 105 top left, 114-115, 116, 117, 118, 119, 120, 121, 122 bottom, 122-123, 129 bottom, 130 center bottom, 135 bottom, 138 top, 139, 164, 165, 168, 172, 173, 174, 175, 221 top right, 230, 266 top.

AKG Photo: pages 220, 221 top left, 221 bottom.

R. Bouquet / Diaf: page 266 bottom left.

British Museum: pages 94 top, 224, 225.

Bruce Coleman: pages 200 bottom, 223 top.

Stephen Coyne / Bruce Coleman: page 250 bottom.

Giovanni Dagli Orti: pages 6-7, 8, 20-21, 22 top, 24 top right, 36, 43 bottom, 60 top, 67 top left, 70, 71, 72, 73, 76 top, 92 bottom, 93, 98, 148, 160-161, 169, 176, 178, 187, 188, 189, 190-191, 229, 236, 264, 265, 267, 270, 271.

Araldo De Luca - Rome: pages 4-5, 9, 12-13, 14-15, 23, 25, 26 center, 35 right, 35 center left, 35 center, 35 center right, 39, 40 bottom, 43 top, 44 top, 45, 46 bottom, 48, 49, 50, 51, 54, 55 bottom, 56-57, 58-59, 60-61, 62 bottom right, 63 top, 63 bottom, 66, 67 bottom, 75 bottom right, 76 center and bottom, 78 bottom, 78-79, 82-83, 84, 85, 89 top, 89 center top, 89 center bottom, 92 top, 96 top, 108, 109, 110, 111, 112, 113, 133 bottom, 140, 141, 142, 143, 144-145, 150, 151, 159 bottom, 170, 171, 180, 181, 192-193.

F.M.R.: pages 26 center left, 27.

Fotografica Foglia: pages 86, 87, 88, 89 center, 89 bottom, 90, 91.

Cesare Galli: pages 266 center, 276, 277, 278, 279, 280, 281.

Jean Paul Garcin / Diaf: pages 255, 268 top, 274.

Cesare Gerolimetto: pages 147 bottom, 228, 262 center and bottom.

Giraudon / Archivio Alinari: page 17.

Johanna Huber / SIE: pages 262, 263.

Archivio IGDA: pages 46 top, 94 bottom, 152 top.

Jürgen Liepe: page 266 bottom right .

Rene Monjoie: pages 67 center left, 152-153, 153 bottom.

Photo Nimatallah / Ag. Luisa Ricciarini: pages 16 bottom, 44 bottom, 62 top, 63 center left, 63 center right, 63 bottom, 67 center right.

Andrea Pistolesi: pages 222-223.

Zev Radovan: pages 47 bottom, 252 center and bottom.

Photo R.N.M.: pag. 268 bottom.

Ag. Luisa Ricciarini: pages 62 bottom left, 64, 75 bottom left.

Roemer & Pelzaus Museum: pages 214 top, 215 bottom.

Rossenbach / Zefa: page 221 center.

Archivio Scala: pages 10-11, 22 bottom, 24 left, 24 bottom right, 26 left, 26 center right, 26 right, 38, 40 top, 41 top, 42, 46, 47 top and center, 58, 60 bottom, 68, 78 top, 152 bottom.

P.G. Sclarandis / SIE: pages 198 bottom, 254, 255.

Alberto Siliotti / Archivio Image Service: page 202 bottom.

Emilio F. Simion - Milan / Ag. Luisa Ricciarini: page 41 center bottom.

Foto Ubu / Ag. Luisa Ricciarini: pages 176-177, 178-179.

MUSEUMS AND ART COLLECTIONS

Antiquarium of the Forum, Rome: page 23 bottom right.

Archaeological Museum, Delphi: page 236 top.

Archaeological Museum, Hama: page 254 left.

Archaeological Museum, Herculaneum: pages 86, 87, 88, 89, 90, 91.

Archaeological Museum, Nîmes: page 216 bottom.

Archaeological Museum, Palmyra: page 265 top.

Archaeological Museum, Sousse: pages 270 top, 270-271.

Archaeological Museum, Suweida: pages 198 bottom, 254 right.

Bardo Museum, Tunisi: page 270 bottom.

Bibliothèque Nationale, Paris: page 1, 17, 35 center left, 37, 40 bottom, 43, 49, 50, 66, 84, 85, 96, 111, 140, 141, 143, 159.

British Museum, London: pages 94 top, 224, 225.

Capitoline Museums, Rome: pages 20-21, 43 bottom, 47 top right, 47 top left, 150, 160-161, 292.

Egyptian Museum, Cairo: page 266 bottom left.

Israel Museum, Jerusalem: pages 47 bottom, 252 center and bottom.

Kunsthistorisches Museum, Vienna: pages 16, 44 bottom, 46 top.

Landesmuseum, Mainz: page 94 bottom.

Louvre Museum, Paris: pages 93, 267, 268 bottom.

Mosaics Museum, Shahba: page 255.

Museo Archeologico, Aosta: page 152.

Museo Civico La Rocca, Riva del Garda: page 67 top left.

Museo della Civiltà Romana, Rome: pages 60 top, 62 bottom left, 64 top, 70 bottom.

Museo Gregoriano Profano, Vatican: pages 58, 60 bottom.

Museo Nazionale Romano, Rome: pages 12-13, 22 top, 26 left, 36 bottom, 58-59, 63 bottom, 76 top, 98, 112, 113, 142-143, 192-193.

Museo Pio Clementino, Vatican: pages 26 right, 41, 45, 108-109, 109.

Museo Prenestino Barberiniano, Palestrina: page 48.

Museo di Villa Giulia, Rome: pages 22 bottom, 23, 24 top, 24 bottom left, 25, 38.

National Archaeological Museum, Florence: page 40 top.

National Archaeological Muesum, Madrid: pages 70 top, 71, 72-73, 73.

National Archaeological Museum, Merida: page 205 bottom.

National Archaeological Museum, Naples: pages 8, 26 center, 39, 67 bottom, 75, 76, 78-79, 82-83, 67 center right, 78 top, 110, 151, 170, 171, 176-177, 178-179, 178, 180, 181, 188-189.

National Archaeological Museum, Venice: pages 26 center right, 41 top.

National Archaeological Museum, Taranto: page 75 left.

National History Museum, Bucharest: pages 92 bottom, 229.

National Museum of Abruzzo, l'Aquila: page 62 top.

Private numismatical collection F. Bourbon: page 35 right.

Roemer - Pelzaeus Museum, Hildesheim: pages 214, 215.

Uffizi Galleries, Florence: pages 63 top left, 63 center.

Vatican Museums, Braccio Nuovo, Vatican: page 9.

292 Jupiter Optimus Maximus was the supreme deity in the Roman pantheon, lord of the sky, daylight, thunder and lightning; a great temple on the summit of the Capitol in Rome was consecrated to him.